PHENOMENON

PHENOMENON

13 Lives of

The Millennium Man

by

Dr. Bob

PHENOMENON

13 Lives of
The Millennium Man

Copyright 2014
      Robert McNary

Cover design
      Curt Perkins
      electricavenuenashville.com

All Rights Reserved

ISBN 978-0-9673499-2-3

Published by

      The Portable School Press
      theportableschool@gmail.com
      www.theportableschool.com
      www.phenom1000man.com

PHENOMENON

The Possible Human

Sedmitchka (Russian for Prodigy)

Explorador (Romanian for Explorer)

Diabolista (Italian for Medium)

Magus (Persian for Savant)

Interprete (Spanish for Interpreter)

Tulku (Tibetan for Vehicle)

Chela (Hindi for Agent)

Hierophant (Greek for Apostle)

Khan (Mongolian for Potentate)

Aenigma (Latin for Enigma)

Helel (Hebrew for Light Bearer)

Phenomene (French for Phenomenon)

Baba (Russian for Grandmother, Hindi for Grandfather)

The Millennium Man

Dedicated to

*
* *

~~~

"Facts are stubborn things."
A.R. Wallace

"There are more things in heaven and earth, Horatio,
Than are dreamt of in your philosophy."
William Shakespeare

" If we rightly understood its power [of the human spirit] ...
nothing would be impossible to us upon the earth."
Paracelsus

PHENOMENON

The Possible Human

"I'll tell you what I think I am.
I think I'm what everybody can be."

George Malley, the *Phenomenon* of the 1996 film, spoke these words to a neurosurgeon who was keen to operate on him and study his living brain. John Travolta played the friendly, wholesome auto mechanic whose life was suddenly changed when he "saw a flash of light" on the evening of his 38th birthday. George quickly developed unusual talents and abilities: like reading piles of library books each week, learning conversational Portuguese in a few minutes, predicting an earthquake, deciphering military codes, gathering information from his neighbors' minds and moving objects with his own.

All these extraordinary talents caused interest and concern among his friends and fellow Californians. Unfortunately, they eventually were shown to be effects of an astrocytoma (malignant brain tumor) which prompted the surgeon to ask permission to open his skull and examine his brain. "You could be our greatest teacher."

George brusquely responded to the Scientist, "I'm the possibility. I think you've got this desperate grasp on technology ... and this grasp on science, and ... you don't have a hand left to grasp what's important.

"If I had to choose between a tumor that got me here ... and some flash of light from an alien craft, I'd choose the tumor. I would, because it's here, within us. What I'm talking about is the human spirit. That's the challenge. That's the voyage. That's the expedition."

George Malley died before his next birthday. Hopefully, he made an impression beyond his moments in the touching movie scenario. Maybe viewers got the hint that George Malley was an embodiment, if only for a few days, of *The Possible Human*. And more importantly, that "everybody can be."

George Malley and the hero of this book are both representations of *The Possible Human*. One was a fabricated film role, the other a flesh-and-blood figure of the 19th century. The two had much in common as well as many differences, but mostly in degree.

Let's briefly compare the movie's George Malley and this book's hero who used the nickname Jack Maloney in repartee among friends. Jack Maloney and George Malley. How do they relate?

George's extraordinary abilities resulted from effects on his brain and a diseased one at that. Jack lived a full life, despite recurring illnesses, produced phenomena at will through an expansive mind, a wholeness of being, and a wide range of additional resources.

George prided himself in "taking on" stacks of books at the local library, reading and digesting them. Jack seemed to read whole libraries of books and also wrote thousands of pages of letters and articles, stories and books without the aid of typewriter, word processor or computer.

George moved pencils and glasses with his insistent and persistent thoughts. Jack did the same and also materialized flowers and cups, books and portraits, and much more - willing them into sight.

George tapped into earthquake energies. Jack communicated with Intelligence and intelligences, elementaries and elementals, spirits and spooks in a host of ways.

George flashed across movie and video screens to the keen interest of viewers in a few recent years. Jack continues to stimulate and confuse seekers and students, thinking and creative minds more than a hundred years since leaving the world stage.

The Real Phenomenon has had a much wider influence than the reader might imagine until he/she reads these pages. Especially since our hero's name is little known by the masses. (The genius Wolfgang Mozart was likewise little recognized beyond the world of musicians until the advent of the play and film *Amadeus*.) Jack has many stories - old and new - yet to be told and retold, travels to be recounted, histories to be reviewed, singular experiences to be recapitulated, and teachings to be resurrected.

Modern youth, raised on *Harry Potter*, may be interested to find that that boy wonder has nothing over our *Phenomenon*. Of possibly more extraordinary interest, the reader may be fascinated, even flummoxed, to discover that, rivaling renowned savants and saviors of history, the greatest *Phenomenon* of the past thousand years and beyond was a WOMAN.

Sedmitchka
(Russian for Prodigy)

"I was an imp of Hell."

Helen Hahn's baptism previewed future events, maybe her whole life. A large room was selected for the ceremony in the equally large family home. But, those who wanted to see the event overflowed the chamber and helped produce the first extraordinary moment in Helen's life. Three sets of sponsors, godparents, family members and a retinue of serfs gathered to celebrate the hour-long rite on the hot summer day. All stood for the whole time as no chairs were used in Orthodox services regardless of their length.

Helen's child-aunt acting as a proxy for a missing relative stood at the front of the group with lighted taper in hand like the rest of the congregation. Near the end of the ceremony as the sponsors were "renouncing the Evil One," the little girl lost control of her candle and set fire to the long robes of the officiating priest. The small conflagration spread so as to injure several people with the old priest incurring severe burns.

Not surprisingly, an omen was taken from the event. The "innocent" babe was considered the ultimate cause and was thenceforth destined according to her family and neighbors to a life of great changes and recurring troubles.

Helen Hahn's whole life from cradle to grave was a whirlwind of action, adventure, and excitement to the view of admirers and enemies alike. Most childhoods are relatively unremarkable, even those of the rich, notable, and powerful. But, a modest-sized volume could have been written about Helen's early days had all the stories been gathered and collated as she was growing up. Even with the lapse of almost two centuries, her formative years are worth an enquiring visit and many pages of text.

Helen was neither born with a caul wrapped round her head nor was she disengaged from a dead twin in the womb. Nor had the babe been the focus of prenatal prophecies. But, she did come into the world in 1831 in the midst of the Asiatic Cholera Pandemic which lasted more than two years decimating populations surrounding her birthplace of Ekaterinoslav, Russia.

The newborn made her entrance close to midnight between July 30 and 31 (Julian - Old Style Calendar) which made her a Sedmitchka (literally, the little seven-numbered one). Because of the epidemic, recent deaths in her family, and prescriptions of the Church - lest the child die with the burden of original sin resting upon her soul, the hurried baptism was performed within hours of her birth.

In later years, Helen laughingly recalled her coming into the world from another angle: "That -- surprisingly enough, I was born with a cigarette of Turkish tobacco in my mouth, and an emerald ring on my left big toe, a small gooseberry bush, moreover growing out of my navel. That I was called Heliona (not Helen as people call me) a Greek name, derived from that of the Sun -- *Helios* -- because (1st) there was an eclipse of the luminary on that day, who knew prophetically, we must infer, that it would be eclipsed for long years by the newly born babe, and also (2nd) because of the possibility it gave the clergy and missionaries of the 19th century to spell it with a double L (thus -- Helliona) and assure the more readily their congregation that I was an imp of Hell."

Little Helen's ancestors on her mother's side included the generals and diplomats of the Dolgoroukov family and the noblemen, statesmen, and military officers of the Fadeyevs. Her mother, also Helen, although only short-lived (1814-1842), was an accomplished writer. She wrote under the pen name of Zeneida and was considered the Russian George Sand (Lucile Aurore Dupin). Her works were published in four volumes in 1843.

Heliona's father, Peter Hahn, traced his own ancestors back to the Carolingian dynasty and German knights and crusaders. Because her father was a horse-artillery officer and also because of her mother's fragile health, the Hahn family moved frequently. The children experienced a broad stretch of southern Russia and bordering states from Romankovo to Odessa, Tula, Kursk, St. Petersburg, Astrakhan, and again to Odessa.

With the death of their mother, the children - Helen, Vera and Leonide - lived with their maternal grandparents in Saratov, Russia, and later in Tiflis, Georgia. During her teens, Helen spent time with an uncle in the Ural Mountains and Semipalatinsk (Kazakhstan), on the boundary of Mongolia. Helen remembered making "numerous excursions beyond the frontiers, and knew all about Lamas and Thibetans before I was fifteen."

From the very first, the willful Hahn child was difficult to manage regardless of who was in charge. Beyond that, her health also vacillated and she was "ever sick and dying," according to the grown woman. Sometimes, even more concerning were Helen's sleepwalking and her psychic gifts which were attributed by her nurses, borne of the Greek Orthodox Church, to "possession by the devil." In later years, she remarked that, "I was drenched during childhood in enough holy water to have floated a ship, and exorcised by priests who might as well have been talking to the wind for all the effect they had."

Helen's fiery temperament caused her to brook little or no authority. Her whims and will generally won out. The young Hahn girl had the habit of telling people what she thought of them -- as well as what she foresaw in their coming days -- to their faces. Still, she became the favorite of relatives and servants alike. Alternately "petted and punished, spoiled and hardened," she continued to be a "difficult child."

From early on, she exhibited a distinctly dual nature. One mischievous and the other mystical. Helen was an inveterate prankster. But, when her deeds had run their course, she was able to put her pug nose to the grindstone and study assiduously. Then, she would be hard pressed to leave her books. "I have always lived a double existence, mysterious, incomprehensible to myself ..."

Mademoiselle Hahn was never typical at anything and did not conform to the ways of governesses, teachers and tutors. Still, her brilliant abilities stood out as she picked up foreign languages easily and demonstrated rare musical talents. Helen loved to read, most especially from the huge library which her grandparents owned. Even then, her craving for knowledge was sometimes left unsatisfied. She read hundreds of books on alchemy, magic, and other occult sciences from the collection which her grandmother had inherited. "Soon neither Paracelsus, Kunrath, nor Cornelius Agrippa would have anything to teach me."

Still, Melle. Hahn discovered her truest senses came to life beyond books in the world of nature - forest, brook and stream, in contact with the catacombs which lay beneath the family mansion, and within her own expansive mind and imagination. From the earliest age, she owned up to a strong belief in the existence of invisible worlds of spirits which blend with the material one of daily life.

The house goblin or Domovoy was real to her as well as to her Russian nurses and maids. A Domovoy was said to be attached to every house and worked silently the year round -- most especially at night -- to watch over the household, to tend animals, and to protect the children. The Domovoy only slipped out of his disciplined role once a year on March 30. On that day, he was prone to disturb and disperse horses and cows as well as upset the entire household who then broke and dropped things and were likely to suffer injury.

Everyone in the house was subject to the Domovoy's misdeeds except for a Sedmitchka. Sedmitchka is an untranslatable Russian word connected with the number SEVEN for one being born in the Seventh month, but particularly on the night between July 30 and 31. The Day of the Sedmitchka is one which was dedicated to the mystery of a special ceremony enacted in great secrecy over the years. Nurses, maids and serfs carried the young child about and made her sprinkle the four corners of house, buildings, stables and cowpens with water while an elder repeated mystic sentences all the while.

Helen was born in the midst of *roussalka* (undine) country, being reared on the shores of the great Dnieper River. She grew up with the green-haired river nymphs nearby. Her Ukrainian nurses passed on local legends and she verified them in her own personal experiences in nature. The shores of the Dnieper which surrounded Ekaterinoslav were one of Helen's favorite places to visit and play. There she saw the roussalka inviting her to follow them. Invulnerable, willful and dynamic, she approached the shores fearlessly. The superior child abused her nurses to let her do her will and have her way on trips to the river until a tragedy occurred.

On one such trip, Helen apparently "scared the life out" of a poor serf named Pavlik. The fourteen year-old boy was dragging her carriage and seemed to incur her displeasure for which Helen told him, "I will have you tickled to death by a roussalka! There's one coming down from the tree ... here she comes...."

Pavlik took off running despite screams from the nurse, and disappeared along the route home. He was not seen alive thereafter, his body being found weeks later when caught in the net of some fisherman. The police pronounced "drowning by accident." He was thought to have been caught in a sand pit which had been created by the rapids of the Dnieper and never got out. However, the verdict of the household was of no death by accident. Nurses and servants believed that Pavlik's death resulted when the child Helen withdrew her protection from the boy and passed him on to the roussalka. The girl corroborated the charge and said that she had handed the disobedient boy over to the water nymphs.

The tragic event led the family to bring a foreign born governess onto the scene. The young English woman lasted just a few months at her job for what were surely obvious reasons. Helen and her younger sister then were sent off to live more closely with their father and to be "raised with the regiment" for some years. "It was only when roaming at leisure in the forests, or riding some unmanageable horse on a Cossack's saddle, that the girl felt perfectly happy."

At the death of their mother from consumption in 1842, the young girls passed again to the care of their grandparents. Helen's sister eventually reflected on their mother's passing and recalled her saying, "Well! Perhaps it is for the better that I am dying: at least, I will not suffer from seeing Helena's hard lot! I am quite sure that her destiny will be not womanly, that she will suffer much."

Vera Hahn (Zhelihovsky), who became an accomplished author in her own right, observed her older sister closely in that time and was able in future years to add greatly to the retelling of Helen's later childhood and adolescence. Helen was well known for her excitability of temperament, fits of passion, and rebellion against authority. At the same time, she readily displayed impulses of kindliness and affection which seemed to mitigate the major irritations caused by her lack of self-control. Sister Vera reported that "she has no malice in her nature, no lasting resentment even against those who have wronged her, and her true kindness of heart bears no permanent traces of momentary disturbances."

Their Aunt Nadya (of similar age, the young proxy at Helen's fiery baptism) also commented freely on her nervous temperament and ungirlish mischief. "She was unlike any other person. Very lively and highly gifted, full of humour, and of most remarkable daring; she struck everyone with astonishment by her self-willed and determined actions."

Helen, by many accounts, was attracted to the dead and keenly curious about the unknown and mysterious, weird and fantastic. The young woman was exuberant, imaginative, sensitive and simply an "exceptional creature." Above all, she had an uncontrollable craving for independent and free action. Outbursts of passion erupted sometimes at the slightest contradiction to her desires. The child was said to possess "the seven spirits of rebellion."

Fortunately, Melle. Hahn possessed many other gifts. Madame Pissarev wrote that, "One of her qualities which exercised a great attraction on her friends and at the same time seriously harmed her, was her well-pointed, brilliant humour, most kindly meant but sometimes ruffling to petty ambitions. Those who knew her in her earlier days remember her with delight -- unswerving, impetuous, merry, sparkling with acute humour and witty conversation. She loved to joke, to tease, to create a commotion."

Other pictures of her behavior were offered, most notably in her "alone" time. "Helen would spend hours and days quietly whispering, as people thought, to herself, and narrating, with no one near her, in some dark corner, marvelous tales of travels in bright stars and other worlds ..."

"The poor, motherless child" eventually rebelled openly against societal customs. Public opinion meant little or nothing to her. Even before her teens, she rode Cossack horses using a man's saddle! She bowed to no authority, prejudice or convention.

Helen did spread her sensitivities and sympathies to young and old alike in the working class. She was quite indifferent to the nobility to which she had been born, often preferring the company of the ragged, the stranger, the servant and his children.

Five years were spent in relative comfort and safety with her grandparents. Governesses followed governesses until Madame Peigneur took on the daunting task of guiding and guarding Helen and her sister. Mme. Peigneur dated from the first French Revolution and repeatedly described to her charges days of glory when she had been chosen by the *citoyen rouges* to act as the Goddess of Liberty at public festivals and in grand processions. Mme. Peigneur was well aged by the time of the retellings and the Hahn sisters ate up the historic repast. Helen was most taken and inevitably pronounced that she intended to be her own "Goddess of Liberty" in the days ahead.

Especially during the time of Madame Peigneur's employment did young Helen make the most of her grandparents' country dacha. The manse was said to be an "old and vast building, full of subterranean galleries, long abandoned passages, turrets, and most weird nooks and corners" and gave the overall impression of a rundown medieval castle. Mme. Peigneur, who had been governess for three generations of children in the same quarters, repeatedly told stories and legends surrounding the dacha about ghosts of martyred serfs, a young woman who was tortured for refusing advances of an old master, and other disturbed and disturbing passages in the history of the ancient villa.

The dacha, its history and layout, was one made to order for young Helen especially after the youngsters had been guided through the Catacombs with torches and lanterns by a half dozen servants. A single visit was hardly enough for Helen. The Underground was her Liberty Hall as well as a refuge from studies. Eventually it was shown that when Mademoiselle Hahn was found missing, she was likely to be discovered in the subterranean reaches of the dacha. A deputation of able-bodied serfs was sent out in search of the miscreant. On one occasion, she was found to have "erected for herself a tower out of old chairs and tables in a corner under an iron-barred window, high up in the ceiling of the vault, and there she would hide for hours, reading a book known as 'Solomon's Wisdom,' in which every kind of popular legend was taught."

According to Sister Vera, Helen was never repentant for either becoming lost or running away or causing extra work and worry for others. Fearless, she alway was. For, "she was never there alone, but in the company of 'beings' she used to call her little 'hunch-backs' and playmates."

When not otherwise occupied and yet corralled in regular quarters of the household, Helen would for hours at a time "narrate to us younger children, and even to her seniors in years, the most incredible stories with the cool assurance and conviction of an eye-witness and one who knew what she was talking about."

She was again fearless. But at times, she claimed to be "persecuted by what she called 'the terrible glaring eyes'" which were quite invisible to all else. She would run wildly from the haunting eyes. At other instances, she would be bowled over in laughing fits because of the amusing pranks of her mysterious companions.

Locks were irrelevant to Helen, she being found at numerous times sleepwalking in apartments and rooms far from the common bedroom. She became more notorious for "talking in her sleep." (See Diabolista.) During the daytime, she might be discovered in a variety of unlikely places other than the Catacombs. Once she was located in a dark loft under the high roof in the midst of pigeons' nests and quite surrounded by hundreds of the birds. Helen was occupied in "putting them to sleep" in accord with the rules of Solomon's Wisdom.

When she was not mesmerizing the pigeons, the young girl let the birds have their own say. They would coo and tell their own personal life stories to her. "For her, all nature seemed animated with a mysterious life of its own. She heard the voice of every object and form, whether organic or inorganic; and claimed consciousness and being, not only for some mysterious powers visible and audible for herself alone in what was to everyone else empty space, but even for visible but inanimate things such as pebbles, mounds and pieces of decaying phosphorescent timber."

Despite or maybe because of the young girl's persistent lone adventures, day and night time expeditions meant to add insect specimens to her grandmother's zoological collection were organized. The nocturnal versions were more exciting and mysterious, and of great charm to all involved. Vera wrote, "Our delightful travels in the neighbouring woods would last from 9 P.M. till 1, and often 2 o'clock A.M. We prepared for them with an earnestness that the Crusader may have experienced when setting out to fight the infidel and dislodge the Turk from Palestine."

Boys and girls twelve to seventeen along with dozens of young serfs set off armed with nets and lanterns. They were followed by older servants, cossacks and armed gendarmes. All in the procession were intent on the collection of the large night-butterflies which were most famous in the forests of the Volga province. The insects soon covered the lantern glasses then to have their lives extinguished by long pins stuck into cork tombs.

But, nothing was simple when Helen was near. She protested and protected from death the dark butterflies known as *sphynxes* which had dark fur-covered heads and bodies which bore the distinct images of a white human skull. Indignantly, Helen tried to make it clear to her brethren that, "Nature having imprinted on each of them the portrait of the skull of some great dead hero, these butterflies are sacred, and must not be killed."

At other times, day trips were taken to a wide sandy tract of land about ten kilometers from the family's villa. It gave the decided appearance of what was once the bottom of a sea or great lake revealing petrified relics of its former inhabitants. This spot was a perfect stage for Helen to unroll countless stories of the antediluvian times. "She never spoke in later years as she used to speak in her childhood and early girlhood.... She had a strong power of carrying away her audiences, with her, of making them see actually, if even vaguely, that which she saw."

Vera well remembered Sister Helen stretched out on the ground with her elbows in the sand and her chin in her palms. She would orate vividly and palpably about the former submarine life that once filled a watery world. Helen added drawings in the sand to vitalize the massive sea monsters. The young girl brought back to life for a few moments the marvelous colors of plants and animals of far distant times.

"Once she frightened all of us youngsters very nearly into fits. We had just been transported into a fairy world, when suddenly she changed her narrative from the past to the present tense, and began to ask us to imagine that all that which she told us of the cool blue waves with their dense populations, was around us, only invisible and intangible so far.... 'Just fancy! A miracle!' she said, 'the earth suddenly opening, the air condensing around us and rebecoming sea waves.... Look, look.... There, they begin already appearing and moving. We are surrounded with water we are right amid the mysteries and the wonders of a submarine world...'

"She had started from the sand, and was speaking with such conviction, her voice had such a ring of real amazement, horror, and her childish face wore such a look of a wild joy and terror at the same time, than when, suddenly covering her eyes with both hands, as she used to do in her excited moments, she fell down on the sand, screaming at the top of her voice, 'There's the wave ... it has come!... The sea, the sea, we are drowning!' Every one of us fell down on our faces, as desperately screaming and as fully convinced that the sea had engulphed us, and that we were no more!"

Recounting tales was not limited to strolls or expeditions. They were really more common at twilight in the midst of grandmother's large, dark and imposing museum. Helen drew the youngsters into her net and kept them spellbound with one weird story after another. Many were adventure stories of which she was the obvious heroine. All of the stuffed animals in the museum played their parts. Having taken her into their confidence, the creatures had revealed to her the histories of their previous incarnations.

"Yet, she would stretch herself on her favourite animal, a gigantic stuffed seal, and caressing its silvery, soft white skin, she would repeat to us his adventures as told to her by himself, in such glowing colours and eloquent style, that even grown up persons found themselves interested involuntarily in her narratives. They all listened to, and were carried away by the charm of her recitals, the younger audience believed every word she uttered."

Young Helen dearly loved to tell and dramatize stories, but she was possibly even more fond of listening to fairy tales retold by others. An old woman servant in the Fadeyev family was famous for her tales. She recounted adventures of Ivan Zarewitch, Kashtey the Immortal, Gray Wolf the wicked magician, Fair Princess Meltressa. Most of the youngsters forgot the stories as quickly as they were told. But, Helen neither forgot them nor saw them as fictions. She took them to heart and considered those wonderful adventures as a matter of natural life.

"People could change into animals and take any form they liked, if they only knew how; men could fly, if they only wished so firmly. Such wise men had existed in all ages, and existed even in our own days, she assured us, making themselves known, of course, only to those who were worthy of knowing and seeing them, and who believed in, instead of laughing at them."

To prove her point - one which she carried all her days, Helen singled out the centenarian sorcerer and seer who lived in a ravine in the neighboring forest to be her friend and mentor. Locals knew Baranig Bouyrak as a benevolent helper who was said to cure all in need who applied to him. But, it was also told that he punished sinners with disease. Bouyrak was a self-taught botanist and beekeeper. Like Helen, he communicated with his plant, animal and insect friends. "Evidently, the golden-winged labourers and their centenarian master understood each other's language."

Helen was convinced of the sorcerer's abilities. Bouyrak was equally taken by his young protegee who visited his fairy kingdom and earnestly questioned him about the language of birds and bees and animals. Sister Vera reported that the 'wise man' constantly told onlookers that, "This little lady is quite different from all of you. There are great events lying in wait for her in the future. I feel sorry in thinking that I will not live to see my predictions of her verified; but they will all come to pass!"

Helen's earliest recollections also included visions of a mature guardian. His imposing appearance dominated her imagination, seeing "... the majestic figure of a Hindu in a white turban, always one and the same. She knew him as well as she knew her own relatives, and called him her Protector, saying that it was He who saved her in dangers." He never seemed to leave her unattended.

Over the years, Helen was wont to repeat a telling story about a curious portrait of one of her ancestors which was always covered by a curtain in her grandparents' castle in Saratov. It was hung high above the floor in a large room. Though small at the time, the little Hahn was determined to see the picture for herself even after being denied permission to do so.

When occasion allowed, Helen "dragged a table to the wall, and contrived to set another small table on that, and a chair on the top of all, and then gradually succeeded in mounting up on this unstable edifice. She could just manage to reach the picture from this point of vantage, and leaning with one hand against the dusty wall, contrived with the other to draw back the curtain. The effect wrought upon her by the sight of the picture was startling, and the momentary movement back upset her frail platform. But exactly what occurred she did not know. She lost consciousness from the moment she staggered and began to fall, and when she recovered her sense she was lying quite unhurt on the floor, the tables and chairs were back again in their usual places, the curtain had been run back upon its rings, and she would have imagined the whole incident some unusual kind of dream but for the fact that the mark of her small hand remained imprinted on the dusty wall high up beside the picture."

There were other moments when Helen's young life was endangered but she seems to have been saved under unusual circumstances. As when nearing the age of fourteen, a horse bolted from under her. She lost control and thought she might have been killed when her foot became entangled in the stirrup. Until the horse was halted, "a strange sustaining power she distinctly felt around her ... seemed to hold her up in defiance of gravity."

Helen Hahn's childhood was practically a picture of her whole life. She was born as the Seven Numbered One and passed her youth as a prodigy. She carried amazing talents from birth and accepted little restraint so as to develop them in extraordinary ways. Signs of the entirely unique life to come were marked for all around her to see.

From her earliest days, Helen Hahn lived in multiple worlds. She communicated with living and non-living creatures and talked incessantly with invisible companions while being cloaked in the aura of a secret protector. Little Helen was born with mediumistic powers and was guided by advanced beings.

Helen searched the worlds around her and was ready to follow the decidedly unusual paths appropriate for a Sedmitchka.

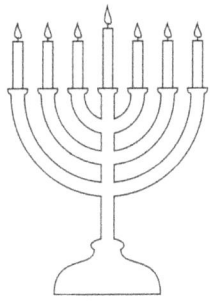

Explorador
(Romanian for Explorer)

"I was in search of the unknown."

In later life, Madame Helen exposed her awesome, steely nature in this brief story from her youth: "I hate dress, finery, and civilized society, I despise a ball room, and how much I despise it will be proved to you by the following fact. When hardly sixteen, I was being forced one day to go to a dancing party, a great ball at the Viceroy's. My protests were not listened to, and my parents told me that they would have me dressed up, or rather according to fashion, undressed for the ball by the servants by force if I did not go willingly. I then deliberately plunged my foot and leg into a kettle of boiling water, and held it there till nearly boiled raw. Of course I scalded it horribly, and remained lame for six months. But I was never forced to go to a ball again. I tell you, that there is nothing of the woman in me."

Woman or not, Helen grew up with advantages which only a few Russians of the time knew. She seemed to lack little in her upbringing beyond the presence of her mother who died when Helen was only eleven years old. Mademoiselle Hahn had ancestry and income, servants and opportunities far beyond the ordinary. Even before reaching her adult years, she saw much of Russia and Central Asia, and also traveled with her father in France, Germany and England. Helen also had the comforts and complications of "attention from the unseen worlds."

The Hahn daughter lived many lives in her singular time on Earth in the 19th century. She was born again and again in a host of ways. Helen's first rebirth occurred in her latter teen years through the rather unlikely means of marrying a much older gentleman -- "thrice her age." (Actually, her husband was little more than twice -- born 1809 -- as old as his young wife.)

Betrothed in the winter, Helen tried to run away from home the next spring. Nonetheless, marriage followed to Nikifor Blavatsky on July 7, 1849 near Tiflis, Georgia. Blavatsky was born into the landed gentry and held a variety of government jobs until he retired from his positions to return to his small estate when aged 55.

According to her Aunt Nadya, Helen's governess, disturbed with her irascible disposition, defied the rebellious girl to find any man who would be her husband. "Even that old man you find so ugly and laugh at so much, 'the plumeless raven,' would refuse you as his wife." Within three days, Helen made that old man propose. The young woman, however, believed that she would be able to "disengage" herself as easily as she had become "engaged."

An alternate version to Helen's taking up with an "old man," which was told in a biographical sketch by Helena Pissarev, relates directly to her occult interests. Young Helen had made the acquaintance of Prince Galitzin who was both a Mason and a magician. He visited her grandparents' home in Tiflis and joined her in long conversations on subjects of mutual interest. The family feared she would run off with Galitzin and therefore arranged her marriage to Blavatsky. Helen acceded to their wishes believing she would be freed from family restraint and be able to strike out on her own soon after her wedding.

Engagement to an "elder" gentleman made more sense to Helen than to accept a proposal from a young man who would have had more expectations of the marital bond. She had acted quite intolerably to all reasonable suitors other than Blavatsky prior to her marriage.

Inevitably, Helen found herself frightened at what she had done and sought a way out. She had accepted a proposal from a man for whom she cared not at all, even hated. She was to be tied to him by the law of the land. A creeping horror came upon her even while she was being impressed with the solemnity of her marriage, her obligations and duties to her soon-to-be husband. The engagement forced a tense wedding which surely gave hints of things to come.

Aunt Nadya recalled how, "A few hours later, at the altar, she heard the priest saying to her: -- 'Thou shalt honour and obey thy husband,' and at this hated word, 'shalt,' her young face ... was seen to flush angrily, then to become deadly pale. She was overheard to mutter in response, through her set teeth 'Surely, I shall not!'

"And surely she has not. Forthwith she determined to take the law and her future life into her own hands, and -- she left her 'husband' for ever, without giving him any opportunity to ever even think of her as his wife."

The whole stories of Helena Hahn's marriage to Blavatsky (and a second one to Betanelly in America) have never been told. However, two things seem to be certain. Becoming Madame Helena Petrovna Blavatsky made it much easier for her to travel the world as a "single" woman on the road. Helena's new name also fit with the powerful nature of her personality. Both H.P.B. and Mme. Blavatsky are much more potent than H.P.H. and Melle. Hahn.

Helena left with her new husband on the same day as the wedding for a mountain resort near Yerevan, Armenia. Not wanting to be anybody's wife anywhere, she attempted another escape from the honeymoon trip but without success.

Despite being an accomplished horsewoman, she was unable to get away. Still, Mme. Blavatsky's horseback riding around Mount Ararat became an important part of that period of her life. She was then accompanied by a Kurdish tribal chief named Safar Ali Bek, who was detailed as her personal escort. Bek is said to have saved her life on one or more occasions.

Helena may have spent more time in the Kurd's company than in that of her husband. Regardless, she firmly insisted that the marriage was never consummated. Helena eventually claimed, with medical certificates as proof, that she remained virginal her whole life. One of her Teachers described H.P.B. as a "Chaste and pure soul -- pearl shut inside an outwardly coarse nature."

Helena eventually did leave her husband on horseback for Tiflis in October to rejoin her relatives. They determined to send her to her father who at the time was living near St. Petersburg after he remarried. Colonel Hahn was to meet her at Odessa. Helena was sent off with two servants to catch the steamer at Poti on the Black Sea. But then, the new Madame Blavatsky contrived to miss the boat. Instead, she boarded the English vessel SS Commodore and took passage for Kerch in the Crimea. At Kerch, Helena sent her servants ashore to prepare for landing the following morning. In the night, she slipped away on the steamer for Constantinople.

At that point, H.P.B. began many years of wandering all over the world. Globetrotting like few have done in any time period. Young Mme. Blavatsky traveled by horseback and simple carriages as well as crude vessel and basic rail transport. Often a lone WOMAN in man's clothing! Attempts have been made to trace her far journeys and "craving for the outlandish." But, gaps and contradictions are common in the history of those treks. Sometimes, mere fragments of her early travels were given out because much of what she experienced was "too sacred to be revealed."

"Then from 17 to 40 I took care during my travels to sweep away all traces of myself wherever I went. When I was at Barri in Italy studying with a local witch -- I sent my letters to Paris to post them from there to my relatives. The only letter they received from me from India was when I was leaving it, the first time. Then from Madras in

1857; -- when I was in South America I wrote to them through, and posted in London. I never allowed people to know where I was and what I was doing. Had I been a common p----- they would have preferred it to my studying occultism. It is only when I returned home that I told my aunt that the letter received from K.H. by her was no letter from a Spirit as she thought. When she got the proofs that they were living men she regarded them as devils or sold to Satan." (See below under 1870.)

1850 - Helena traveled in Greece, Eastern Europe, Egypt and Asia Minor, probably in the company of Countess Kisselev for part of the time. "So I was in Egypt with the old Countess who liked to see me dressed as a man student, 'gentleman student' she said. Now you understand my difficulties? That which would pass with any other as eccentricity, oddity, would serve now only to incriminate me in the eyes of the world." H.P.B. met and studied at Cairo with the Copt occultist, Paulos Metamon, during the year. Her life was saved -- again -- in Greece by the Irishman Johnny O'Brien.

Helena was for a time in Paris and London - with Princess Bagration-Muhransky - as well as making short tours on the Continent. Later while traveling with her father, she saw her Master for the first time (in the physical) on her 20th birthday in London. The "tall Hindu in the street with some Indian princes" met with her on two occasions and asked for the young woman's help which would require preparation of at least three years in Tibet. Helena took three days to consider the proposal before accepting. Her direct training and time with the Masters remained in the future as she left for Canada in the fall of 1851 "to study the Indians" and stayed in Quebec.

1852 - From Canada, she traveled to Nauvoo, Missouri, to investigate the Mormons. Thereafter, she continued on to New Orleans to look into Voodoo practices. Proceeding through Texas to Mexico, she encountered Pere Jacques, an old Canadian, who saw her through "some difficult moments." At this time, H.P.B. received a legacy of 80,000 rubles from "one of her godmothers" with which she bought some land in America. Inevitably, she forgot where the purchase was made and lost the related papers as well. Helena admitted at one point to having "squandered" her inheritance.

Her travels continued on as she explored Central and South America widely, visiting ancient ruins. In Copan, H.P.B. contacted a Hindu chela. She wrote of "doing business" with an old native priest and to having traveled with the Peruvian in the interior of the land.

She pressed onward to the West Indies. "A certain Englishman" of an earlier encounter and the Hindu chela joined her there. The three quested together via the Cape to Ceylon and then to India.

The group split in Bombay and H.P.B. continued on her own, "bent on Tibet" through Nepal. The attempt failed likely because of the opposition of the British Resident. Helena was stopped from crossing the Ranjit River by Captain Murray. She then stayed with Captain and Mrs. Murray for a month, departed and was heard from as far as Dinajpur. H.P.B. is said to have traveled in India "nearly two years, receiving money each month from an unknown source."

After a turn in Southern India, she passed through Java and Singapore on her way back to England. She took passage on the SS Gwalior "which was wrecked near the Cape." H.P.B. was saved - again - along with about twenty others.

1854 - Madame Blavatsky was detained in England during the Crimean War. That summer, she met her Master "in the house of a stranger in England, where he had come in the company of a dethroned native prince." In the fall, Helena carried herself back to America via New York. She traveled west to Chicago and over the Rockies to San Francisco with emigrants in a covered wagon. H.P.B. also may have spent some time in South America in that year.

In the fall of '55, she sailed for India via Japan and the Straits, landing at Calcutta. H.P.B. traveled widely throughout India. At Lahore she met a friend of her father, a German ex-Lutheran minister by the name of Kuhlwein, and his two companions. "Were I to describe my visit to India only in that year that would make a whole book, but how can I NOW say the truth. Suppose I were to tell that I was in man's clothes (for I was very thin then) which is solemn truth, what would people say?"

The four formed a plan to penetrate Tibet and journeyed together through Kashmir to Leh. Part of the time, they were accompanied by a Tartar shaman who was on his way home to Siberia. But, H.P.B. and the shaman crossed into forbidden Tibetan territory alone. The others were foiled in making their own entry.

Providing Madame Blavatsky with appropriate disguise, the shaman conducted her across the frontier into forbidden lands. The man carried mystery with him in the form of a talisman. He was repeatedly asked about it, but paid little heed. At a precarious moment in their travels, H.P.B. was rescued through the aid of the talisman and the man's psychic powers. H.P.B. recounted that story in *Isis Unveiled*.

"Of what use is it to you, and what are its virtues?" was the question we often offered to our guide. To this he never answered directly, but evaded all explanation, promising that as soon as an opportunity was offered and we were alone, he would ask the stone to answer for himself. With this very indefinite hope we were left to the resources of our own imagination.

But the day on which the stone 'spoke' came very soon. It was during the most critical hours of our life; at a time when the vagabond nature of a traveller had carried the writer to far-off lands where neither civilisation is known nor security can be guaranteed for one hour. One afternoon, as every man and woman had left the yourta (Tartar tent) that had been our house for over two months, to witness the ceremony of the Lamaic exorcism of Tshoutgour (elemental demon), accused of breaking and spiriting away every bit of the poor furniture and earthenware of a family living about two miles distant, the Shaman who had become our only protector in those dreary deserts, was reminded of his promise. He sighed and hesitated, but after a short silence, left his place on the sheepskin, and, going outside, placed a dried-up goat's head with its prominent horns over a wooden peg, and then dropping down the felt curtain of the tent, remarked that now no living person would venture in, for the goat's head was a sign that he was 'at work.'

After that, placing his hand in his bosom he drew out the little stone, about the size of a walnut, and, carefully unwrapping it, proceeded, as it appeared, to swallow it. In a few moments his limbs stiffened, his body became rigid, and he fell, cold and motionless as a corpse. But for a slight twitching of his lips at every question asked, the scene would have been embarrassing, nay dreadful. The sun was setting, and were it not that the dying embers flickered at the centre of the tent, complete darkness would have been added to the oppressive silence which reigned. We have lived in the prairies of the West, and in the boundless steppes of Southern Russia; but nothing can be compared with the silence at sunset on the sandy deserts of Mongolia; not even the barren solitudes of the deserts of Africa, though the former are partially inhabited, and the latter utterly void of life. Yet, there was the writer, alone with what looked no better than a corpse lying on the ground. Fortunately this state did not last long.

"Mahaudu!" uttered a voice which seemed to come from the bowels of the earth, on which the Shaman was prostrated. "Peace be with you. What would you have me do for you?"

Startling as the fact seemed, we were quite prepared for it, for we had seen other Shamans pass through similar performances.

"Whoever you are," we pronounced mentally, "go to K, and try to bring that person's thought here. See what that other party does, and tell what we are doing and how situated."

"I am there," announced the same voice. "The old lady (kokona) *is sitting in the garden... she is putting on her spectacles and reading a letter."*

"The contents of it, and hasten," was the hurried order, while preparing notebook and pencil. The contents were given slowly, as if, while dictating, the invisible presence desired to afford us time to put down the words phonetically, for we recognised the Vallachian language, of which we knew nothing beyond the ability to recognise it. In such a way a whole page was filled.

"Look west ... toward the third pole of the yourta," pronounced the Tartar in his natural voice, though it sounded hollow, and as if coming from afar. 'Her thought is here."

Then with a convulsive jerk the upper portion of the Shaman's body seemed raised, and his head fell heavily on the writer's feet, which he clutched with both his hands. The position was becoming less and less attractive, but curiosity proved a good ally to courage. In the west corner was standing, life-like, but flickering, unsteady, and mist-like, the form of a dear old friend, a Roumanian lady of Vallachia, a mystic by disposition, but a thorough disbeliever in this kind of occult phenomena.

"Her thought is here, but her body is lying unconscious. We could not bring her here otherwise," said the voice.

We addressed and supplicated the apparition to answer, but all in vain. The features moved and the form gesticulated as if in fear and agony, but no sound broke forth from the shadowy lips; only we imagined -- perchance it was a fancy -- hearing, as if from a long distance, the Roumanian words, "Non se pote -- It cannot be done."

For over two hours the most substantial, unequivocal proofs that the Shaman's astral soul was travelling at the bidding of our unspoken wish were given us. Ten months later, we received a letter from a Vallachian friend in response to ours, in which we had enclosed the page from the note-book, inquiring of her what she had been doing on that day, and describing the scene in full. She was sitting, she wrote, in the garden on that morning (the hour in Bucharest corresponded perfectly with that of the country in which the scene had taken place), prosaically occupied in boiling some conserves; the letter sent to her was word for word the copy of the one received by her from her brother; all at once, in consequence of the heat she thought, she fainted, and remembered distinctly dreaming she saw the writer in a desert place, which she accurately described, and sitting under a 'gipsy's tent,' as she expressed it. "Henceforth," she added, "I can doubt no longer."

But our experiment was proved better still. We had directed the Shaman's Inner Eye to the same friend heretofore mentioned in this chapter, the Kutchi of Lha-Ssa, who travels constantly to British India and back. We know that he was apprized of our critical situation in the desert; for a few hours later came help, and we were rescued by a party of twenty-five horsemen, who had been directed by their chief to find us at the place where we were, which no living man endowed with common powers could have known. The chief of this escort was a Shaberon, an 'adept,' whom we had never seen before, nor did we after that, for he never left his sotimay *(lamasary), and we could have no access to it.... But he was a personal friend of the Kutchi.*

H.P.B. is said to have made two other "unsuccessful" attempts to enter Tibet. Entrance into Tibet, Land at the Top of the World, was tenaciously protected in the 19th and early twentieth centuries from *philings.* The borders were guarded from foreigners of most any extraction, but especially blue-eyed, white-faced ones. The security was motivated for a number of reasons. China, Russia, and Britain all had geopolitical intentions for the region. The Tibetans feared for the future of their lands, in part, because of ancient prophecies about foreigners entering and destroying the Buddhist Dharma. Tibetan leaders also wanted to contain, hold and manage their feudal properties.

For generations, outsiders - adventurers, missionaries, mystics - had been trying to enter the forbidden territory which surrounded Shangri-La. Tibetans, sometimes with British intrusion or guidance, endeavored to keep the gates closed to all who would enter. In Madame's day, numbers of foreigners continued to try to bypass restrictions. But, few ever achieved noteworthy results.

Mme. Blavatsky's just cited travels on the borders of Tibet were at an end. She would be back. H.P.B. had not penetrated into the Forbidden Land, but it seems she did make contact with her Teachers and began her training and probation as a chela during this time period.

H.P.B. was returned to the Tibetan frontier by a route of which she had no previous knowledge. After more travels in India, she was directed by her guardian to leave the country before the troubles which began in India in 1857. Ever the inveterate explorer, H.P.B. traveled into Burma, Siam and Assam and contracted a "fearful fever" after flooding of the Irrawaddy River. Leaving the Indian subcontinent ahead of the Sepoy Mutiny, Helena took a Dutch vessel from Madras to Java "for a certain business."

1858 - H.P.B. journeyed to Europe traveling through France and Germany before returning to Russia in February. She appeared unexpectedly on Christmas Night at her sister's house at Rougodevo in the province of Pskov. "We embraced each other, overcome with joy ... I took her at once to my room, and that very evening I was convinced that my sister had acquired strange powers. She was constantly surrounded, awake or asleep, with mysterious movements, strange sounds, little taps which came from all sides -- from the furniture, from the window-panes, from the ceiling, from the floor, and from the walls. They were very distinct and seemed intelligent into the bargain; they tapped three times for 'yes,' twice for 'no.'" Helena stayed only a short time, but long enough for her growing powers to be recognized and produce quite a stir among the neighbors.

In the spring of 1859, she traveled with her father to St. Petersburg before going back to live with her sister in Pskov. Quiet reigned only for brief periods around Madame Blavatsky. H.P.B. suddenly succumbed to a severe illness. Her symptoms focused around a remarkable and mysterious wound she had received in the steppes of Asia. The wound was prone to re-open spontaneously. Madame then suffered intensely, sometimes leading to convulsions and a death-like trance, lasting up to four days. The ailment recurred while Helena stayed with her sister in Rougodevo. "A physician was sent for from the neighbouring town; but he proved of little use, not so much indeed through his ignorance of surgery, as owing to a remarkable phenomenon which left him almost powerless to act through sheer terror at what he had witnessed. He had hardly examined the wound of the patient prostrated before him in complete unconsciousness, when suddenly he saw a large, dark hand between his own and the wound he was going to anoint. The gaping wound was near the heart, and the hand kept slowly moving at several intervals from the neck down to the waist. To make his terror worse, there began suddenly in the room such a terrific noise, such a chaos of noises and sounds from the ceiling, the floor, window-panes, and every bit of furniture in the apartment, that he begged he might not be left alone in the room with the insensible patient."

1860 - H.P.B. departed for Tiflis with her sister to be with her grandparents for about a year. Traveling by coach, they stopped in the territory of the Cossack Army of the Don at Zadonsk, a place of pilgrimage. Vera prevailed on her "lazy sister" to attend mass to be conducted by Isidore, the Metropolitan of Kiev (one of the three "Popes" of Russia). Isidore was a long-time friend of the family and had known the sisters from their childhood.

The prelate recognized the young women at the Archi-Episcopal Church and sent a monk to invite them for a visit after the service. They barely had made their entrance into the drawing room of the Holy Metropolitan when "a terrible hubbub, noises, and loud raps in every conceivable direction burst suddenly upon us with a force to which even we were hardly accustomed: every bit of furniture in the big audience-room cracked and thumped -- from the huge chandelier under the ceiling, every one of whose crystal drops seemed to become endowed with self-motion, down to the table, and under the very elbows of his holiness, who was leaning on it."

While Vera was confused and embarrassed, Helena smirked and held back laughing aloud. But the Metropolitan Isidore was shrewd as well as courteous. He "knew" what was going on, having read about "spiritual manifestations." When he saw a huge arm chair glide toward him, he could but smile.

Isidore expressed his interest in the phenomena and asked, "Which one of you is responsible? I must know when and how you have come to these powers?"

Helena admitted her "guilt" and explained as much as she could under the circumstances. The Metropolitan listened closely then asked, "Will you permit me to offer your 'invisible' a mental question?"

The query received a precise and pointed answer at which the holy man was amazed. He became anxious and even more interested in Helena's abilities. He detained the young women for more than three hours. The Metropolitan forgot all about his dinner and gave orders not to be disturbed. He was entirely astonished by the *vsezna'isivo* (all-knowledge) of the unseen presences.

When the women departed, the Venerable Isidore blessed them on their journey. He turned to H.P.B. and addressed her in this way: "As for you, let not your heart be troubled by the gift you are possessed of, nor let it become a source of misery to you hereafter, for it was surely given to you for some purpose, and you could not be held responsible for it. Quite the reverse! For if you but use it with discrimination, you will be enabled to do much good to your fellow creatures."

During her time in Tiflis, H.P.B. became somewhat reconciled with Nikifor Blavatsky while living for a year or so with her grandfather. Still, in later years, she referred to him as her "hated husband."

1863 - Helena left Tiflis for a while to Zugdidi and Kutais, Georgia, eventually returning to Tiflis again to live for another year with her grandfather. During these years, H.P.B. traveled and lived for periods in Imeretia, Guriya and Mingrelia, in the forests of Abkhasia, and along the Black Sea Coast. She studied with native *kudyani,* or magicians, and became widely known for her healing powers. She is said to have bought a house in Mingrelia and engaged in commercial enterprises, floating lumber and exporting nut-tree-spunk.

While at Ozurgety, Helena developed another severe illness and was apparently near death when ordered by the local physician to be taken in a native boat down the river Rion to Kutais. (See Diabolista.) She was then transported in a carriage to Tiflis. Soon after, she experienced another sudden cure. Like others of her ailments, this one seemed to be of an occult nature as there was said to have been an "unbridgeable gulf" between H.P.B. before and after 1865.

1865 - In those years, H.P.B. was always traveling, traveling. She rarely settled for any length of time. Passing through Italy, she journeyed in the Balkans, Serbia, and the Carpathian Mountains. Later, she went to Greece and Egypt as well as Syria, Lebanon and Persia. She wandered with Bedouin Arabs and sat with the Marabout of Damascus. During this time, she danced with Dervishes, became a member of the secretive Druzes of Mt. Lebanon and took other mystic orders of Asia Minor. She admitted to "studying with a witch" while in Italy and learned of necromancy, astrology, crystal gazing, spiritualism but "encountered not the Red Virgin."

1867 - H.P.B. amazingly appeared in settings of war and conflict. She was at Belgrade when the Turkish garrison yielded to Austro-Hungary and the commander, Al Rezi Pasha, withdrew from Serbian territory on April 13, 1867. H.P.B. traveled by boat on the Danube, and by coach between various towns of Hungary and Transylvania.

After her time in the Balkan states, she journeyed to Venice and was present at the Battle of Mentana, November 2, 1867. Madame was generally quiet on the subject of her involvement in the Second War of Italian Independence. But, she did tell the Corson family (next chapter) that she slept in the Pontine marshes and fought with the Italian volunteers of Giuseppe Garibaldi. Garibaldi was known as "The Hero of Two Worlds" for his efforts to unify Italy and extract Rome from the hands of French-Papal forces. General Garibaldi was defeated and also wounded in the Battle of Mentana. During that same engagement, H.P.B. suffered five of her own wounds. Her left arm was broken in two places by the stroke of a saber. She had musket bullets imbedded in her right shoulder and another in her leg. But, nothing seemed to hold H.P.B. back for very long. Not even five battle scars and a mystery wound at her heart.

1868 - At the beginning of the year, Helena traveled through Florence and Constantinople en route to India. She spent time again in the Carpathian Mountains and in Serbia before returning through Constantinople. H.P.B. went on to India which was then her pathway to various parts of Tibet, including Shigatse, the Kuenlun and Karakorum Mountains, and time with the Masters. Details of this very important period of her life are lacking and surely for a purpose. H.P.B., however in later years, did emphatically synopsize her time in the Himalayas. "... I have lived at different periods in Little Tibet as in Great Tibet, and ... these combined periods form more than seven years ... What I have said, and repeat now, is, that I have stopped in Lamaistic convents; that I have visited Tzi-gadze [Shigatse], the Tashi-Lhünpo territory and its neighbourhood, and that I have been further in, and in such places of Tibet as have never been visited by any other European, and that he can ever hope to visit."

In later years, Major Cross of the British Army was able to certify Madame Blavatsky's Tibetan travels in that period. For, he had traced "the progress of a white woman" through difficult country to a lamasery in the far north and identified her as Helena Blavatsky. Aunt Nadya also was able to put her stamp of approval to Madame's claim to be in the Himalayas.

1870 - She, who early on regarded Helena's Masters as devils, much later wrote about "a certain note, received by me phenomenally when my niece was at the other side of the world, and not a soul knew where she was -- which grieved us greatly. All our researches had ended in nothing. We were ready to believe her dead, when -- I think it was about the year 1870, or possibly later -- I received a letter from him, whom I believe you call 'K.H.,' which was brought to me in the most incomprehensible and mysterious manner, by a messenger of Asiatic appearance, who then disappeared before my very eyes. This letter, which begged me not to fear anything, and which announced that she was in safety - I have still at Odessa."

The note to Nadya was written upon brittle Chinese rice-paper, backed with glassy Kashmiri hand-made paper, and enclosed in a similar envelope. It was addressed "To the Honorable, Very Honorable Lady Nadejda Andriewna Fadeeff, Odessa," and received on November 11, 1870. The brief letter says, "The noble relatives of Madame H. Blavatsky have no cause to mourn. Their daughter and niece has not departed from this world. She lives and wishes to make known to those she loves, that she is well and feels very happy in the distant and unknown retreat that she has chosen.... Let the ladies of her family comfort themselves. Before 18 new moons have risen, she will have returned to her home."

Helena began her return to Europe via the Suez Canal in December 1870 stopping in Cyprus and Greece. Then embarked for Egypt at the port of Piraeus (Athens), on the SS Eunomia. Protecting against pirates in those days, ships were provided with guns and gunpowder. But protection is not always safe. Plying between the islands of Dokos and Hydra, the ship's powder magazine blew up on July 4, 1871, with wholesale loss of life. H.P.B., however, was uninjured.

Survivors (sixteen of 400 original passengers) were conducted to their intended destination. H.P.B. eventually reached Alexandria with few means of her own. She won some money, however, on what she called "No. 27" and moved on to Cairo where she stayed until April 1872. Madame was aided at the time by Emma Cutting (later Coulomb) who eventually became an "important" figure in her life. During her time in Cairo, Helena attempted to organize what she called the Societe Spirite. It failed quickly and dramatically.

H.P.B. continued on to Syria, Palestine and Constantinople. She also spent time at Palmyra and went on to Dair Mar Maroon which lay between the Lebanon and the Anti Lebanon Mountains.

Helena reached Odessa and her family in July 1872, which figured to be some "18 moons" after the receipt of K.H.'s letter. There are suggestions that she opened an ink factory and artificial flower shop at Odessa during her stay. More surely, H.P.B. made a piano-playing tour in Russia and Europe as "Madame Laura" during 1872-73.

1873 - She left Odessa in April going first to Bucharest and proceeding on to Paris, staying with a cousin. To some, H.P.B. appeared to be almost "settled" as she spent her time in painting and writing, and establishing friendships and ties.

But suddenly, H.P.B. "received orders" to go to New York. Her voyage to America was made not only precipitately but also uncomfortably as she ended up traveling below decks in steerage. (See Baba.) Arriving in New York City on July 7, 1873, short of money, she took up residence in a new tenement house on Madison Street, an experiment in cooperative living launched by some forty women workers. Helena was soon designing illustrated advertising-cards and doing ornamental leather work to pay her way. Before long, she abandoned those trades and moved on to making artificial flowers for a "kindhearted Hebrew" shop-keeper. Within months, H.P.B. was drawn into her life's real work.

Though most of her sailing and galavanting days were over, H.P. Blavatsky could lay claim to be a grand world traveler. She had by the age of 42 circled the globe three times unaccompanied.

Still, the year 1873 hardly saw the end of her world travels. Vera Zhelihovsky remembered, "All her life was passed in restlessness and in travelling; she was ever, as it were, seeking some unknown goal, some task which it was her duty to discover and to fulfil. Her wandering life and unsettled ways did not end until she found herself face to face with the scientific, the humanitarian and spiritual problems presented by Theosophy; then she stopped short, like a ship which after years of wanderings finds itself safe in port, the sails are furled and for the last time the anchor is let go."

Diabolista
(Italian for Medium)

"Spiritualism, in the hands of an adept, becomes Magic ...
In the hands of an inexperienced medium, Spiritualism becomes
UNCONSCIOUS SORCERY."

From age eight until fifteen, young Helena entertained the spirit of an old German woman by the name of Tekla Lebendorff "who came every night to write through me, in the presence of my father, aunts and many other people.... She gave a detailed account of her life, stated where she was born, how she married, and gave the history of all her children ..." as well as the long romance of her daughter and the suicide of her son.

Over that period of time, ten volumes of material in peculiar handwriting and grammar came through H.P.B. They were scribed in old-fashioned German, a language foreign to the young girl. The manifestations were all quite impressive, but not what they appeared to be.

H.P.B. was a medium and she was not, as this narrative will show. She readily admitted to having "unfortunately passed at one period of life personally through such (mediumistic) experiences." Helena was well known to have "played with spooks," "danced with demons," and "followed the will o' the wisp." This propensity set her apart and stretched her boundaries in many directions. It also had stressed her family, household servants, and others to keep tabs on her.

But, those early psychic faculties were merely in developmental stages during her childhood and adolescence. When she returned to Russia in 1858 after almost ten years of worldly travels, Helena produced many more phenomena to the wonder of all those around her. According to Sister Vera, her time particularly in Tibet taught her about "mediumistic phenomena ... caused by quite another agency than that of *spirits*; mediumship proceeding, they say, from a source, to draw from which, my sister thinks it degrading to her human dignity; in consequence of which ideas she refuses to acknowledge such a force in herself. From letters received by me from my sister, I found she had been dissatisfied with much that I had said of her in my 'Truth about H.P. Blavatsky.' She still maintains, now as then, that in those days (of 1860) she was influenced as well as she is now by quite another kind of power, -- namely, that of the Indian sages, the Raj-Yogis, -- and that even the shadows (figures) she sees all her life are no phantoms, no ghosts of the deceased, but only the manifestations of her powerful friends in their astral envelopes. However it may be, and whatever the power that produced her phenomena only, during the whole time that she lived with us at the Yahontoffs, such phenomena happened constantly before the eyes of all -- believers and unbelievers (relatives and outsiders) -- and they plunged everyone equally into amazement."

Helena seemed to turn the whole Pskov countryside (where Vera lived) upside down with the help of her spooks (*kikimorey*). The phenomena demonstrated to her friends, family and neighbors were generally far beyond simple rappings, noises and untimely intrusions of previous years. H.P.B. showed them that she could quite easily read minds and penetrate thoughts and memories of bygone days. Fashionable visitors began to appear in hope of tasting the "psychic cuisine" and usually went away satisfied.

Initially, Helena responded to questions by answering via raps. (For some unstated reason, she decided to communicate through that simple method rather than verbal or handwritten messaging which she had used in earlier years and at other places.) The responses occasionally turned into discourses sometimes in languages other than Russian and even ones said to be unknown to the "poor medium." H.P.B. submitted to all kinds of tests, however absurd they sometimes appeared.

Much of the time, Helena embroidered while sitting on the sofa or in an arm chair and seemed to take little interest in the "psychic activity" around her. One person offered a question, another recited the alphabet while waiting for a rap, while still another wrote down answers as they were sounded out. Sometimes, even unspoken queries received quite unexpected responses.

There were times when mistrust and doubts arose, but Sister Vera insisted that Madame Blavatsky handled such moments patiently and nonchalantly. She accepted skeptics and challengers as easily as fawners. Helena even allowed herself to be searched, have her hands and feet tied or held fast under pillows. Then, she produced rappings at the other end of the room, on the ceiling, on window sills, and on pieces of furniture in nearby rooms.

But, H.P.B. sometimes got revenge on her doubters. She once projected raps into the eyeglasses of a young professor while sitting at the opposite end of the room. The fellow's glasses were nearly knocked off his nose and made him blanch in fear.

A prim and proper lady asked, "What is the best conductor for these raps that you do? Are there any limits on where they can be done?"

"Gold," was soon rapped out, followed by, "We prove it to you immediately."

Hardly had the answer been given out when the woman became quite pale, jumped out of her chair, and wrapped her hand around her mouth. She then was convulsed with both fear and astonishment and raced out of the room. There was a gale of laughter shared at her expense. Long before the mortified woman's eventual confession, all around her had understood that the lady had felt raps in the gold of her artificial teeth!

Sister Vera recalled the numerous gifts which Helena displayed in that time period to include "thought-reading" - direct written answers to mental questions; prescriptions (in Latin) for diseases with eventual cures; divulgence of private secrets; instant changes in weights of furniture and of persons; appearance (*apports*) of objects unknown and unclaimed by anyone; musical sounds projected into the air wherever desired; letters with answers to queries appearing in mysterious places.

"A governess, named Leontine, who wanted to know the fate of a certain young man, she had hoped to be married to, learnt what had become of him; his name, that she had purposely withheld, being given in full -- from a letter written in an unknown handwriting she found in one of her locked boxes, placed inside a trunk equally locked."

An incident involving their brother Leonide helped to solidify Helena's standing in her own family. The young, muscular and independent university student listened in at one point to H.P.B. telling about how mediums could make heavy objects light as well as reverse the process turning light ones into substantial pieces.

Leonide asked his sister, "And you mean to say that you can do it?"

"Mediums can, and I have done it occasionally; though I cannot always answer for its success," replied Madame.

"But would you try?" came the call from several in the room.

"I will try," she said, "but I beg of you to remember that I promise nothing. I will simply fix this chess-table, and try.... He who wants to make the experiment, let him lift it now, and then try again after I shall have fixed it."

"After you shall have fixed it?" said a voice, "And what then? Do you mean to say that you will not touch the table at all?"

"Why should I touch it?" answered Mme. Blavatsky, with a smile.

One of the young men in attendance went over to the small chess-table lifting it as it were light as a feather.

"All right," she said. "Now kindly leave it alone, and stand back!"

The order was obeyed and a silence fell upon the company. All held their breath watching for H.P.B.'s next movement. But, she seemed to do nothing at all. She just fixed her big eyes upon the table and kept looking at it with an intense gaze. Then without removing her gaze, she motioned to the same young man to remove it. He approached and grasped the table with one hand and proceeded to lift it ... But, the table would not be moved!

He then took it with both his hands and gave it a yank. The table stood as though screwed to the floor.

Then the young man crouched down using all the strength of his broad shoulders to lift. His face turned red as he grimaced and groaned in exasperation. But his efforts were in vain! The table acted as if rooted to the carpet and would not be moved. Applause burst through the crowd of watchers. The confused and exasperated young man abandoned his job and stood aside.

He folded his arms, elbows akimbo and slowly spewed forth, "Well, this is a good joke!"

"Indeed, it is a good one!" echoed Brother Leonide who suspected that the young visitor of acting as a secret confederate for his sister.

"May I give it a try?" he suddenly asked Helena.

"Please do, my dear," was her snickering response.

Leonide then approached and seized the little table by its leg with his strong arm. But the smile quickly disappeared giving place to an expression of dumb amazement. He stepped back a bit and re-examined the suspicious chess table. Then he walloped it with his foot, but the little table would not budge.

In a fit, he put his whole powerful chest and arms to work, trying to shake it. The wood cracked, but the table stood in place as if screwed to the floor. Abandoning the innocent table and stepping aside with a frown, he exclaimed but two words, "How strange!" He then turned with an expression of astonishment toward his sister.

Many others in the group followed suit and tried to lift or simply budge the obstinate little chess table. They all failed.

Upon seeing her brother's astonishment, and desiring to destroy any final doubts, Mme. Blavatsky addressed him with a muffled laugh, "Try to lift the table now, one more time!"

Leonide approached the little thing with disdain and pulled with a quick tug. The table came up like a feather and almost dislocated his arm because of his excessive effort.

Helena had gotten her brother's attention and some level of credulity. That left her father as the lone disbeliever. But, change eventually came on a trip to Saint Petersburg. Colonel Hahn and his daughters stayed in a hotel while attending business related to Vera's property in Pskov.

One evening they were visited by two friends of their father. Both were old gentlemen, Baron M. and Mr. K.W. Both were interested in mediumship and anxious to see Helena produce something unusual.

After a few phenomena were demonstrated, the visitors admitted to being positively delighted and amazed. They were quite at a loss what to make of Madame's powers. Neither could they account for her father's indifference in the presence of such manifestations. He persisted in playing Patience (cards) while seemingly wonderful phenomena were taking place around him. The old man was taken to task and responded in turn.

"Why it's all bosh! I would rather not hear of such nonsense. My daughter spends much too much time on these things which are frivolous and hardly worthy of serious people. At least, it is to my mind."

The other gentlemen insisted that Colonel Hahn should, for old friendship's sake, join in their experiments before totally denying the possibility of his daughter's abilities. They asked him to test the intelligences by writing a word in another room, secret from everyone. Then, he was to request the powers to reveal it to them.

Expecting a hearty laugh and the chance to "get" his old mates, Peter gave in and consented to the experiment. He put up his cards and went into an adjoining room. There he deliberated and wrote a word on a piece of paper. He placed the paper in his pocket and returned to his Patience. He waited silently, smiling behind his gray moustache.

"What shall you say, old friend, if the word written by you is correctly repeated? Will you not feel compelled to believe in such a case?" asked the Baron on the Colonel's return.

"What I might say, if the word were correctly guessed, I could not tell at present. One thing I could answer, however, from the time I can be made to believe your alleged spiritism and its phenomena, I shall be ready to believe in the existence of the devil, undines, sorcerers, and witches -- in the whole paraphernalia -- in short, of old women's superstitions; and you may prepare to offer me as an inmate of a lunatic asylum."

He returned again to his cards. The rest of the retinue began to listen to the loud and persistent raps coming from a plate brought out for the purpose. Vera went through the alphabet, the letters were marked down. Mme. Blavatsky did nothing at all. Or, so it seemed.

The group, less the old man, were filled with expectations of a complicated sentence or at least something with the appearance of import. When a single word was repeated, everyone around the table became doubtful. They wondered whether it should be read aloud. Further questioning was made with affirmative sounds fitting the present code. "Yes! yes, yes, yes!!!"

Colonel arose and approached the group, "Well! Have you any answer? It must be something very elaborate and profound indeed."

Vera sheepishly replied, "We only got one word, Father."

"And what is it?"

"Zaitchik."

A wave passed over the old man's face at the single word! He turned pale. His hand trembled as he adjusted his spectacles. Then, he stretched his limb forward, saying, "Let me see it! Hand it over. Is it really so?"

He caressed the paper and read in an agitated voice, "Zaitchik. Yes, zaitchik; so it is. How very strange!" He then removed from his pocket the paper upon which he had written in the adjoining room. He handed it over in silence to his daughter and guests.

They found on it the question offered and the anticipated answer: "What was the name of my favourite war-horse which I rode during my first Turkish campaign?" Lower down, in parenthesis was written "Zaitchik."

Everyone was thrilled, most especially the old officer. The single word, Zaitchik (little rabbit), had an enormous effect upon the old gentleman. After being so long a skeptic, he had to conclude that there was indeed something in his elder daughter's claims. Convinced of this lone fact, he proceeded into the realm of phenomena with ardent zeal.

Peter Hahn soon began to experiment with his daughter's powers. Genealogy became his chief focus after inquiring and receiving the date of an event in his family history hundreds of years past. Thence, he set himself and his daughter to the task of restoring the family chronology. The Hahn genealogical tree had been lost in the darkness of the first crusades. "It must be restored."

First, the legend of Count von Rottenstern, the Knight Crusader, was given. Then followed a series of figures, dates of years and months, hundreds of names by connection and side marriages, in the long line of descent from the Knight Crusaders down to contemporary events which had occurred relevant to family history. They were given rapidly and unhesitatingly.

There were many missing links in their genealogical tables. But, the few documents that had been preserved among the various branches of the family in Germany and Russia corroborated details furnished through Mme. Blavatsky's helpers. The "invisibles" were never found to make a mistake.

During the course of one of their lengthy "investigations," the superintendent of the district police passed through Vera's village. He stopped to make inquiries related to a murder committed not far from her property. A man had been found killed in a gin shop.

The question arose as to why the police-superintendent should not seek the name and whereabouts of the murderer from her sister's invisible agents. The officer smiled incredulously and shrugged his shoulders. He was ready to bet that those "horned and hoofed gentlemen" would prove insufficient for such a task.

"They would hardly betray and inform against their own kind."

That seemed to be a slap at Madame's invisible "powers." H.P.B.'s color changed as she felt the impulse to "humble the ignorant fool, who hardly knew what he was talking about."

She rose up retorting, "And suppose I prove to you the contrary?"

"Then, I would resign my office, and offer it to you, Madame; or, still better, I would strongly urge the authorities to place you at the head of the Secret Police Department."

"Now, look here, Captain. I do not like meddling in such a dirty business, and helping you detectives. Yet, since you defy me, let my father say over the alphabet, and you put down the letters, and record what will be rapped out. My presence is not needed for this, and with your permission I will even leave the room." Helena retreated to the balcony with a book, seeming unconcerned about the details.

Colonel Hahn was keen to make a convert and began repeating the letters of the alphabet. The communication gave the name of Samoylo Ivanof as the murderer and told that he had crossed over to the next district before daylight. "He is hiding under a bundle of hay in the loft of a peasant, named Andrew Vlassoff, of the village of Oreshkino. Go there immediately to secure the criminal."

The Stanovoy (district officer) was shaken. He admitted that Oreshkino was a likely spot for the culprit to be hiding. "Allow me, however, to enquire, how come you -- whoever you are -- can know anything of the murderer's name, or of that of the confederate who hides him in his loft? And who is Vlassof, for I know him not?"

The answer was clear and condescending. "Very likely that you should neither know nor see much beyond your own nose. We, however, who are now giving you the information, have the means of knowing everything we wish to know. Samoylo Ivanof is an old soldier on leave. He was drunk, and quarrelled with the victim. The murder was not premeditated; it is a misfortune, not a crime."

The superintendent rushed out of the house and raced towards Oreshkino, more than thirty miles from Rougodevo. The Stanovoy later confessed that he had no doubt that the rest of the details would be shown accurate because the new information agreed with points he had already collected and furnished the last word to the mystery of the names given.

The next morning a messenger sent by the officer on horseback appeared with a letter to Colonel Hahn. Events in Oreshkino had proved every word of the information to be correct. The murderer was found and arrested in his hiding-place at Andrew Vlassof's cottage. He was identified as a soldier on leave and his name was Samoylo Ivanof.

That quite extraordinary event produced a sensation in the district. Future messages received through H.P.B. were sure to be viewed in a more serious light. To Vera and her father, Madame denied any intervention of "spirits" in the case. She explained that she had the picture of the whole tragedy and its developments before her from the moment the Stanovoy entered Vera's house. Helena knew the names of the murderers, of the confederate, and of the village. She saw them all interlaced in her visions. Then, she merely guided the raps to give out the information.

Phenomena persisted regardless of intrusions of outside influences and company. But when the family was alone, the "pressure was off" and there was no one to convince. Then, the most extraordinary things tended to unfold. Manifestations produced themselves at their own impulse and pleasure. Or, so it seemed.

Madame repeatedly explained to her kin that the invisible forces at work were of decided and distinct categories. The lowest on the scale produced most of the physical phenomena. The highest beings rarely appeared or communicated and only when the family was alone and serenity reigned. Harmony was said to be a keen catalyst in the manifestation of mediumistic force. Physical manifestations generally depend but little on the will of the medium.

Gradually, such feats as that accomplished with the little chess-table at Pskov became rarer. More frequently, H.P.B. refused to entertain opportunities to prove or convince intellectual visitors and investigators. Likewise, requests for high-flown answers usually got impertinent rebuttals.

Friends traveled great distances with the expressed purpose of witnessing phenomena, to "hear with their ears and see with their eyes" the strange gifts of Mme. Blavatsky. H.P.B., in turn, often gave mocking assurance, "Well, I am doing all that I can." Sometimes, absolutely nothing happened for visitors to carry home as memories. Helena explained this situation by describing herself as tired and perturbed with the unquenchable public thirst for "miracles."

Dissatisfied visitors were hardly out the door and ... "the bells of their horses (were) yet merrily tinkling in the last alley of the entrance park, when everything in the room seemed to become endowed with life. The furniture acted as though every piece of it was animated and gifted with voice and speech, and we passed the rest of the evening and the greater part of the night as though we were between the enchanted walls of the magic palace of some Scheherazade."

We sat at supper in the dining-room, there were loud accords played on the piano which stood in the adjoining apartment, and which was closed and locked, and so placed that we could all of us see it from where we were through the large open doors. Then at the first command and look of Mme. Blavatsky there came rushing to her through the air her tobacco-pouch, her box of matches, her pocket-handkerchief, or anything she asked, or was made to ask for.

Then, as we were taking our seats all the lights in the room were suddenly extinguished, both lamps and wax candles, as though a mighty rush of wind had swept through the whole apartment; and when a match was instantly struck, there was all the heavy furniture, sofas, arm-chairs, tables, cupboards, and large side-board standing upside down, as though turned over noiselessly by some invisible hands, and not an ornament of the fragile carved work, nor even a plate broken. Hardly had we gathered our senses together after this miraculous performance, when we heard again someone playing on the piano a loud and intelligible piece of music, a long marche de bravoure *this time. As we rushed with lighted candles to the instrument (I mentally counting the persons to ascertain that all were present), we found, as we had anticipated, the piano locked, the last sounds of the final chords still vibrating in the air from beneath the heavy closed lid.*

After this, notwithstanding the late hour, we placed ourselves around our large dining-table, and had a seance. The huge family dining-board began to shake with great force, and then to move, sliding rapidly about the room in every direction, even raising itself up to the height of a man.

Two even more striking phenomena took place on that memorable night. After the family chose to first use "spook (mediumistic) raps," numerous distinguished phantoms appeared. Most prominent among them was the spirit of Alexander Poushkine whose remains rested on the "holy mountain" near Rougodevo.

By that time, the family quite understood that the true spirit of Poushkine was far away in devachan *and that the spook was but the shade of its former owner. Still, the group was taken in by the poet's spook who seemed to be in the midst of a dark, melancholy time. To family queries, the entity responded with a poem for the moment.*

Vera preserved the piece, but remarked that its "character and style are beneath criticism." Nonetheless, the spook orated for a time that his sufferings were secret and not to be shared. He had only one desire "to rest on the bosom of Death, instead of which he was suffering in great darkness for his sins, tortured by devils, and had lost all hope of ever reaching the bliss of becoming a winged cherub ..."

"Poor Alexander Sergeitch!" exclaimed old Colonel Hahn who immediately rose searching for something while the family asked what he was looking for.

"My long pipe! I have had enough of these cigars, and I cannot find my pipe; where can it be?"

"You have just smoked it, after supper, father," Vera replied.

"I did; and now Helen's spirits must have walked off with it or hidden it somewhere."

"One, two, three! One, two, three!" affirmed triple raps, as though mocking the old gentleman.

"Indeed? Well, this is a foolish joke. Can not our friend Poushkine tell us where he has hidden it? Do let us know, for life itself would be worthless on this earth without my old and faithful pipe."

"One, two, three! One, two, three!" knocked the table.

"Is this you, Alexander Sergeitch?" they asked.

"*Who is it, then?*"
"*It is me; your old orderly, your honour: Voronof.*"
"*Ah, Voronof! very glad to meet you again, my good fellow.... Now, try to remember old times: bring me my pipe.*"
"*I would be very happy to do so, your honour, but I am not able; somebody holds me fast. But you can take it yourself, your honour. It is now swinging over your head on the lamp.*"
Everyone raised their heads. Moments before there was just an old lamp shade. But of a sudden, a huge Turkish pipe appeared. It was resting on the alabaster shade hanging over the dining table.

Vera and all the rest were increasingly amazed by Madame's mediumistic wonders. "The new physical demonstration filled with astonishment even those of us who had been accustomed to live in a world of marvels for months. Hardly a year before we would not have believed even in the possibility of what we now regarded as perfectly proved facts."

Later in her most colorful life, Helena Blavatsky adamantly and repeatedly denied ever being a medium. "If people (referring to Colonel Olcott), ignorant of the psychological laws, were hallucinated enough to take me for a 'wonderful medium' I am not responsible for it. I, at least, neither practised mediumship nor pretended to it."

Practicing mediumship and being paid for such a gift was the major sticking point. Madame decried simple sorcery, dull diabolism, and the ordinary occupation of mediumship. Furthermore, she found disturbing the drains on paid mediums and disgusting the temptations to cheat so as to fulfill requests of sitters and patrons. It is also clear that H.P.B.'s talents were refined over the years as she developed from being a willful medium to becoming a willing mediator. Still, the difference between the two were and are not easily discerned by the uninitiated.

Sister Vera was aware of the difference. "She never made a secret that she had been, ever since her childhood, and until nearly the age of twenty-five, a very strong medium; though after that period, owing to a regular psychological and physiological training, she was made to lose this dangerous gift, and every trace of mediumship, outside her will, or beyond her direct control, was overcome."

Vera explained the two methods Madame used in those days to produce communications through raps. In the first case, H.P.B. was a relative bystander and permitted the influences to act at their will. The "brainless Elementals" (shells were not invited to participate, owing to the danger of intercourse with them) basically reflected the thoughts of those present. They also responded to the suggestions found by them in Madame B.'s mind.

The second method was rarely used because she disliked dealing with the "currents of thought" from true departed entities. Then, H.P.B. "sat in the astral light" to receive impress of some well-known departed entity. "Thus, if the rapping 'spirit' pretended to be a Shakespeare, it was not really that great personality, but only the echo of the genuine thoughts that had once upon a time moved in his brain and crystallised themselves, so to say, in his astral sphere whence even his shell had departed long ago -- the imperishable thoughts alone remaining. Not a sentence, not a word spelt by the raps that was not formed first in her brain, in its turn the faithful copier of that which was found by her spiritual eye in the luminous Record Book of departed humanity. The, so to express it, crystallised essence of the mind of the once physical brain was there before her spiritual vision; her living brain photographed it, and her will dictated its expression by guiding the raps, which thus became intelligent."

Madame considered herself a conscious mediator as opposed to the run-of-the-mill paid medium who acted as an entirely unconscious avenue for spooks, *bhutas*, and *pisachas*. H.P.B. respected and sympathized with the lot of reputable mediums who lived difficult lives and suffered for their "gifts," but she refuted that they ever conducted seances with real personalities of the recently deceased. Mediums typically extended themselves to allow free play of unspent forces of shades and shells of unremarkable souls which generally had long since passed onto higher and deeper and happier realms.

Still, Vera Zhelihovsky considered her sister to be a "good writing medium." She was quite able - rather than resorting to raps - to scribe the answers to queries while conversing with those around her on any number of topics. Although writing was a much simpler and faster means of communication, Helena rarely consented to use it. Raps apparently required fewer explanations and kept visitors occupied.

From childhood, Melle. Hahn often *saw* the thoughts of persons asking questions. Alternately, she engaged the reflections of an event or a name which collected around the inquirers of the shadow world. H.P.B. had only to see the "picture" to proceed to an acute response. No helpers were needed for the work after years away from Russia.

To the outsider, the rapping part of the process had to seem much more difficult and tedious compared to the method of direct writing.

She had to read the thought, interpret and memorize it, keep track of the letters of the alphabet as they were called, and direct a current of force to strike and sound at the exact moment. But, it apparently became easy for her.

Madame not only had extraordinary mediumistic gifts, but also was clairvoyant from childhood. She could hear and see ghosts and phantoms as well as elementals constantly active most everywhere. On walks with Vera on her new properties in Pskov, H.P.B. would point out shades of the dead who populated the area in large number.

"It is very interesting, the more so since I now see them so rarely. I wish I were still a real medium, as the latter ... are constantly surrounded by a host of ghosts, and that I see them now but occasionally, not as I used to years ago, when a child....

"They are harmless unless encouraged. Then I am too accustomed to such sights to experience even a passing uneasiness. If anything, I feel disgust, and a contemptuous pity for the poor spooks! In fact, I feel convinced that all of us mortals are constantly surrounded by millions of such shadows, the last mortal image left of themselves by their ex-proprietors....

"How often, how earnestly, have I tried to see and recognise, among the shadows that haunted me, some one of our dear relatives, or even a friend!... Stray acquaintances, and distant relatives, for whom I care little, I have occasionally recognised, but they never seemed to pay any attention to me, and whenever I saw them, it was always unexpected, and independently of my will. How I longed from the bottom of my soul, how I have tried -- all in vain! As much as I can make out of it, it is not the living who attract the dead, but rather the localities they have inhabited, those places where they have lived and suffered, and where their personalities and outward forms have been most impressed on the surrounding atmosphere."

"Say, shall we call some of your old servants, those who have been born and lived in this place all their lives. I feel sure, that if we describe to them some of the forms I have just seen, that they will recognise in them people they knew, and who have died here."

Helena's suggestion to Vera was immediately put into action. A servant was sent to find the oldest serfs on the property. Timothy the tailor who was bent and retired from old age, along with the just as-old Oulyan, once chief gardener, soon appeared. Vera then de-scribed to the elders the strange being with terribly long fingernails, high black *headgear, and a long gray coat which H.P.B. had pointed out to her in their recent investigations.*

She quickly followed on, asking, "Has there ever been a worker resembling those features who lived on this compound?"

The two old peasants, interrupted each other as they went, and fought to respond to the question. "Knew well who it was whom the young mistress described."

"Don't we know him? Of course we do -- why, it is our late barrin! Just as he used to be -- our deceased master Nikolay Mihaijlovitch!"

"But why did he wear such a strange-looking cap, and, never cut his nails?"

"This was owing to a disease, mistress -- an incurable disease, as we were told, that the late master caught while in Lithuania, where he had resided for years. It is called the Koltoun.... *He could neither cut his hair nor pare his nails, and had to cover constantly his head with a tall velvet cap, like a priest's cap."* (Koltoun - Polish plait - is a severe skin complaint, once common in northern Europe. The hair becomes grievously diseased and the nails of the fingers and toes cannot be touched. Cutting of the nails can lead to grave bleeding.)

The old gentlemen corroborated Madame's occult espionage. The woman, in her semi-Flemish costume, was Mina Ivanovna, a German housekeeper, who had resided in the house for over twenty years; and the young man, who looked like a German student in his velvet blouse, was really such a student who had come from Gottingen....

"This was not all, moreover. We found out that the corner room in which H.P.B. had seen ... the phantoms of all these deceased personages of Rougodevo, had been made to serve for every one of them, either as a death-chamber when they had breathed their last, or had been converted for their benefit into a mortuary-chamber when they had been laid out awaiting burial. It was from this suite of apartments, in which their bodies had invariably passed from three to five days, that they had been carried away into yonder old chapel, on the other side of the lake, that was so well seen, and had been examined by us from the windows of our sitting-room."

In the following days, H.P.B. continued to see the restless ghosts gliding about the old out-house. Nine-year-old Lisa, the elder women's half sister, also recognized the strange forms. She accepted them innocently for living persons and was only concerned with "where they had come from, who they were, and why no one except her 'old' sister and herself ever consented to notice them."

Lisa's "talent" with ghosts and death left her in later years, but Madame's long persisted. Helena almost always knew, without being informed by letter, of the moment of death of relatives, friends, and old servants of the family. "We have given up advising her of any such sad events, the dead invariably precede the news, and tell her themselves of their demise; and we receive a letter in which she describes the way she saw this or that departed person, at the same time, and often before the post carrying our notification could have reached her...."

Mme. Blavatsky was apt to see ghosts and ghouls in some of the least expected places. Sister Vera recounted one of her ghost stories from the trip in which they encountered the Metropolitan of Kiev. At one of the station stops, the women were told that no fresh horses were available to speed them on their journey. This greatly disturbed the travelers, especially since roads were good and a full moon was rising. They then were looking at several hours of sitting and waiting.

It seemed that nothing could be done because the station master was not only drunk but also refused to parlay with his supposed customers. The latter had no choice but to try to settle in for the night. But even that became a problem because the one-roomed station house was locked and could not be opened except on special orders.

"Well, this is fine," said H.P.B. losing patience. "We are refused horses and even the room we are entitled to is shut for us! Why is it shut? Now, I want to know and insist upon it."

But the station house seemed totally empty, and there was no one about. H.P.B. probed more deeply. She stared at the locked room through its little low windows and flattened her broad face against the window panes.

"A-ha! That's what it is! Very well then. Now I can force the drunken brute to give us horses in five minutes."

H.P.B. immediately charged off in search of the station master. Vera was more than curious as to what secret the little station house held. But, here "uninitiated eyes" could discover nothing out of the ordinary when she pressed her own face to the windows.

Still in ten rather than five minutes, three fresh and strong post horses appeared with the station master himself in the lead. The man, just recently brutish and uncooperative, magically had changed into a polite and helpful attendant. The carriage was readied and the travelers soon continued on their way.

"What kind of sorcery did you have to perform on that man to get his attention and help?"

Madame was silent until the next day when she deigned to share the story with her sister. "The wretch must have taken me for a witch. I found him in a backyard and shouted to him that the person whose body had been just standing in the coffin in the travelers' room was there again. I asked him not to detain us any further. Else we would insist upon our right to enter the room and disturb the spirit. The man's eyes bulged incredulously. I told him that I was speaking of his deceased wife whom he had just recently buried. She was there and would remain until we were gone away. I described the ghost to the sad widower who became pale as death itself. Then, he hurried on to get our fresh horses!"

In later days when Madame lived and roamed through the Trans-Caucasus territories of Imeretia, Georgia, and Mingrelia, she met with superstitious Pagans, half-savage Abkhasians, as well as supposed descendants of the ancient Greeks who came with Jason in search of the Golden Fleece.

Not long past, many of the nomads in the area had been outlaws and highwaymen. In Madame's day, they retained much of their predilections and stood "fanatical as Neapolitan monks and ignorant as Italian noblemen."

Mme. Blavatsky likewise became renowned with the locals as a witch when not a beneficent magician. She attracted many friends and sometimes more enemies. Her reputation as a healer spread. Helena bewitched and cured those in need and made adversaries of others who had thought to take advantage of their own kind. She warded off the evil eye only to reap contempt or bribes from the dark ones. But, she never stooped to accept money for any of her healing works.

The list of H.P.B.'s enemies began in Mingrelia and Imeretia and grew years later to include church-goers and missionaries, spiritists and spiritualists, scientists and psychics. But, she defied them all and would not bend to public opinion preferring to "avoid society" and stand for truth and goodwill.

Her sympathies went out to tabooed portions of humanity which society avoids and abhors -- the witches and the wizards, the obsessed and possessed, and other misunderstood beings. In her travels, she took under protection the native *Koodiani* (magicians, sorcerers), Persian thaumaturgists, and old Armenian hags -- healers and fortune-tellers.

There was a price to pay for her curiosities and searches, her loyalties and commitments.

Madame's occult powers became stronger as she began to subject all kinds of manifestations to her direct will. "The whole country was talking of her. The superstitious Gouriel and Mingrelian nobility began soon to regard her as a magician, and people came from afar to consult her about their private affairs."

By then, H.P.B. had given up communication through raps, and used the far more rapid and satisfactory method of giving answers verbally or through direct writing. With eyes wide open and in full consciousness yet deeply concentrating, Madame B. watched people's thoughts. They simply "evolved out of their heads in spiral luminous smoke, sometimes in jets of what might be taken for some radiant material, and settled in distinct pictures and images around them. Often such thoughts and answers to them would find themselves impressed in her own brain, couched in words and sentences in the same way as original thoughts do. But so far as we are all able to understand, the former visions are always more trustworthy, as they are independent and distinct from the seer's own impressions, belonging to pure clairvoyance, not 'thought transference,' which is a process always liable to get mixed up with one's own more vivid mental impressions."

In that time period as at other key points in her life, Madame was likely to be taken ill and seriously to the point that all doctors were entirely incapable of understanding her physical condition. While living near a military settlement in the forests and woods of remote Mingrelia, she again became incapacitated with another "mysterious nervous disease" which baffled those who attended her.

"Whenever I was called by name, I opened my eyes upon hearing it, and was myself, my own personality in every particular. As soon as I was left alone, however, I relapsed into my usual, half-dreamy condition, and became somebody else (who, namely, Mme. B. will not tell). I had simply a mild fever that consumed me slowly but surely, day after day, with entire loss of appetite, and finally of hunger, as I would feel none for days, and often went a week without touching any food whatever, except a little water, so that in four months I was reduced to a living skeleton. In cases when I was interrupted, when in my other self, by the sound of my present name being pronounced, and while I was conversing in my dream-life, -- say at half a sentence either

spoken by me or those who were with my second me at the time, -- and opened my eyes to answer the call, I used to answer very rationally, and understood all, for I was never delirious. But no sooner had I closed my eyes again than the sentence which had been interrupted was completed by my other self, continued from the word, or even half the word, it had stopped at. When awake, and myself, I remembered well who I was in my second capacity, and what I had been and was doing. When somebody else, i.e., the personage I had become, I know I had no idea of who was H.P. Blavatsky! I was in another far-off country, a totally different individuality from myself, and had no connection at all with my actual life."

The army surgeon could come to no conclusions as to her ills, but it was obvious she was in rapid decline. So, he sent her down river in a native boat, a four-day journey with four native servants. It must have been a disturbing journey for all involved: a single boat on a narrow river enclosed on both sides by ancient forests.

H.P.B.'s servants may well have been confused and "out of their wits." Still, their reports fit with many other "phenomena" in Madame B.'s colorful life. During consecutive nights on the river as Helena lay in the bottom of the boat, the man towing the canoe "saw the form of the mistress gliding across the waters." He shrieked in fear and ran away for a time while an old faithful servant held things together. On the last night out, the old servant himself attested to seeing two ethereal figures attend to Madame as she rested in the boat.

The nerve-wracking journey was more than the natives could stand. Upon depositing Madame with a distant relative at Kutais, all the servants excepting the faithful one disappeared. H.P.B., still near death, was then transported to Tiflis by carriage.

That strange episode apparently opened to her further profound occult powers. H.P. Blavatsky began even more so "to lead a double life." Many might have suspected she already had been living so for many years prior, but a decided change occurred in those days.

From that period onward, Madame Blavatsky suggested that she was no longer subject to unwitting and irritating intrusions of spooks and *bhuts, diaki* and demons. "The last vestiges of my psycho-physical weakness is gone, to return no more. I am cleansed and purified of that dreadful attraction to myself of stray spooks and ethereal affinities. I am free, free, thanks to Those whom I now bless at every hour of my life," Madame wrote in a letter to a relative.

In past times, it was common for spooks to act outside of her control. Manifestations came and went. After H.P.B.'s illness in the wilderness (1866) and another great transition when she returned to Europe (1870), Helena consistently was able to defy and subject the invisibles to her indomitable will.

(Or so it seemed. Because the invisibles were apparently not *always* tame and docile. A story was told from H.P.B.'s days living in a cooperative house for women in New York City in 1873. "One morning Madame did not appear for breakfast, and her friend finally went to her bedroom to see what was the matter; there she found H.P.B. unable to rise because her night-gown was securely sewed to the mattress, and sewed in such a manner that it would have been impossible for Madame to have done it herself, and so thoroughly had the sewing been done that the stitches had to be cut before Madame could rise. This was the work of the *diaki*.")

H.P.B.'s mediumistic and witch-like talents were superseded by far greater abilities then practically unknown to the western world. H.P. Blavatsky had largely completed her wide, deep and passionate search for occult knowledge.

Madame B. was long aware that she had work to do in the world. The moment to share the knowledge and mysteries of the ancients was not far off. But, the details for manifesting them eluded her for yet a time. How to use her psychic gifts, massive experience, wide knowledge, and iron will to bring westerners to the doorstep of spiritual understanding?! And how to do it while moving around a complex, skeptical, masculine world - seemingly all alone - in the body of a Russian woman?

Materialistic spiritualism and phenomena were the obvious but messy means to gain interest and attention. After being saved from the explosion of the SS Eunomia in Mediterranean waters, Madame found her way to Egypt and made a brief attempt to establish a society for the investigation of spiritualistic phenomena. She endeavored to create a Societe Spirite to investigate mediumship and phenomena according to the spiritistic theories of the Frenchman Allan Kardec (1804-1869). Helena intended to start with Kardec's somewhat accepted teaching and then find ways to go beyond what she knew to be a limited view of the "spirit world."

H.P.B. was prepared, if necessary, to take on the role of a hapless medium. "They know no better, and it does me no harm -- for I will very soon show them the difference between a passive medium and an active doer," she explained in a letter to family. Within weeks, she was disgusted with the undertaking. It quickly failed when she was unable to obtain the services of a professional medium. Amateur female spiritist mediums came to her unfortunate rescue. But, they turned out to be "beggarly tramps, when not adventuresses in the rear of M. de Lesseps's army of engineers and workmen on the canal of Suez."

"They steal the society's money. They drink like sponges, and I now caught them cheating most shamefully our members, who come to investigate the phenomena, by bogus manifestations. I had very disagreeable scenes with several persons who held me alone responsible for all this. So I ordered them out.... The Societe Spirite has not lasted a fortnight -- it is a heap of ruins -- majestic, but as suggestive as those of the Pharaoh's tombs.... To wind up the comedy with a drama, I got nearly shot by a madman -- a Greek, who had been present at the only two public seances we held, and got possessed, I suppose, by some vile spook."

The Societe Spirite was for a short time not merely a failure but also a source of ridicule and claims of fraud and charlatanry made by new enemies. Such were mostly the French women she had fired. Nonetheless, H.P. Blavatsky continued on -- armed with increased powers and sense of the work to be done.

Magus
(Persian for Savant)

"There never was genius but was cracked.
And I am a genius - so Williams says at least."

Other stories persist from H.P.B.'s Egypt days. One shows her magical and moralistic self in action after dinner at a hotel in Alexandria. Madame and a gentleman remained behind when others went off to the theater. Mr. N. took a glass of wine from their table and was about to put it to his lips when it suddenly broke into many pieces.

Instead of frowning, Madame laughed loudly and remarked that she detested liqueurs and wines, and didn't like being around those who used them. The man was flabbergasted to think she could have been responsible. It simply had to be an accident. Or at least he wanted to think so. Still, he later admitted that he thought it strange that a thick and strong glass should disintegrate in his hand.

So, he drew her out. "She looked at me very seriously, and her eyes flashed. 'What will you bet,' she asked, 'that I do not do it again?'

"'Well, we will try on the spot. If you do, I will be the first to proclaim you a true magician. If not, we will have a good laugh at you or your spirits tomorrow at the Consulate....'

"And saying so, I half filled the tumbler with wine and prepared to drink it. But no sooner had the glass touched my lips than I felt it shattered between my fingers, and my hand bled, wounded by a broken piece in my instinctive act at grasping the tumbler together when I felt myself losing hold of it." Madame made a comment about spirits and left the room with a sneer on her face.

Arriving in America in 1873, H.P.B. carried the same mission which she had briefly attempted while in Egypt in 1870. Mme. Blavatsky was directed to attempt to put a new light on the phenomena and philosophy surrounding the current entity called Spiritualism. "I was sent from Paris on purpose to America to prove the phenomena and their reality and -- show the fallacy of the Spiritualistic theories of 'Spirits.' But how could I do it best? I did not want people at large to know that I could produce the same thing at will. I had received ORDERS to the contrary, and yet, I had to keep alive the reality, the genuineness and possibility of such phenomena in the hearts of those who from Materialists had turned Spiritualists and now, owing to the exposure of several mediums fell back again, returned to their skepticism."

H.P.B. knew much, but could tell little. Only over time was she allowed to reveal bits and pieces of a puzzle which is far from complete even more than a century later. Many of the puzzle pieces continue to be disputed or entirely ignored into the present day.

Mme. Blavatsky was not new to America nor to New York City. And she had more than twenty-five years of experience traveling diverse parts of the globe which certainly had required much more courage. She also had her invisible helpers, when all else failed. But most of the time, she was probably like the rest of us. Having to fend for ourselves as best we can while believing that we are "doing it all on our own."

Helena arrived physically quite alone in that massive, sprawling congregation of humanity in New York City. She surely thought a time or two, "Could they not have come up with another more congenial place for me to do the Work?"

Still, America was the hotbed of Spiritualism. The Fox sisters -- Margaret and Kate and Leah -- had started the ball rolling in 1848 in Hydesville, NY, with rappings. Their work with the "spirits" attracted wide attention and modern spiritualism was born. The Fox sisters had a long run in the spotlight and made careers as paid mediums in the spiritualist movement. Dr. William Crookes, discoverer of thallium and the cathode ray tube, eventually studied them and vouched for their gifts. "I have tested them (their phenomena) in every way that I could devise, until there has been no escape from the conviction that they were true objective occurrences not produced by trickery or mechanical means."

But, the younger sisters eventually fell on hard times, became alcoholics and "exposed" themselves to be frauds. A reporter plied them with $1500 to stand in front of an audience of 2000 people in New York City in 1888 and to confess to their supposed misdeeds. Margaret recanted her confession a year later. Within five years, they both died penniless and were buried in paupers' graves.

Madame B. surely had her own explanations for the Fox sisters' demise and the sad state of affairs which surrounded mediums like them. First, she knew that space and matter are filled with spooks and spirits. They have many names and means of attaching themselves to human beings. Helena herself had been obsessed and oppressed by demons for many years. Thanks to her Teacher, she was eventually freed of them. But, that was hardly the case for the likes of Margaret and Kate Fox.

"The whole universe is filled with spirits. It is nonsense to suppose that we are the only intelligent beings in the world. I believe there is latent spirit in all matter. I believe almost in the spirits of the elements. But all is governed by natural laws. Even in cases of apparent violation of these laws the appearance comes from a misunderstanding of the laws. In cases of certain nervous diseases it is recorded of some patients that they have been raised from their beds by some undiscoverable power, and it has been impossible to force them down. In such cases it has been noticed that they float feet first with any current of air that may be passing through the room. The wonder of this ceases when you come to consider that there is no such thing as the law of gravitation as it is generally understood. The law of gravitation is only to be rationally explained in accordance with magnetic laws as Newton tried to explain it, but the world would not accept it."

Second, mediumship requires very large expenditures of energy. That expenditure itself can lead to all manner of bodily distress and depletion. Even in her later years as a "mediator," Madame carried a burden similar to that of the Fox sisters and other mediums. H.P.B.'s myriad medical problems were in part due to her acting as a conduit for the Masters. The motives and results may have been quite different, but the bodily effects over periods of time of "pumping energy" seem to have been similar. "Do you know one medium who has made a profession of it and who has not had some serious physical disease, or has not become a drunkard, or a lunatic, or something horrible? What the medium accomplishes is at his or her own expense, it is an expenditure of their vital energy, it is demoralizing both to themselves and to the entities -- call them spirits or shells or spooks, or what you will -- who seek such persons in order to obtain a temporary vitality. In other cases the phenomena are produced solely by means of what I call a psychological trick, which, however, is not jugglery as commonly understood, but which likewise implies a large expenditure of energy on the part of the medium and can only be done by reserving and storing up the energy ..."

Third, mediums become so in part because their inner bodies do not mesh properly with their outer forms. Madame B. was a point in case. "It will be remembered that I was weak and sickly, and that I inherited capacities for such abnormal exercise of mind -- capacities which subsequent training might develop, but which at that age would have been of no avail, had not feebleness of physique, a looseness of attachment, if I may so phrase it, between the matter and spirit, of which we are all composed, abnormally, for the time, developed them. As it was, as I grew up, and gained health and strength, my mind became as closely prisoned in my physical frame as that of any other person, and all these phenomena ceased."

Fourth, mediums are just not like the rest of their human kin. Both for good and for ill. "In some way or another, mediums are all imperfect. The spirits which are forever seeking a body to inhabit seize on those which are defective, being unable to control those which are not. So in the East, insane persons are regarded with peculiar veneration, as being possessed of spirits - daimons." Having a daimon or spirit can create problems for even the best of humans. Socrates is well known for having his own daimon. And, like many others, the little daimon (devil) got him into trouble.

Fifth, "mediumship is most dangerous; and psychic experiences when accepted indiscriminately lead only to honestly deceiving others, because the medium is the first self-deceived victim." The astral world with which typical mediums unwittingly deal can disturb, distress and derange not only the mediums but others it touches through them.

Sixth, when money came into the equation "all bets were off." Professional mediums had to perform regularly and dramatically for their customers. If the energy was not flowing for one reason or another, there was the recurrent temptation to cheat. And, cheaters eventually got caught in their games. Which looked bad for the moment and could tarnish a whole career as well as cast negative reflections on other upright mediums.

Madame had the background and experience, training and Teachers to take on the world of "spirits" and of Spiritualism. Despite all her efforts, her work turned out to be incomplete and inconclusive. Investigators still wonder, even as H.P.B. did. "Did I do wrong? The world is not prepared yet to understand the philosophy of Occult Science -- let them assure themselves first of all that there are beings in an invisible world, whether 'Spirits' of the dead or Elementals; and that there are hidden powers in man, which are capable of making a God of him on earth."

The task was daunting and effects were modest. Most Spiritualists were convinced of their beliefs and not ready to listen to H.P.B.'s dissenting views on the essentials of the subject to which they held so dearly. They, too, believed in their experiences and interpretations. Even while most had no real training and lacked spiritual discernment. Furthermore, they wanted terribly to believe that Aunt Maude and

Uncle Joe were intact and eternally happy in the Summerland, waiting for their kin to join them in heavenly bliss, and trying to communicate with them in the meantime.

H.P.B. not only contended with "believers" but also with the almost totally non-believing materialistic scientists of the day. For a time, she imagined that she could "demonstrate spiritualism mathematically, to force it upon science." But, few in the scientific community cared to listen at all. Fewer still dared to study and experiment. Renowned scientists like physicist William Crookes and naturalist A.R. Wallace, who took mediums and phenomena seriously, were treated as pariahs by their colleagues. They were denigrated, demeaned and shunned for deigning to stoop to the level of the "charlatanry of mediums."

Still, Madame B. continued to preach her own gospel denouncing the "bogus spirits of seances" and denying the possibility of real spirits manifesting in the physical world. Nonetheless, H.P.B. *KNEW* through many long years of intense and guided experience that Spiritualistic phenomena were valid. It was only their interpretation which needed serious adjustment. Spooks (remnants of living beings) worked through mediums. Spirits (Egos of the deceased) ascended to the true heaven realms and were quite unable to hold intercourse with the physical plane. The latter don't descend again until rebirth, but they can be reached by the highly evolved in sincere and persistent efforts and by others in the sleep state.

Madame was no simple diabolist. If there was such a thing. Stainton Moses thought of her as a medium "in the sense of the postman who brings a letter from one living person to another; in the sense of an assistant electrician whose master tells him how to turn this screw and arrange that wire in the battery ..." She was an active and aware participant, not a passive machine. Mme. Blavatsky plodded on in her loyal "postal" efforts to give the public, scientists, and spiritualists honest glimpses of the Other World.

H.P.B. inevitably found aid in her endeavors when she encountered Henry Olcott at Chittenden, Vermont. Colonel Henry Steel Olcott already had had his own varied career as an agriculturist, decorated Civil War officer, and lawyer to boot. He met Madame B. in another one of his occupations. He was then on his own mission as a journalist, working for the *New York Daily Graphic* and charged with getting the real story on the Eddy brothers. The Eddys hosted nightly mediumistic seances on the second floor of their remote farmhouse. They opened the doors to all seekers for modest lodging costs, feeding their visitors as well. But having been mistreated by many "investigators" along the way, they were suspect of the Colonel and his reporting.

His journalistic work for *The Daily Graphic*, which eventually led to writing *People from the Other World*, caused Olcott to do diligent research on his subject and the Eddy brother mediums. He found that the Eddys' work was really nothing new as "belief in the ministration of good and evil spirits prevailed among all peoples in all times." It could be studied in "the Hindoo Vedas, Puranas, Bhagavat-Gita, and Ramayanas; the Chinese Confucian writings; the Koran; the discourses of the Roman and Grecian sages; the Egyptian records; the Persian Zend-Avesta; the Jewish Kabbala; and, lastly, the Christian Bible."

Sadly he concluded that the Eddys were like slaves and machines. They had "everything to gain and nothing to lose by abandoning the fraud (as the media supposed) and being like other folk." Olcott was more than sympathetic to the lot in life which had fallen to the Eddy brothers and became acutely aware that it was "hardly good luck to be a medium."

Many years later in writing his *Old Diary Leaves*, reporter Olcott retained a vivid remembrance of his first experiences of Madame Blavatsky on October 14, 1874.

The dinner hour at Eddys was noon, and it was from the entrance door of the bare and comfortless dining-room that Kappes and I first saw H.P.B. She had arrived shortly before noon with a French Canadian lady, and they were at table as we entered. My eye was first attracted by a scarlet Garibaldian shirt the former wore, as in vivid contrast with the dull colours around. Her hair was then a thick blond mop, worn shorter than the shoulders, and it stood out from her head, silken-soft and crinkled to the roots, like the fleece of a Cotswold ewe. This and the red shirt were what struck my attention before I took in the picture of her features. It was a massive Calmuck face, contrasting in its suggestion of power, culture, and imperiousness, as strangely with the commonplace visages about the room as her red garment did with the grey and white tones of the walls and woodwork and the dull costumes of the rest of the guests. All sorts of cranky people were continually coming and going at Eddy's to see the mediumistic phenomena, and it only struck me on seeing this eccentric lady that this was but one more of the sort. Pausing on the door-sill, I whispered to Kappes [newspaper artist], "Good gracious! look at that specimen, will you." I went straight across and took a seat opposite her to indulge my favourite habit of character-study. *The two ladies conversed in French, making remarks of no consequence, but I saw at once from her accent and fluency of speech that, if not a Parisian, she must at least be a finished French scholar. Dinner over, the two went outside the house and Madame Blavatsky rolled herself a cigarette, for which I gave her a light as a pretext to enter into conversation.*

"*Permettez moi, Madame,*" *I said, and gave her a light for her cigarette; our acquaintance began in smoke, but it stirred up a great and permanent fire.*

My remark having been made in French, we fell at once into talk in that language. She asked me how long I had been there and what I thought of the phenomena; saying that she herself was greatly interested in such things, and had been drawn to Chittenden by reading the letters in the Daily Graphic: *the public were growing so interested in these that it was sometimes impossible to find a copy of the paper on the book-stalls an hour after publication, and she had paid a dollar for a copy of the last issue.*

"*I hesitated before coming here,*" *she said,* "*because I was afraid of meeting that Colonel Olcott.*"

"*Why should you be afraid of him, Madame?*" *I rejoined.*

"*Oh! because I fear he might write about me in his paper.*" *I told her that she might make herself perfectly easy on that score, for I felt quite sure Col. Olcott would not mention her in his letters unless she wished it. And I introduced myself. We became friends at once.*

Madame's arrival at the Eddy farmhouse and seance parlor brought dramatic changes to the nightly works of the Eddy brothers. In *People from the Other World*, Olcott recounted in detail his experience of the Eddy seances and the spooks which appeared through their agency. Olcott and the other sitters could not help but be fascinated by the nightly visitors and their activities. But, those gradually became repetitious, almost tiresome to the reporter. The only changes appeared due to the different visitors who desperately wanted to know about their loved ones and sometimes drew unexpected company with them.

Madame Blavatsky brought her own entourage with her. Prior to her appearance, the spooks which showed themselves at the seances were recognized as Red Indians, Americans, and others of European ancestry similar to the sitters of the evening. On Madame's first night, the "western" pattern changed to include a servant boy from Georgia, a Muslim merchant from the Ukraine, and a Russian peasant girl. At succeeding seances, there appeared a Kurdish cavalier armed with scimitar, pistols, and lance, a black African sorcerer with a horned coronet, and a European gentleman wearing the cross and collar of St. Anne. H.P.B. recognized the latter as her uncle. Such unexpected and unusual figures in the seance-room of the poor Eddy brothers fully convinced Olcott and the rest of the sitters that the apparitions were genuine.

The evening of October 24th was as bright as day with the light of the moon, and, while there was a good deal of moisture in the air, the atmospheric conditions would, I suppose, have been regarded as favorable for manifestations. In the dark-circle, as soon as the light was extinguished, George Dix (a spook), addressing Mme. de Blavatsky, said: 'Madame, I am now about to give you a test of the genuineness of the manifestations in this circle, which I think will satisfy not only you, but a skeptical world beside. I shall place in your hands the buckle of a medal of honor worn in life by your brave father, and buried with his body in Russia. This has been brought to you by your uncle, whom you have seen materialized this evening.' Presently I heard the lady utter an exclamation, and, a light being struck, we all saw Mme. de B. holding in her hand a silver buckle of a most curious shape, which she regarded with speechless wonder.

When she recovered herself a little, she announced that this buckle had, indeed, been worn by her father, with many other decorations, that she identified this particular article by the fact that the point of the pin had been carelessly broken off by herself many years ago; and that, according to universal custom, this, with all his other medals and crosses, must have been buried with her father's body. The medal to which this buckle belongs, was one granted by the late Czar to his officers, after the Turkish campaign of 1828. The medals were distributed at Bucharest, and a number of the officers had buckles similar to this made by the rude silversmiths of that city. Her father died July 15th, 1873, and she, being in this country, could not attend his obsequies. As to the authenticity of this present, so mysteriously received, she possessed ample proof, in a photographic copy of her father's oil portrait, in which this very buckle appears, attached to its own ribbon and medal.

Colonel Olcott eventually came to understand Madame Blavatsky "had evoked them [foreign spooks] by her own developed and masterful power." H.P.B. explained those phenomena which were quite unusual even for a seance in the heart of spiritualist country. They were like unto portraits of dead people, but not spirits at all. "Even the materialized form of my uncle at the Eddys' was the picture; it was I who sent it out from my own mind, as I had come out to make experiments without telling it to any one. It was like an empty outer envelope of my uncle that I seemed to throw on the medium's astral body. I saw and followed the process. I knew Will Eddy was a genuine medium, and the phenomenon as real as it could be, and, therefore, when days of trouble came for him, I defended him in the papers."

Helena and Henry continued on from Vermont to become friends and chums. They acted as "Jack and Harry" for each other as well as mutual helpers and eventual co-founders for the Theosophical Society. Before the Chittenden experience, Colonel Olcott was a confirmed Spiritualist. After seeing H.P.B. at work, "I gradually discovered that this lady, whose brilliant accomplishments and eminent virtues of character, no less than her exalted social position, entitle her to the highest respect, is one of the most remarkable mediums in the world.

"At the same time, her mediumship is totally different from that of any other person I ever met; for, instead of being controlled by spirits to do their will, it is she who seems to control them to do her bidding. Whatever may be the secret by which this power has been attained, I cannot say, but that she possesses it, I have had too many proofs to permit me to doubt the fact."

H.P.B. made further explanation of the phenomena: "Spiritualism, in the hands of an adept, becomes Magic, for he is learned in the art of blending together the laws of the Universe, without breaking any of them and thereby violating Nature. In the hands of an inexperienced medium, Spiritualism becomes UNCONSCIOUS SORCERY; for, by allowing himself to become the helpless tool of a variety of spirits, of whom he knows nothing save what the latter permit him to know, he opens, unknown to himself, a door of communication between the two worlds, through which emerge the blind forces of Nature lurking in the astral light, as well as good and bad spirits."

H.P.B. remembered years later finding "Olcott in love with spirits." But, his eyes were quickly opened to see the real magic at which his previous spiritualistic experiences had only hinted. "I proved to him that all that mediums could do through spirits others could do at will without any spirits at all...." H.S.O. was one of the few in the early New York years to receive close personal instruction from Madame. Over time, he was given attention and interviews with a number of the

Masters. He became a companion and co-worker along the way. Despite other failings, his loyalty was never to falter. The work of the First Theosophists suffered from human frailties. But, they accomplished much on three continents in the tenure of their hard labors.

H.S.O. must have had extraordinary karma to bring Madame Helena Blavatsky and the Masters into his life. He didn't have to travel to Tibet, beat a path through the Himalayas, and spend several years of probation to be admitted into audience with the Teachers. Yet, he paid dearly for his "good fortune." From his reporting days at Chittenden and onward, he was exposed like few others to Madame's unfolding life, experiences and talents. He was given intimate details - many surely never published - of H.P.B.'s incredible journeys and gifts.

Working and traveling, living and training with Mme. B. at close quarters for years allowed him to see those "... special elements about H.P.B. which gave her power over others, viz.: (a) Her amazing occult knowledge and phenomena-working powers, together with her relation to the hidden MASTERS. (b) Her sparkling talents, especially as a conversationist, with her social accomplishments, wide travels, and extraordinary adventures. (c) Her insight into problems of philology, racial origins, fundamental bases of religions, and keys to old mysteries and symbols; certainly not the result of study, for a more restless and eccentric student, there never was. She was not all smoothness or courtesy -- far from it: when the mood was on her she was all that, but at other times she spared nobody, no matter how rich, powerful, or highly placed they might be. As to trained literary faculty, she had none; she wrote under inspiration, thoughts flashed through her brain like meteors, scenes painted themselves before her mental vision and died out often when but half caught, parenthesis bristled through her paragraphs so as to sometimes interminably stretch out her sentences, and she would -- as it now appears -- catch up and use other men's writings as though they were her own -- intent only on fitting their formulated thoughts into the working out of her theme. In short, she was a genius in the same sense as Shakespeare and others, who took materials as they were found, and worked them into the amalgam upon which they put the stamp of their own individuality."

Helena Blavatsky had not been subjected to the slightest formal education. Yet, she had gained *WORLDS* of experience which put her in good stead as she entered the unique realm of New York City. She already had gathered the qualities of wit and intellect and character which allowed her to act as artist and artisan, musician and medium, translator and teacher and tale teller, linguist and writer, soldier and leader, advocate and polemicist. Helena could have filled most any job or profession, if she so desired.

Helena Blavatsky was a polymath, much like her fellow Russian, G.I. Gurdjieff, who lived a generation after her and confounded so many. While neither as accomplished nor renowned, Gurdjieff was able to take on any job, do most anything. If not, he was able to make people think he could.

Madame B. did much the same and responded to the need at hand. She could "psychologize" people around her, if necessary. Or better yet, get the work done herself. H.P.B. was successful in practically every field of the day except those consciously avoided: religion, politics and sports.

Still it has been told that Madame B. was a superb horsewoman. She was fearless in the saddle as she was in practically every arena of life. Helena rode with Cossacks and Kurds, nomads and Mongols, and in covered wagons and caravans in locations all over known and unknown stretches of world. Across prairies and deserts, through rivers, and over mountains on five continents.

Helena generally had little time for common sport. But, traveling the world around a number of times was surely a grand substitute. H.P.B. eschewed politicians and clerics both for much the same reason. She suggested that they so often did not practice what they preached. They handed down rules and laws and codes for others to follow. Madame "followed the rules." The rules of Caesar as well as those of the Great Ones whom she revered.

Helena Blavatsky was not afraid of work. She was much like Abraham Lincoln who once said, "My father taught me how to work. But, he didn't teach me to like it."

Helena filled most any bill as the time and need arose. She acted as a business woman in diverse locations. H.P.B. harvested and shipped logs from Central Asia while at Mingrelia. She eventually published a number of magazines which circled the world as she had. In America, she showed herself as a master of needlework and skilled in making beautiful artificial flowers. She also designed some of the first advertising cards in New York City.

Few details are known about her work as an artisan and maybe less as an artist. But, a number of her pen-and-ink sketches exist which show that eye and hand worked together just as well in artistic as in her other magical endeavors.

H.P.B. told Constance Wachtmeister how she produced a number of art pieces phenomenally: "In New York I was given a test which created a great sensation at the time. A sheet of clean note paper was brought to me from a certain club-room, having the heading of the club stamped on it. I laid my hand on the paper, and concentrating my mind on the features of an Eastern Yogi, with whose physiognomy I was intimately acquainted, I presently removed my hand, and there was seen the portrait of the man on whom I had concentrated my thoughts and then projected on the paper by means of my will power. This portrait was examined by some of the leading artists in New York, and in sworn evidence they said that it was impossible for them to tell by what means the portrait was impressed on the paper; it was not done by any of the processes with which they, as experts, were familiar, and, moreover, with regard to the artistic qualities of the representation, it was such as could only have been produced by the greatest master in the art of portraiture who had ever lived."

This incident occurred in 1878 before a number of witnesses who signed affidavits to authenticate the event. Noted artists of the time followed suit in commenting on the quality of H.P.B.'s production. William Donovan, a well-known American sculptor, considered her work to be "of a kind that could not have been done by any living artist known to any of us. It has all the essential qualities which distinguish the portraits by Titian, Masaccio, and Raphael: namely, individuality of the profoundest kind, and consequently breadth and unity of as perfect a quality as I can conceive."

Thomas LeClear, a portrait painter with fifty years' experience, remarked that the portrait was "entirely unique. It would require an artist of very extraordinary power to reach the degree of ability which is expressed in this work. There is a oneness of treatment difficult to attain, with a pronounced individuality, combined with great breadth. As a whole, it is an individual. It has the appearance of having been done on the moment -- a result inseparable from great art.... Madame Blavatsky ... must possess artistic powers not to be accounted for on any hypothesis except that of magic.... No human being, however much genius he might have, could produce the work, except with much time and painstaking labour ..."

Helena's talents were versatile as well as unusual. It is not certain that Madame ever took to the stage to act or perform. If she did, H.P.B. surely would have filled any role uniquely. In later years, she "held court" with a wide variety of admirers and sycophants, students and curiosity seekers. But, Madame B. was not known to stand at a podium or give formal lectures for "people in the seats."

She did, however, play piano for the public in Europe during her sojourns. Helena took a "few music lessons" when she accompanied her father to London in 1845. In later years, she studied with the noted pianist-composer Ignaz Moscheles (once assistant to Beethoven) at the Leipzig Conservatory. Helena eventually became a member of the Philharmonic Society in England.

Of greater interest may be that at another point, H.P.B. took on the name of Madame Laura. She used the title when she gave concerts in England, Italy and Russia. Little was revealed of that period in her life, but a few friends got to witness her musical talents in later times. Mrs. Hiram Corson related how "H.P.B. would sit down at the piano and improvise with great skill, showing a remarkable efficiency for one who played but at odd times as the spirit might move her."

Henry Olcott remembered in *Old Diary Leaves* her extraordinary musical gift. "She was a splendid pianist, playing with a touch and expression that were simply superb. Her hands were models -- ideal and actual -- for a sculptor, and never seen to such advantage as when flying over the keyboard to find its magical melodies.... when in London as a young girl, with her father, [she] played at a charity concert with Mme Clara Schumann and Mme Arabella Goddard in a piece of Schumann's for three pianos....

"During the time of our relationship she played scarcely at all.... There were times when she was occupied by one of the Mahatmas, when her playing was indescribably grand. She would sit in the dusk sometimes, with nobody else in the room beside myself, and strike from the sweet-toned instrument improvisations that might well make one fancy he was listening to the Gandharvas, or heavenly chorister."

Even in her late and ailing years and but months before her death, Madame B.'s musical talents remained intact. William Kingsland, one of her early biographers, recalled a visit she made to his London home in 1889: "She sat down at the piano and played Schubert's *Erlkonig*, to my great surprise and delight, as I had never even heard that she had ever been a pianist." Madame had hardly touched a piano in a dozen years at the time.

Madame Laura (Helena) was not just an ethereal musician, but also a magician who could bridge worlds and blend spirit and matter. Helena Hahn Blavatsky was born an artist with seemingly whole worlds as her media. She obviously had mastered many fields of life even before entering her 19th-century incarnation. (Much of knowledge, according to Socrates, is mere recollection.) H.P.B. was so versatile that her talents spread in practically all directions.

She not only lived with senses attuned to inner worlds and ancient times, but she also extended herself widely through her extraordinary gift for languages. Her linguistic abilities both symbolized and energized her as a mediator throughout her life.

H.P.B.'s facility with language seemed to know few bounds. The list of tongues which she either wrote, read, or at least understood is quite long. It varies from source of information and the angle from which her work was viewed. Madame admitted to "knowing" only a few languages, but the many stories told about her suggest that her abilities went far beyond those which she claimed.

The New York Mercury reported in 1875 that Madame B. "converses and writes fluently in Russian, Romaic (modern Greek), Low Dutch, German, French, Spanish, Italian, Portuguese and English." H.P.B. did not deny that statement, while she took to task other parts of that *Mercury* newspaper article.

When Madame Blavatsky worked with mediums in New York City and Vermont, the manifestations were said to have spoken French, Spanish, German, Russian, Latin and Greek as well as Georgian, Persian and Tartar. The implication is that the medium or someone else in the room where the seance was held had some facility with those languages. The prime suspect was Madame Blavatsky.

It is probable that she developed some fluency in Kurdish when riding with Safar Ali Bek. She seems to have understood Wallachian (Romanian dialect) and very likely spoke it. (See Explorador.)

In a letter of 1872 to a Russian official, she wrote, "I can speak French, English, Italian, as well as Russian, I easily understand German and Hungarian and a little bit of Turkish."

Countess Wachtmeister recalled that she spoke English, Russian, French, Italian and "drooped into Hindustanee." In a letter of 1878 to Hurry Chintamon in India, H.P.B. told her correspondent that she intended to study Hindustani again. "I will be at my post -- however much (like an old idiot that I am) I have forgotten Hindustani."

That was hardly all despite Helena's unwillingness to make claims regarding her phenomenal linguistic abilities. In her later writings, she used ancient Greek, Hebrew, Sanskrit and Senzar terms freely, showing her familiarity with them. "The Senzar and Sanskrit and other occult tongues, besides other potencies, have a number and colour and distinct syllable for every letter, and so also has ancient Hebrew."

In *Old Diary Leaves,* Colonel Olcott mentioned that, "... when H.P.B. wrote to the Masters or they to her, on business that was not to be communicated to third parties, it was in an archaic language, said to be 'Senzar,' which resembles Tibetan, and which she wrote as fluently as she did Russian, French or English."

She told A.P. Sinnett how in Tibet in the early 1870s, she spent much of her studies there learning Senzar along with re-learning (then, she knew not for what future use) conversational English. Helena had been taught English by a Yorkshire governess whose accent was laughable. Hence, H.P.B. spoke with the same stressed English till corrected in Tibet, of all places. Surely, she picked up Tibetan at the same time.

H.P.B. appeared to be, from the vantage point of those who should have known, not only a linguist but also a philologist (expert in word origins). When in America writing to Dr. Alexander Wilder, himself a noted philologist, she discussed with him the "name of God" as it had been given in Russian, Slavonian, Semitic, Sanskrit, Assyrian. She went on to say, "I have studied some of the old Turanian words ... in Samarkand with an old scholar ..."

So, she could understand, read and write many, many languages! So, H.P.B. put those talents to use certainly when she traveled and in her own private studies. But, she also went on to translate whole books from one language to the other.

Most of her writings over the years were done in English, French and Russian. She freely and regularly translated her own pieces from one to the other language so that they could be available for readers in distant lands. H.P.B.'s first major translating job involved interpreting Henry Olcott's writings on spiritualism for use in Russian newspapers.

Newspapers were common ground for Blavatsky's own writings from the time of her arrival in the USA in 1873, but probably even before that. She told a reporter for *The Daily Graphic* in New York in 1874 that she was a contributor to the *Revue des Deux Mondes* and had been a correspondent to the *Independence Belge* and Parisian Journals.

H.P.B. also translated the whole of Buckles's *History of Civilization in England* and Darwin's *Origin of the Species* into Russian. Madame Blavatsky re-wrote her own book *Isis Unveiled* into French while at sea on the ship Chandernagore in 1884 as it steamed from Bombay, India, to Marseilles, France.

While living in the USA, she endeavored to complete Dickens's *Edwin Drood*. In correspondence with a publisher in Moscow, H.P.B.

reported, "I have translated this second part, and it is lying ready before me...." In 1882, Helena did a partial translation of *The Brothers Karamazov* into English. That part is entitled *The Grand Inquisitor* and tells of Dostoevski's views on the Society of Jesus: the Jesuits.

The final writing project of Madame Blavatsky's life was a translation, or so she described it. H.P.B. worked with extracts from the ancient text called *The Book of Golden Precepts* which she had learned in Telugu, a southern Indian tongue. The modern version became a classic piece which she entitled *The Voice of the Silence*.

As she became a sought-after teacher and respected writer in the USA, Madame B. would quote "to them (students and colleagues) whole sentences in ancient Hebrew." At her writing desk, she took dictation from adepts for letters in English, Russian, French - and Marathi, Bhasha, and other Hindustani dialects.

Regardless of what she said and wrote about herself, H.P.B. was clearly, like other savants and genii and masters of thought, a *rara avis*. She lived more than others could ever realize in two or three or more worlds. They included the obvious outer one, another in the inner realm where she set about to accomplish her assigned work, and yet another - a world of her own, one with a language peculiar to herself.

A reporter visiting H.P.B. remarked, "Glancing at a pile of letters which the servant had just brought, we exclaimed, 'What an immense correspondence must be yours, madame! And in so many different languages! Tell us! What language do you think in?'

"'In a language of my own! which is neither Russian, French, nor any you know.'" *Hartford Daily Times*, December 2, 1878

Interprete
(Spanish for Interpreter)

"I am but the humble interpreter of
the more or less veiled truths and symbols,
well known to all who have studied their Virgil
and their Horace, as well as their Ovid."

Helena Blavatsky was not one to take credit even when it was due. She objected when praised for many of her linguistic exhibitions and gave a totally different view of those talents in a letter to Aunt Nadya. "When I tell these people that I have never been in Mongolia, that I don't understand either Sanskrit, Hebrew or the ancient European languages, they simply laugh at me and say, 'How does it come that you can describe everything so exactly, if you have never been there?' They believe that I have some reason for not admitting the truth, and I feel embarrassed when I must say that I have no knowledge of languages, while at the time everyone can hear me speaking different Indian dialects with a learned man, who has lived 20 years in India ..."

There seemed, at times, a wide disparity between what H.P.B. thought of her own wide-ranging talents and what interviewers and bystanders, colleagues and fellow writers, students and professors took from her expositions and exhibitions. Earlier in the same letter of 1877 cited just above, H.P. Blavatsky took on both sides of the debate: "A pupil of Faraday's, a certain Professor H., who has been christened 'the Father of experimental physics' [referring to Faraday] by the voice of a thousand mouths, having spent the last evening with me, now assures me that I am well qualified to 'put Faraday in my pocket.' Can it be that friends and enemies alike have leagued together to make of me a savant, if all that I do is to prove superficially certain wild theories of my own? And if it were only my own devoted Olcott and other Theosophists who had such a high opinion of me it could be said: '*Dans le pay des aveugles les borgnes sont rois*' [In the land of the blind, the one-eyed are kings]. But I continually have a whole crowd from morning till night of all kinds of Professors, Doctors of Science, and Doctors of Divinity ... for instance, there are two Hebrew Rabbis here, Adler and Goldstein, who are both of them thought to be the greatest Talmudists. They know by heart both the Quabalah of Shimon ben Yohai and the Codex Nazaraeus of Bardesanes. They were brought to me by A., a protestant clergyman and commentator on the Bible, who hoped they would prove that I am mistaken on the subject of a certain statements in the Chaldean Bible of Onkelos. And with what result? I have beaten them. I quoted to them whole sentences in ancient Hebrew and proved to them that Onkelos is an authority of the Babylonian school...."

Madame Blavatsky was incredibly versatile and often as active as several persons. She could carry on conversations in two languages, play her evening game of patience, and be mentally and astrally busy elsewhere all at the same time. Madame's intellect and repartee as well as her many talents tended to make heads swim from Russia to America, England to India, and many places in between. However since she departed the physical world, H.P.B. is probably most remembered for her prolific pen.

"Prolific pen" only hints at the prodigious output of writing which came through her expansive mind and busy fingers. Helena Blavatksy surely ranks with history's very most productive writers, doing so in a wide range of genres while creating products of depth and lasting value. Her writing began for recounting purposes in 1874 early in her New York City days and ended with her death in London in 1891: a relatively brief 17 years compared to other productive authors. Before that period, she was mostly engaged in growing up and traveling the world, training for and discovering her niche in life. The most prolific of writers generally spend their whole adult lives working with words and crafting their arts. Not so for H.P.B.

Still, Madame Blavatsky wrote millions of words in many thousands of pages of letters and editorials, articles and books with merely pen and ink and foolscap paper for her tools. Forget computers or word processors with which moderns can quickly write, cut and paste. (Even using electronically-assisted methods, authors of recent history still say that writing is real and daunting work.)

Forget as well the typewriter which was just beginning to be used toward the end of Helena's life. It is said that Mark Twain was the first American to submit a typewritten novel for publication in 1883. That book was *Life on the Mississippi* and Twain dictated the story to a typist. Apparently, he had a devil of time dealing with typewriters even though he got credit for their early use.

The publishing and printing processes were also quite slow and crude in the time of Mark and Madame. They have gone through many stages of improvement since Gutenberg came up with the first press with moveable type. But most of them have occurred in recent times, so that we don't readily realize how tedious and involved writing and producing papers and books was in generations past.

H.P.B. was not so lucky to have a typewriter nor a typist taking her dictation. (She did have help typing her works into manuscript form in the last years of her life.) Generally, she wrote by hand, day and night, leaving piles of foolscap to be studied, edited and re-written the next work day. And if anyone was taking "dictation," it was Madame.

Beyond that, Russian-born Blavatsky wrote most of her material in one of her adopted languages, usually English. For Mme. B. to become an accomplished writer of English non-fiction in the United States of America was a phenomenon in itself. In her very last article on "My Books" which she penned shortly before her death, H.P.B. stated,

(1). When I came to America in 1873, I had not spoken English -- which I learned in my childhood colloquially -- for over 30 years. I could understand when I read it, but could hardly speak the language.
(2). I had never been at any College, and what I knew I had taught myself; I have never pretended to any scholarship in the sense of modern research; I had then hardly read any scientific European works, knew little of Western philosophy and sciences. The little which I had studied and learned of these disgusted me with its materialism, its limitations, narrow cut-and-dried spirit of dogmatism and air of superiority over the philosophies and sciences of antiquity.
(3). Until 1874, I had never written one word in English, nor had I published any work in any language. Therefore:—
(4). I had not the least idea of literary rules. The art of writing books, of preparing them for print and publication, reading and correcting proofs, were so many close[d] secrets to me.
(5). When I started to write that which developed later into Isis Unveiled, *I had no more idea than the man in the moon what would come of it. I had no plan; did not know whether it would be an essay, a pamphlet, a book or an article.*

Isis Unveiled, begun in late 1874, was her first great writing effort. It followed her early articles to newspapers and journals printed in diverse places, her name eventually appearing in print all around the globe. She first devoted her pen to issues surrounding then-popular Spiritualism and Mediumship. Many of her articles were published in Boston's *Spiritual Scientist* and *Banner of Light*. She made frequent contributions to the *Religio-Philosophical Journal* (Chicago) as well as *The Spiritualist* (London) and *La Revue Spirite* (Paris). At the same time, she wrote fascinating occult stories for leading New York City newspapers, including *The World*, *The Sun* and *The Daily Graphic*.

Madame Blavatsky put her power and prowess into purposeful action only in high-minded and fervent-hearted works. They were meant not just to be read but to be studied and pondered and studied again. She soon passed beyond those long and pointed letters to editors. H.P.B. took on Science and Theology in her grand two-volume, 1200-page *Isis Unveiled*.

Many paradoxes surround the writing of *Isis Unveiled*. It was Mme. Blavatsky's first major writing effort in any language -- and a foreign one at that. Still, reviewers thought it a "monumental work." H.P.B. considered it "my worst book," even while *Isis* contained an awesome "mass of original and never hitherto divulged information on occult subjects." Much of the material was drawn and translated from eastern languages and placed before western readers. A mountain of references and quotations were used to support the arguments in her writing. That part of her work is surely unprecedented.

Still, it seems that *Isis*, like her later *The Secret Doctrine*, was never completed. *Isis Unveiled* was written, written and re-written. H.P.B. was the amanuensis for the book and Henry Olcott took on the job of "Englishing" the material to make it palatable to its intended audience. Only a small portion of the material that Madame Blavatsky collected, wrote and re-wrote was ever put into print. Olcott's descriptions of the writing of *Isis Unveiled* (further details follow below) make for fascinating reading. "We had laboured at the book for several months and had turned out 870-odd pages of manuscript when, one evening, she put me the question whether, to oblige -- (our "Paramaguru "), I would consent to begin all over again! I well remember the shock it gave me to think that all those weeks of hard labour, of psychical thunder-storms and head-splitting archaeological conundrums, were to count -- as I, in my blind-puppy ignorance, imagined -- for nothing. However, as my love and reverence and gratitude to this Master, and all the Masters, for giving me the privilege of sharing in their work was without limits, I consented, and at it we went again. Well for me, was it, that I did; for, having proved my steadfastness of purpose and my loyalty to H. P. B., I got ample spiritual reward."

H.S.O. capped his reminiscence telling about how in the process of composition, "... we had prepared almost enough additional MS to make a third volume, and this was ruthlessly destroyed before we left

America; H.P.B. not dreaming that she should ever want to utilise it in India, and the *Theosophist, Secret Doctrine,* and her other subsequent literary productions, not even being thought of. How often she and I mingled our regrets that all that valuable material had been so thoughtlessly wasted!"

Still, within those two volumes, "the explanations of a hundred mysteries lie but half buried.... only waiting for the application of intelligence guided by a little Occult knowledge to come into the light of day." *Isis* was keen to make known the wonders that ancient sages have preserved for all times in a variety of ways. Symbols lay unexposed for ages. And even when uncovered they have been misread because of the smallness of human minds.

Dr. Alexander Wilder, physician and scholar, was drawn into the *Isis* project to help with the editing and to create its massive index. Some critics tried to give the degreed professor credit for the work, implying that an unschooled, Russian-born woman was incapable of composing such a tome. Wilder would have none of it. He said that *Isis* was "a truly ponderous document and displayed research in a very extended field (particularly occultism and philosophy), requiring diligence and familiarity with various topics ... as far as related to current thinking, there was a revolution in it, but I added that I deemed it too long for remunerative publishing."

Despite its ponderosity and length, a 50-page index in which 1339 works were referenced, and a plethora of quotations from a dozen or more languages, *Isis* was published in 1877 to plentiful plaudits and repeated printings. The first edition of 1000 copies sold out in nine days. New York City newspapers declared it "one of the remarkable productions of the century" and "one of the most extraordinary works of the nineteenth century."

Isis Unveiled was itself a reflection of the phenomenal aspects of life upon which H.P.B. lectured. She not only transcribed *Isis*. She lived *Isis*. Madame wrote and wrote, day and night. Seven days a week, she put pen to paper to produce typically twenty-five closely written foolscap pages each day. Even though hundreds of references originating in a dozen languages were cited in the book, Helena had practically no library to draw upon.

Parts of the composition of *Isis* were done in Ithaca, New York, at the home of Professor Hiram Corson who noted, "She would write in bed, from nine o'clock in the morning, smoking innumerable cigarettes, quoting long verbatim paragraphs from several languages ..."

"She herself told me that she wrote them (quotations) down as they appeared in her eyes on another plane of objective existence ... never have I seen such an intense creature, intense in her purpose, intense in her endeavour; nothing round her mattered ... she clearly saw the page of the book, and the quotation she needed, and simply translated what she saw in English.... The hundreds of books quoted were certainly not in my library, many of them not in America, some of them very rare and difficult to get in Europe, and if her quotations were from memory, then it was an even more startling feat than writing them from the ether. The facts are marvelous, and the explanation must necessarily bewilder those whose consciousness is of a more ordinary type."

Eventually, Professor Corson was given further *pictures* on one of Madame B.'s favored writing methods. Once she returned to New York City to do the bulk of the work on *Isis*, H.P.B. sent letters about how the work passed through her and how she *suffered* for it. "I am nailed up like a slave to my chair writing all days as I did at your [Corson's] place. I am writing *Isis*; not writing, rather copying out and drawing that which she (*Isis*) personally is showing me. I live in a kind of permanent enchantment, a life of visions and sights with open eyes, and no trance whatever to deceive my senses! I sit and watch the fair goddess constantly. And as she displays before me the secret meaning of her long lost secrets, and the veil becoming with every hour thinner and more transparent, gradually falls off before my eyes, I hold my breath and can hardly trust to my senses.... For several years in order not to forget what I have learned elsewhere, I have been made to have permanently before my eyes all that I need to see. Thus, night and day, the images of the past are ever marshalled before my inner eye. Slowly, and gliding silently like images in an enchanted panorama, centuries after centuries appear before me ... and I am made to connect these epochs with certain historical events, and I know there can be no mistake. Races and nations, countries and cities, emerge during some former century, then fade out and disappear during some other one, the precise date of which I am then told by ____. Hoary antiquity gives room to historical periods; myths are explained by real events and personages who have really existed; and every important and often unimportant event, every revolution, a new leaf turned in the book of life of nations -- with its incipient course and subsequent natural results -- remains photographed in my mind as though impressed in indelible colours.... When I think and watch my thoughts, they appear to me as though they were like those little bits of wood of various shapes and colours, in the game known as the *casse tete*: I pick them up one by one, and try to make them fit each other, first taking one, then putting it aside, until I find its match, and finally there always comes out in the end something geometrically correct.... I certainly refuse point-blank to attribute it to my own knowledge or memory, for I could never arrive alone at either such premises or conclusions.... I tell you seriously I am helped. And he who helps me is my Guru...."

A few other intimates got glimpses of how she worked hour after hour with pen and paper. Staring off into space with a keen eye, as if searching for something in the distance. H.P.B. reported to her sister by letter, "When I wrote *Isis,* I wrote it so easily that it was actually no labour, but a real pleasure.... ever I am told to write, I sit down and obey, and then I can write easily upon almost anything; metaphysics, psychology, philosophy, ancient religions, zoology, natural sciences -- or what not. ... all essential matter is dictated to me.... All that I write will not be my own; I shall be nothing more than the pen, the head which will think for me will be that of one who knows all ..."

H.P.B. related in more detail about the help that she received: "I see this Hindu every day, just as I might see any other living person, with the only difference that he looks to me more ethereal and more transparent. Formerly I kept silent about these appearances, thinking that they were hallucinations. But now they have become visible to other people as well. He (the Hindu) appears and advises us as to our conduct and our writing. He evidently knows everything that is going on, even to the thoughts of other people, and makes me express his knowledge. Sometimes it seems to me that he overshadows the whole of me, simply entering me like a kind of volatile essence penetrating all my pores and dissolving in me. Then we two are able to speak to other people, and then I begin to understand and remember sciences and languages -- everything he instructs me in, even when he is not with me any more."

Colonel Olcott recalled Madame's *modus operandi* during her early writing days. "H.P.B. was, all the world knows, an inveterate smoker. She consumed an immense number of cigarettes daily, for the rolling of which she possessed the greatest deftness. She could even roll them with her left hand while she was writing 'copy' with her right. While she was writing *Isis Unveiled*, at New York, she would not leave her apartment for six months at a stretch. From early morning until very late at night she would sit at her table working. It was not an uncommon thing for her to be seventeen hours out of the twenty-four at her writing. Her only exercise was to go to the dining-room or bath-room and back again to her table."

Olcott stayed in close physical proximity to Blavatsky during nearly two years of the writing and editing, collating and proofing of *Isis Unveiled*. He had keen and prolonged opportunity to watch Helena at work as well as assist in the copying and pasting and correcting. His general critique of the process included these remarks:

Whence did she get this knowledge? That she had it, was unmistakable ... Not from her governesses in Russia; not from any source known to her family or most intimate friends; not on the steamships or railways she had been haunting in her world-rambles since her fifteenth year; not in any college or university, for she never matriculated at either; not in the huge libraries of the world. To judge from her conversation and habits before she took up this monster literary task, she had not learnt it at all, whether from one source or another; but when she needed it she had it, and in her better moments of inspiration -- if the term be admissible -- she astonished the most erudite by her learning quite as much as she dazzled all present by her eloquence and delighted them by her wit and humorous raillery.

One might fancy, upon seeing the numerous quotations in Isis Unveiled *that she had written it in an alcove of the British Museum or of the Astor Library in New York. The fact is, however, that our whole working library scarcely comprised one hundred books of reference.*

Unfamiliar with grammatical English and literary methods, and with her mind absolutely untrained for such sustained desk-work, yet endowed with a courage without bounds and a power of continuous mental concentration that has scarcely been equalled, she floundered on through weeks and months towards her goal, the fulfilment of her Master's orders. This literary feat of hers far surpasses all her phenomena.

The glaring contrasts between the jumbled and the almost perfect portions of her MS quite ... prove that the same intelligence was not at work throughout; and the variations in hand-writing, in mental method, in literary facility, and in personal idiosyncracies, bear out this idea.

Regardless of her method and inspiration, H.P.B. wrote and wrote and wrote. When the Theosophical Society moved to India, Madame Blavatsky continued to be fully occupied with writing despite the travails of the foreign, impoverished and seemingly ignorant land. She soon went to work through *The Theosophist*. But, she also made time for travelogues for Russian newspapers, which eventually became *From the Caves and Jungles of Hindustan,* and her *Nightmare Tales*. Those stories were "written in leisure moments, more for amusement than with any serious design. Broadly speaking, the facts and incidents are true; but I have freely availed myself of an author's privilege to group, colour and dramatize them ..." From 1879 to 1886 (while fully occupied in India), she wrote her serials for the Russian newspaper, *Moskovskiya Vedomosty* (Moscow), and the periodical, *Russkiy Vestnik* (Moscow), as well as for lesser newspapers, such as *Pravda* (Odessa), *Tiflisskiy Vestnik* (Tiflis), *Rebus* (St. Petersburg), and others.

At the same time from 1879 onward, she contributed to *The Indian Spectator, The Deccan Star, The Bombay Gazette, The Pioneer, The Amrita Bazaar Patrika*, and other newspapers. Once H.P.B. got her pen racing over pages of foolscap, she was like an untamable dynamo.

The Theosophist became Madame's own journal through which she could pour her ardent beliefs and compassionate aspirations. It was inaugurated when Olcott and Blavatsky strategically removed themselves from America to India to build and broaden the fledgling Theosophical Society established in New York City in 1875. Leaving the USA in December 1878, Madame opened the pages of *The Theosophist* in October 1879. She acted as editor and chief writer until departing for Europe 1884 and handing the day-to-day business of the journal to Headquarters staff in Adyar, India.

Writing through *The Theosophist*, H.P.B. went beyond religion, spiritualism and the occult. She tackled such diverse subjects as prehistory and history (especially Russian and Indian), geology, paleontology, anthropology and cosmology. Blavatsky continued to cover legends and myths, fakirs and yogis, elementals and elementaries, Kabbalah and Freemasonry, numerology and cycles, electricity and magnetism, miracles and magic, the zodiac and astrology, saints and philosophers, lamas and druzes, adepts and brothers, death and satan, and on and on. There was hardly a topic of interest in the nineteenth century which Madame Blavatsky shied away from other than politics. She even had a few prophetic things to say about western nations and their governments in the twentieth century.

Religions of the world, especially from the East, were regular fare in the journals which she created once the Theosophical Society had been birthed. She was capable of writing with authority on any religion or tradition, East and West, past and present. Animism and Deism, Hinduism and Buddhism, Christianity and Judaism.

Those pieces were not snippets, but detailed expositions of depth knowledge on both common denominational religion as well as their esoteric counterparts. Madame "investigated" all religions and their founders. She often found the former far from conforming to the ideals of the latter. At one point, H.P.B. sent out an open letter to the Archbishop of Canterbury taking him and his Church of England to task for failing to live up to the Gospel of the Christ. "The time is approaching when the clergy will be called upon to render an account of their stewardship. Are you prepared, My Lord Primate, to explain to YOUR MASTER why you have given His children stones, when they cried to you for bread?"

Science, history and philosophy formed the broad umbrella of subjects for writing which she did with knowledge and sagacity. Blavatsky's truncheon was always Truth. She did not shirk from it and went about bringing leaders and followers to stand face to face with it. "There is no Religion higher than Truth" was adopted early on as the motto of the Theosophical Society. It most truly suited its co-founder and her attitude to life and fellow creatures.

Years passed with Helena producing thousands more pages of writing in her newspaper articles and journal contributions before another major project developed. When she took on the composition of her *The Secret Doctrine*, close scrutiny again was paid to her routines and methods.

At that time, Countess Wachtmeister, Franz Hartmann, W.Q. Judge and others kept tabs on her work and assisted as possible. By that time in her life, H.P.B. was plagued by recurrent, often life-threatening illnesses. Despite her ills, she plodded on writing wherever she could find space, paper and ink. As in other times, Madame Blavatsky wrote while traveling on ship. En route to Naples in 1885, Dr. Hartmann reported that even while at sea there were often piles of sheets with notes on *The Secret Doctrine* waiting for Madame before she set to work each morning.

Dr. Wilhelm Hubbe-Schleiden, lawyer and author himself of *The Sphinx* magazine, called on Madame a number of times when she was settled in Germany and began to compose *The Secret Doctrine*. "When I visited her in October, 1885 ... she had scarcely any books, not half a dozen ... I saw her write down sentences as if she were copying them from something before her, where, however, I saw nothing.... I remember well my astonishment one morning when I got up to find a great many pages of foolscap covered with that blue pencil handwriting lying on her own manuscript, at her place on the desk. How these pages got there I do not know, but I did not see them before I went to sleep and no person had been bodily in the room during the night, for I am a light sleeper."

Countess Constance Wachtmeister was aide and assistant to Mme. Blavatsky for much of her latter years. She, too, wondered at "the poverty of her traveling library. Her manuscripts were full to overflowing with references, quotations, allusions, from a mass of rare and recondite works on subjects of the most varied kinds...." By her side in Germany, Wachtmeister was asked on occasion by Madame to verify certain passages in *The Secret Doctrine*. One of her contacts visited the Bodleian Library at Oxford and another went to the Vatican to verify H.P.B.'s work. The former found her reference totally correct. The latter discovered errors in two words, but those two were said to be blurred on the original manuscript and "difficult to decipher."

H.P.B. was prone to common errors which occur when reading via the Astral Light. She would reverse numbers and letters. When she made a mistake in her transcription, H.P.B. likely had failed to make allowance for "reading the reflection" of physical material.

Bertram Keightley, another theosophical aide, experienced Madame Blavatsky's amazing range of literary resources. He remembered how H.P.B. fancied putting a quotation at the top of her *Lucifer* editorials. That often produced troubles because she seldom gave a reference.

One day she handed me as usual the copy of her contribution, a story for the next issue headed with a couple of four line stanzas. I went and plagued her for a reference and would not be satisfied without one. She took the MS and when I came back for it, I found she had just written the name 'Alfred Tennyson' under the verses. Seeing this I was at a loss: for I knew my Tennyson pretty well and was certain that I had never read these lines in any poem of his, nor were they at all in his style. I hunted up my Tennyson, could not find them: consulted every one I could get at -- also in vain. Then back I went to H.P.B. and told her all this and said that I was sure these lines could not be Tennyson's, and I dared not print them with his name attached, unless I could give an exact reference. H.P.B. just damned me and told me to get out and go to Hell. It happened that the Lucifer copy must go to the printers that same day. So I just told her that I should strike out

Tennyson's name when I went, unless she gave me a reference before I started. Just on starting I went to her again, and she handed me a scrap of paper on which were written the words: *The Gem -- 1831.* 'Well, H.P.B.,' I said, 'this is worse than ever: for I am dead certain that Tennyson has never written any poem called *The Gem.*' All H.P.B. said was just: Go out and be off.'

So I went to the British Museum Reading Room and consulted the folk there; but they could give me no help and they one and all agreed that the verses could not be, and were not Tennyson's. As a last resort, I asked to see Mr. Richard Garnett, the famous Head of the Reading Room in those days, and was taken to him. I explained to him the situation and he also agreed in feeling sure the verses were not Tennyson's. But after thinking quite a while, he asked me if I had consulted the Catalogue of Periodical Publications. I said no, and asked where that came in. 'Well,' said Mr. Garnett, 'I have a dim recollection that there was once a brief-lived magazine called the *Gem*. It might be worth your looking it up.' I did so, and in the volume for the year given in H.P.B.'s note, I found a poem of a few stanzas signed 'Alfred Tennyson' and containing the two stanzas quoted by H.P.B. verbatim as she had written them down. And anyone can now read them in the second volume of *Lucifer*: but I have never found them even in the supposedly most complete and perfect edition of Tennyson's Works.

Uncle Archibald Keightley appeared for a time and was requested to "emendate, excise, alter the English, punctuate (*The SD* manuscript)" During his short stay and occupation he was most struck by "the enormous number of quotations from various authors. I knew that there was no library to consult and I could see that H.P.B.'s own books did not amount to thirty in all, of which several were dictionaries and several works counted two or more volumes."

For those who have eyes to see, with or without astral vision, Madame Blavatsky's referencing work alone was phenomenal. Any librarian before the digital era would have required years to track down and verify the quotations and references H.P.B. used in her major works. Even with modern computers, the task would be daunting.

Sister Vera appeared for a time during *The Secret Doctrine* project. Like most other visitors, she was struck by several seeming contradictions in H.P.B.'s extraordinary works.

During these readings two characteristic points struck me especially, viz., the wonderful picturesqueness of language and detailed descriptions when Helena Petrovna spoke, giving explanations on all kinds of questions asked her by specialists, and at the same time her perfect inability to keep to a purely scientific presentation of the evidences and the formulas.

Her talk was always entrancing, but as soon as she came to mathematical data, it constantly occurred that she was not able to read the algebraical and geometrical conclusions written down by her personality. Very often when left alone with her, I expressed astonishment to her: "How can it be, that you, having calculated and written all this down yourself, can't read it?"

To this question my sister always replied, with hearty laughter, "Do you expect me to know the problems of the higher mathematics? Your daughters are bas bleus and have learnt all these erudite matters, but, as to you and myself, have not we learned side by side, and did not we have the greatest trouble to master the first four rules of arithmetic?"

"Then how is it that you have written all this without knowing anything about it?"

"Come, now, don't be so naive! As if you don't know there are many things in my writings of which I never dreamed before. I do not write them, I only copy out what is ready made before my eyes. I know that you always disbelieved me, but in this you see one more proof that I am only the tool and not the master."

Vera's daughter, Vera Johnston, topped that story with an episode which occurred when Madame called for help one morning: "Vera, do you think you could tell me what is a pi?"

Rather astonished at such a question, I said I thought a pie was some kind of an English dish. "Please don't make a fool of yourself," she said rather impatiently, "don't you understand I address you in your capacity of a mathematical pundit...."

I looked at the page that lay before her on the table, and saw it was covered with figures and calculations, and soon became aware that the formula $\Pi = 3\text{-}14159$ was put down wrongly throughout them all. It was written $\Pi = 31\text{-}4159$. With great joy and triumph I hastened to inform her of her mistake.

"That's it!" she exclaimed. "This confounded comma bothered me all the morning. I was rather in a hurry yesterday to put down what I *saw, and to-day at the first glance at the page I intensely but vaguely felt there was something wrong, and do what I could I could not remember where the comma actually was when I saw this number."*

Knowing very little of Theosophy in general and my aunt's ways of writing in particular at that time, I of course was greatly struck with her not being able to correct such a slight mistake in the very intricate calculations she had written down with her own hand.

"You are very green," she said, "if you think that I actually know and understand all the things I write. How many times am I to repeat to you and your mother that the things I write are dictated to me, that sometimes I see manuscripts, numbers, and words before my eyes of which never knew anything."

Helena eventually finished the composition of the two volumes of *The Secret Doctrine (Cosmogenesis* and *Anthropogenesis*) in 1888. To the open-minded, Bertram Keightley suggested that its 1600-page text "will be found of incalculable value, and will furnish suggestions, clues, and threads of guidance, for the study of Nature and Man, such as no other existing work can supply."

Christmas Humphreys, British Buddhist, attorney and author, took on the task of making *An Abridgement of The Secret Doctrine* in the 1960s. He noted, "In these 250 pages is to be found enough for a lifetime's study and application and, in the two volumes, more as I have found, than in all the scriptures of the world available in English."

The Secret Doctrine will only be attractive to small fractions of the reading population for centuries to come. Yet, the first edition in the the 19th century quickly sold out requiring further printings. *The Secret Doctrine* has continued in publication for over a century (as have most of H.P.B.'s books) and in a variety of editions including recent electronic versions. Many commentators believe that students of the text have just begun to mine the treasures found within its pages.

Madame and her weighty *Doctrine* have profoundly influenced scientists and thinkers, artists and writers for generations now. And certainly will for many more to come even as further installments are made when the times and Teachers permit. (See Helel.)

Yet there is always the other hand, as when pedants and nitpickers criticized *The Secret Doctrine* and its writer for "plagiarism." But, Madame beat critics to the punch in the introduction to her volumes: "To my judges, past and future, therefore -- whether they are serious literary critics, or those howling dervishes in literature who judge a book according to the popularity or unpopularity of the author's name, who, hardly glancing at its contents, fasten like *lethal bacilli* on the weakest points of the body -- I have nothing to say. Nor shall I condescend to notice those crack-brained slanderers -- fortunately very few in number -- who, hoping to attract public attention by throwing discredit on every writer whose name is better known than their own, foam and bark at their very shadows. These, having first maintained for years that the doctrines taught in the *Theosophist*, and which culminated in 'Esoteric Buddhism [written by A.P. Sinnett],' had been all invented by the present writer, have finally turned round, and denounced 'Isis Unveiled' and the rest as a plagiarism from Eliphas Levi (!), Paracelsus (!!), and, *mirabile dictu*, Buddhism and Brahmanism (!!!) As well charge Renan with having stolen his *Vie de Jesus* from the Gospels, and Max Muller his 'Sacred Books of the East' or his 'Chips' from the philosophies of the Brahmins and Gautama, the Buddha. But to the public in general and the readers of the 'Secret Doctrine' I may repeat what I have stated all along, and which I now clothe in the words of Montaigne: Gentlemen, 'I HAVE HERE MADE ONLY A NOSEGAY OF CULLED FLOWERS, AND HAVE BROUGHT NOTHING OF MY OWN BUT THE STRING THAT TIES THEM.'"

Madame Blavatsky was hardly done after completing what would have been a terribly exhausting task for any human, hale and able-bodied. Some few months after finishing *The Secret Doctrine*, Madame B. moved from the Continent to London and soon decided another journal was in order. She then put her considerable force and weight into *Lucifer: A Theosophical Magazine*, designed to "bring to light the hidden things of darkness."

Inaugurated on September 15, 1887, the *Lucifer* title likely scared more than a few. But, H.P.B. was not deterred. Helena knew quite what she was about and finally had sufficient help at hand in London as well as her everpresent invisible aides to guide her works. In the same time period, her editorial and authorial works were also channeled through *Revue Theosophique* and *Le Lotus Bleu* in Paris and *The Path* in New York. How she managed to write and edit for journals in two European capitals and the great American metropolis is one of those questions which must point to her phenomenal talents for an answer.

Madame Blavatsky's book-writing days continued in the midst of her editorial and teaching work in England. Her physical body became a greater and greater burden in a number of ways in latter years. Yet, she persisted despite being at death's door, many times. She stayed on to see *The Secret Doctrine* published, write many more journal articles, teach more students, and compose a few more texts.

Her final book may be the greatest gem of all her works. *The Voice of the Silence* was based on writings she had studied while in India at least a score years past. She composed it from three fragments of the most ancient *Book of Golden Precepts*. Madame took great pride in that accomplishment. She had memorized 39 slokas (verses) and carried them with her for decades before putting them down on paper for the western readers. *The Voice* text is approximately 10,000 words. What a phenomenal memory! That one little book shines out as yet another wonderful gift that H.P.B. passed on to her fellows, then and now and into the future. Her followers in 1891 were delighted with the result and the little book has become a classic.

Ten thousand words make only a modest-sized book, but *The Voice of the Silence* is another one of those study-and-ponder productions which Madame B. penned. It supplemented her previous tomes of *Isis Unveiled* (1877) and *The Secret Doctrine* (1888), *The Keys to Theosophy* (1889) which is a concise volume on basic principles of the Ageless Wisdom, *Transactions of the Blavatsky Lodge* (1890), *The Theosophical Glossary* (1892), a calendar of *Gems of the East* (1892), and the fascinating collection of stories called *Nightmare Tales* (1892).

H.P.B.'s travelogue *From the Caves and Jungles of Hindustan*, which tied together her serial newspaper articles into book form, was published in Russia in 1883 and eventually translated into English by her niece, Vera Johnston, in 1892. Vera also did the same for Helena's stories about *The Enigmatical Tribes of the Azure-Blue Hills* which became *The People of the Blue Mountains* in English in 1893. All those writings were penned under the pseudonym of Raddha-Bai (one possible meaning is "perfect in magical powers").

In her books, Madame filled several thousand pages of print beginning with her quill pen and ink and foolscap. Her newspaper and journal articles were eventually compiled after her death and fill fourteen volumes, approximating 8000 pages including indexes and supporting information. Two volumes of her letters have been published. A 400-page book of *The Letters of H.P. Blavatsky to A.P. Sinnett* was collated and printed long ago. A decade ago, *The Letters of H.P. Blavatsky: Volume I - 1861-1879* (500 pages) was collected and published. Two further volumes will follow. One might wonder about pages never printed, consigned to wastebaskets and fireplaces.

To top it all off over 120 years after her death, Helena Blavatsky is widely read and studied. Biographies continue to be written. And, we might well expect revivals of her teaching to appear over the coming years while much of her thinking and many of her predictions are verified as philosophic and scientific study press on.

While the foregoing is rather phenomenal in itself, the even more amazing part of Madame's writing talents comes in the details as to how she composed her articles and books. To begin, she was a talented descriptive writer as can be readily seen for those who delve into *From the Caves and Jungles of Hindustan* and *Nightmare Tales*. Helena might have been a pop writer of the day had she produced more such page-turners for Americans and Englishers as well as Russians.

But, H.P.B. neither wrote stories and books nor collected references and interviews to simply create attractive material for readers of the late 19th century. Her versatility is really unparalleled as foregoing and following details make apparent. She wrote with a mission.

Much of Madame Blavatsky's writing work was done "on orders." On many mornings during her authorial career, she would be met by written slips of paper in blue or red ink on her work table. This was the case even though her desk had been tidied the night before. Whence came the slips and what were they for? She would simply respond, "These are my writing assignments, placed there by my Teachers."

How to proceed with her assignments? Madame utilized at least five main methods to "get the work done." She took dictation remotely, was impressed by the thoughts of distant helpers and Teachers, read astrally from books and libraries around the world, received written assistance by precipitation, and was overshadowed in her capacity as a *Tulku*. All of these require explanation.

CLAIRAUDIENCE: Helena Blavatsky lived much of her adult life at the end of an astral "on-call" button which made her immediately accessible to her Superiors when needed. She was note only attuned to the inner world and her Teachers, but at their beck and call practically all day long. Countess Wachtmeister related how H.P.B. kept her ear open to the "spiritual telegraph" and her pen to paper. "Day after day she would sit there writing through all the long hours, and nothing could be more monotonous and wearisome than her life regarded from an outside point of view. But, I suppose, at that time she lived much in the inner world, and there saw sights and visions which compensated for the dreariness of her daily life. She had, however, a distraction of rather a peculiar nature. In front of her writing table, attached to the wall, was a cuckoo clock, and this used to behave in a very extraordinary manner. Sometimes it would strike like a loud gong, then sigh and groan as if possessed, cuckooing in the most unexpected way. Our maid, Louise, who was the most dense and apathetic of mortals, was very much afraid of it, and told us solemnly one day that she thought the devil was in it. 'Not that I believe in the devil,' she said, 'but this cuckoo almost speaks to me at times.' And so it did. One evening I went into the room and saw what appeared to me like streams of electric light coming out of the clock in all directions. On telling H.P.B. she replied, 'Oh, it is only the spiritual telegraph, they are laying it on stronger to-night on account of tomorrow's work.'"

H.P.B. literally heard her Masters speak across the miles through her spiritual telegraph and telephone. She *merely* used a subtler version of sound reception than most humans do, one which called for much heightened sensitivity of her astral and mental bodies. Helena had highly developed inner senses. Ones which we all use in sleep states while free in our inner vehicles. For good or ill, we presently are unable to translate our nightly subtle sense experiences into conscious awareness. In distant rounds, we all will have evolved into practical use of these advanced abilities.

"... to do this, not only have one's spiritual senses to be abnormally opened, but one must himself have mastered the great secret -- yet undiscovered by science -- of, so to say abolishing all the impediments of space; of neutralising for the time being the natural obstacle of intermediary particles of air and forcing the waves to strike your ear in reflected sounds or echo. Of the latter you know as yet only enough to regard this as an unscientific absurdity.... But then, may there not be people who have found more perfect and rapid means of transmission, from being somewhat better acquainted with the occult powers of air (*akas*) and having plus a more cultivated judgment of sounds?"

TELEPATHY: H.P.B. not only responded to subtle sounds but she also tuned into and received the directed thoughts of her Master and his helpers. "... every word of information found in this work [*Isis Unveiled*] or in my later writings, comes from the teachings of our Eastern Masters; and ... that many a passage in these works has been written by me under their dictation. In saying this no supernatural claim is urged, for no miracle is performed by such a dictation. Any moderately intelligent person, convinced by this time of the many possibilities of hypnotism (now accepted by science and under full scientific investigation), and of the phenomena of thought-transference, will easily concede that if even a hypnotized subject, a mere irresponsible medium, hears the unexpressed thought of his hypnotizer, who can thus transfer his thought to him -- even to repeating the words read by the hypnotizer mentally from a book -- then my claim has nothing impossible in it. Space and distance do not exist for thought; and if two persons are in perfect mutual psycho-magnetic rapport, and of these two, one is a great Adept in Occult Sciences, then thought-transference and dictation of whole pages, become as easy and as comprehensible at the distance of ten thousand miles as the transference of two words across a room."

"An electro-magnetic connection, so to say, exists on the psychological plane between a Mahatma and his chelas, one of whom acts as his amanuensis. When the Master wants a letter to be written in this way, he draws the attention of the chela, whom he selects for the task, by causing an astral bell (heard by so many of our Fellows and others) to be rung near him just as the despatching telegraph office signals to the receiving office before wiring the message. The thoughts arising in the mind of the Mahatma are then clothed in word, pronounced mentally, and forced along the astral currents he sends towards the pupil to impinge on the brain of the latter. Thence they are borne by the nerve-currents to the palms of his hand and the tips of his finger, which rest on a piece of magnetically prepared paper. As the thought-waves are thus impressed on the tissue, materials are drawn to it from the ocean of *akas* (permeating every atom of the sensuous universe), by an occult process, out of place here to describe, and permanent marks are left."

CLAIRVOYANCE: Being impressed by distant thoughts is not all that uncommon. But sadly in the modern day, such "talents" can become problematic and attached to the label of lunatic (past) or psychotic (present). H.P.B. fit neither of those categories, although many in her time would have liked to make her out to be so.

Madame Blavatsky also developed the ability, now active in only a rare few, to accurately view the inner worlds. Clairvoyance generally involves people who tune into remotely occurring events in distressing times. Other "clairvoyants" view the auras of associates and attempt to describe what they sense. But, H.P.B.'s skill was much more directive. She pointed her mind at will and collected exotic information.

Henry Olcott was privileged to see her in the process while he was at her side as *Isis Unveiled* was written and re-written. "To watch her at work was a rare and never-to-be-forgotten experience. We sat at opposite sides of one big table usually, and I could see her every movement. Her pen would be flying over the page, when she would suddenly stop, look out into space with the vacant eye of the clairvoyant seer, shorten her vision as though to look at something held invisible in the air before her, and begin copying on her paper what she saw. The quotation finished, her eyes would resume their natural expression, and she would go on writing until again stopped by a similar interruption."

Css. Wachtmeister got H.P.B.'s own explanation when writing *The Secret Doctrine*, "Well, you see, what I do is this. I make what I can only describe as a sort of vacuum in the air before me, and fix my sight and my will upon it, and soon scene after scene passes before me like the successive pictures of a diorama, or, if I need a reference or information from some book, I fix my mind intently, and the astral counterpart of the book appears, and from it I take what I need. The more perfectly my mind is freed from distractions and mortifications, the more energy and intentness it possesses, the more easily I can do this."

In sum, Helena Blavatsky had the exceedingly rare gift of reading the Akashic Records: "The (to us) invisible tablets of the Astral Light, 'the great picture-gallery of eternity' -- a faithful record of every act, and even thought of man, of all that was, is, or ever will be, in the phenomenal Universe. The Book of Life."

Her methods were neither simple nor static, but varied with writing project, her age and health, and other influences. "There's a new development and scenery, every morning. I live two lives again. Master finds that it is too difficult for me to be looking consciously into the astral light for my *S.D.* and so, it is now about a fortnight, I am made to see all I have to as though in my dream. I see large and long rolls of paper on which things are written and I recollect them. Thus all the Patriarchs from Adam to Noah were given me to see — parallel with the Rishis; and in the middle between them, the meaning of their symbols — or personifications."

Dr. Hubbe-Schleiden watched her at work for extended periods with *The Secret Doctrine*. He recognized H.P.B. using two methods. "I also saw her write down sentences as if she were copying them from something before her, where, however, I saw nothing. I did not pay much attention to the manner of her work from the standpoint of a hunter of phenomena, and did not control it for that purpose; but I know that I saw a good deal of the well-known blue K.H. handwriting as corrections and annotations on her manuscripts as well as in books that lay occasionally on her desk. And I noticed this principally in the morning before she had commenced to work."

PRECIPITATION: With regard to H.P. Blavatsky's writing, precipitation entailed the phenomenon of making words or pictures appear on some medium without the application of a pen or pencil or brush. Besides having her "assignments" detailed in that manner on slips posted at her work table in the morning, H.P.B. was fortunate enough to find on occasion some chores done for her. As if the elves in a fairy tale came to her rescue and completed some of the mountain of work laid upon her feeble frame. "Most perfect of all were the manuscripts which were written for her while she was sleeping. The beginning of the chapter on the civilisation of Ancient Egypt of Isis (vol. i, chap. xiv) is an illustration. We (Olcott and Blavatsky) had stopped work the evening before at about 2 A.M. as usual, both too tired to stop for our usual smoke and chat before parting; she almost fell asleep in her chair while I was bidding her good-night, so I hurried off to my bedroom. The next morning, when I came down after my breakfast, she showed me a pile of at least thirty or forty pages of beautifully written H.P.B. manuscript, which, she said, she had had written for her by _____ well, a Master ..."

In a letter to A.P. Sinnett, K.H. explained how the precipitation of messages was accomplished. "Of course *I have to read* every word you write: otherwise I would make a fine mess of it. And whether it be through my physical or spiritual eyes the time required for it is practically the same. As much may be said of my replies. For, whether I 'precipitate' or dictate them or write my answers myself, the difference in time saved is very minute. I have to *think* it over, to photograph every word and sentence carefully in my brain before it can be repeated by 'precipitation.' As the fixing on chemically prepared surfaces of the images formed by the camera requires a previous arrangement within the focus of the object to be represented, for otherwise -- as often found in bad photographs -- the legs of the sitter might appear out of all proportion with the head, and so on, so we have to first arrange our sentences and impress every letter to appear on paper in our minds before it becomes fit to be read. For the present, it is *all* I can tell you. When science will have learned more about the mystery of the *lithophyl* (or *lithobiblion*) and how the impress of leaves comes originally to take place on stones, then will I be able to make you better understand the process. But you must know and remember one thing: we but follow and *servilely copy nature* in her works."

Helena Blavatsky made clear to interested readers that her inspiration as well as direction came from the Elder Brothers and she was their flawed but fiercely loyal and persistent amanuensis. They gave her orders, direction, and dictation. She was delegated to get material onto paper in some usable manner, published and available for the 19th century reading public. Helena was an imperfect channel for the work to be done, but the best that could be found at the time. Still, she brought forth ideas and information which had been relatively hidden for ages, much of it guarded in secrecy by religious sects. She also attracted help in America and Europe to get those earth-shaking contributions into print.

Madame took orders and dictation and followed the path set before her. The precipitation process may be considered a symbol for the whole of her works, written and otherwise. Henry Olcott related that, "they were asking H.P.B. to explain the scientific rationale of the process of precipitating upon paper, cloth, or any other surface, a picture or writing, then invisible to the onlooker, and without the help of ink, paints, pencils, or other mechanical agents. ... she explained that inasmuch as the images of all objects and incidents are stored in the Astral Light, it did not require that she should have seen the person or known the writing, the image of which she wished to precipitate; she had only to be put on the trace and could find and see them for herself and then objectivate them."

H.P.B.'s final method of composition was one in which she was much more the instrument than the writer. That most fantastic method involved the grand phenomenon called Tulku.

Tulku
(Tibetan for Vehicle)

"All that I can say is that someone positively inspires me ... more than this: someone enters me."

Early in the present century a Florentine scientist, a skeptic and a correspondent of the French Institute, having been permitted to penetrate in disguise to the hallowed precincts of a Buddhist temple, where the most solemn of all ceremonies was taking place, relates the following as having been seen by himself. An altar is ready in the temple to receive the resuscitated Buddha, found by the initiated priesthood, and recognized by certain secret signs to have reincarnated himself in a new-born infant. The baby, but a few days old, is brought into the presence of the people and reverentially placed upon the altar. Suddenly rising into a sitting posture, the child begins to utter in a loud, manly voice, the following sentences: 'I am Buddha, I am his spirit; and I, Buddha, your Dalai-Lama, have left my old, decrepit body, at the temple of ... and selected the body of this young babe as my next earthly dwelling.' Our scientist, being finally permitted by the priests to take, with due reverence, the baby in his arms, and carry it away to such a distance from them as to satisfy him that no ventriloquial deception is being practiced, the infant looks at the grave academician with eyes that 'make his flesh creep,' as he expresses it, and repeats the words he had previously uttered. A detailed account of this adventure, attested with the signature of this eye-witness, was forwarded to Paris, but the members of the Institute, instead of accepting the testimony of a scientific observer of acknowledged credibility, concluded that the Florentine was either suffering under an attack of sunstroke, or had been deceived by a clever trick of acoustics.

This incident, retold in the first volume of *Isis Unveiled*, gives clues to one of the most extraordinary lamaistic capacities which Helena Blavatsky was trained to manifest. The ability became particularly important in her writing and teaching life.

Madame B. "brought through" information in the astounding ways already described. But, there is much more. At times, she wrote and even spoke with associates and students in the most incredible method of all. Suggested on a few occasions in the previous chapter, the method has been called Tulku.

Tulku is an almost entirely foreign - and possibly abhorrent - concept to western thought and imagination. But, it holds a place of high value and honor in some Asian countries, most especially Tibet.

Tulku is commonly equated with the idea of an exalted reincarnation in the land Tibetans call Bod-Las. The current Dalai Lama is thought to be the Tulku for the spirit of the Buddha Avalokiteshvara which was passed on to him from his predecessor the 13th Dalai Lama. In a similar manner, Panchen Lamas, Karmapas and other high-born divines in Tibetan lineages are said to be the vehicles for the essence of a Buddha or Bodhisattva.

The Great Lamas must "prove" themselves as infants or toddlers to be exponents of tulku, but generally not in the manner told above. Typically, they do this through a long-held tradition in which regents and colleagues of the recently deceased Guru go out in search of the newly-reborn vehicle of the divine spirit. Using information from dreams and oracles as well as hints left by the previous lama, the seekers scout likely locations for the new tulku. Once a potential child candidate is discovered, he is tested with some secrecy and ingenuity to determine if the young one has carried sufficient memories from his most recent existence. If and when the authorities are satisfied, the new "Living Buddha" is proclaimed.

H.P.B. encountered the tulku phenomenon on an early excursion into Tibet. While trekking with her Shaman guide (see Explorador) and Mr. K (Kuhlwein), she witnessed a tulku similar to the previous story.

Years ago, a small party of travellers were painfully journeying from Kashmir to Leh, a city of Ladahk (Central Thibet). Among our guides we had a Tartar Shaman, a very mysterious personage, who spoke Russian a little and English not at all, and yet who managed, nevertheless, to converse with us, and proved of great service. Having learned that some of our party were Russians, he had imagined that our protection was all-powerful, and might enable him to safely find his way back to his Siberian home, from which, for reasons unknown, some twenty years before, he had fled, as he told us, via Kiachta and the great Gobi Desert, to the land of the Tchgars. With such an interested object in view, we believed ourselves safe under his guard. To explain the situation briefly: Our companions had formed the unwise plan of penetrating into Thibet under various disguises, none of them speaking the language, although one, a Mr. K----, had picked up some Kasan Tartar, and thought he did. As we mention this only inci-

dentally, we may as well say at once that two of them, the brothers N----, were very politely brought back to the frontier before they had walked sixteen miles into the weird land of Eastern Bod; and Mr. K----, an ex-Lutheran minister, could not even attempt to leave his miserable village near Leh, as from the first days he found himself prostrated with fever, and had to return to Lahore via Kashmere. But one sight seen by him was as good as if he had witnessed the reincarnation of Buddha itself. Having heard of this 'miracle' from some old Russian missionary in whom he thought he could have more faith than in Abbe Huc, it had been for years his desire to expose the 'great heathen' jugglery, as he expressed it. K---- was a positivist, and rather prided himself on this anti-philosophical neologism. But his positivism was doomed to receive a death-blow.

About four days journey from Islamabad, at an insignificant mud village, whose only redeeming feature was its magnificent lake, we stopped for a few days' rest. Our companions had temporarily separated from us, and the village was to be our place of meeting. It was there that we were apprised by our Shaman that a large party of Lamaic 'Saints,' on pilgrimage to various shrines, had taken up their abode in an old cave-temple and established a temporary Vihara therein. He added that, as the 'Three Honorable Ones' were said to travel along with them, the holy Bikshu (monks) were capable of producing the greatest miracles. Mr. K-----, fired with the prospect of exposing this humbug of the ages, proceeded at once to pay them a visit, and from that moment the most friendly relations were established between the two camps.

The Vihar was in a secluded and most romantic spot secured against all intrusion. Despite the effusive attentions, presents, and protestations of Mr. K----, the Chief, who was Pase-Budhu (an ascetic of great sanctity), declined to exhibit the phenomenon of the 'incarnation' until a certain talisman in possession of the writer was exhibited. Upon seeing this, however, preparations were at once made, and an infant of three or four months was procured from its mother, a poor woman of the neighborhood. An oath was first of all exacted of Mr. K----, that he would not divulge what he might see or hear, for the space of seven years. The talisman is a simple agate or carnelian known among the Thibetans and others as A-yu, and naturally possessed, or had been endowed with very mysterious properties. It has a triangle engraved upon it, within which are contained a few mystical words.

Several days passed before everything was ready; nothing of a mysterious character occurring, meanwhile, except that, at the bidding of a Bikshu, ghastly faces were made to peep at us out of the glassy bosom of the lake, as we sat at the door of the Vihar, upon its bank. One of these was the countenance of Mr. K----'s sister, whom he had left well and happy at home, but who, as we subsequently learned, had died some time before he had set out on the present journey. The sight affected him at first, but he called his skepticism to his aid, and quieted himself with theories of cloud-shadows, reflections of tree-branches, etc., such as people of his kind fall back upon.

On the appointed afternoon, the baby being brought to the Vihara, was left in the vestibule or reception-room, as K---- could go no further into the temporary sanctuary. The child was then placed on a bit of carpet in the middle of the floor, and every one not belonging to the party being sent away, two 'mendicants' were placed at the entrance to keep out intruders. Then all the lamas seated themselves on the floor, with their backs against the granite walls, so that each was separated from the child by a space, at least, of ten feet. The chief, having had a square piece of leather spread for him by the desservant, seated himself at the farthest corner. Alone, Mr. K---- placed himself close by the infant, and watched every movement with intense interest. The only condition exacted of us was that we should preserve a strict silence, and patiently await further developments. A bright sunlight streamed through the open door. Gradually the 'Superior' fell into what seemed a state of profound meditation, while the others, after a sotto voce short invocation, became suddenly silent, and looked as if they had been completely petrified. It was oppressively still, and the crowing of the child was the only sound to be heard. After we had sat there a few moments, the movements of the infant's limbs suddenly ceased, and his body appeared to become rigid. K---- watched intently every motion, and both of us, by a rapid glance, became satisfied that all present were sitting motionless. The superior, with his gaze fixed upon the ground, did not even look at the infant; but, pale and motionless, he seemed rather like a bronze statue of a Talapoin in meditation than a living being. Suddenly, to our great consternation, we saw the child, not raise itself, but, as it were, violently jerked into a sitting posture! A few more jerks, and then, like an automaton set in motion by concealed wires, the four months' baby stood upon his feet! Fancy our consternation, and, in Mr. K----'s case, horror. Not a hand had been outstretched, not a motion made, nor a word spoken; and yet, here was a baby-in-arms standing erect and firm as a man!

The rest of the story we will quote from a copy of notes written on this subject by Mr. K----, the same evening, and given to us, in case it should not reach its place of destination, or the writer fail to see anything more.

"After a minute or two of hesitation," writes K----, "the baby turned his head and looked at me with an expression of intelligence that was simply awful! It sent a chill through me. I pinched my hands and bit my lips till the blood almost came, to make sure that I did not dream. But this was only the beginning. The miraculous creature, making, as I fancied, two steps toward me, resumed his sitting posture, and, without removing his eyes from mine, repeated, sentence by sentence, in what I supposed to be Thibetan language, the very words, which I had been told in advance, are commonly spoken at the incarnations of Buddha, beginning with 'I am Buddha; I am the old Lama; I am his spirit in a new body,' etc. I felt a real terror; my hair rose upon my head, and my blood ran cold. For my life I could not have spoken a word. There was no trickery here, no ventriloquism. The infant lips moved, and the eyes seemed to search my very soul with an expression that made me think it was the face of the Superior himself, his eyes, his very look that I was gazing upon. It was as if his spirit had entered the little body, and was looking at me through the transparent mask of the baby's face. I felt my brain growing dizzy. The infant reached toward me, and laid his little hand upon mine. I started as if I had been touched by a hot coal; and, unable to bear the scene any longer, covered my face with my hands. It was but for an instant; but when I removed them, the little actor had become a crowing baby again, and a moment after, lying upon his back, set up a fretful cry. The superior had resumed his normal condition, and conversation ensued.

"It was only after a series of similar experiments, extending over ten days, that I realized the fact that I had seen the incredible, astounding phenomenon described by certain travellers, but always by me denounced as an imposture."

The expression of tulku, detailed in *Isis Unveiled*, is not restricted to the transference of consciousness or "spirit" from one form or incarnation to another as in the Great Lamas. (Note: All of us are incarnations of our persisting soul.) Tulku is a concept with wider implications and manifestations than involve Great Lamas or those demonstrated in the story of the Shaberon enveloping and speaking through the small child in H.P.B.'s recollection. Tulku is, according to the profound teachings of the East, one of the conscious spiritual faculties of Raja Yoga called Siddhis.

Siddhis are listed in various ways according to the tradition or teacher involved. The following are given from the Bhagavata Purana: Being unaffected by hunger, thirst, bodily needs; Hearing things far away; Seeing things far away; Projecting the astral form; Assuming any form desired; Entering the bodies of others; Dying when one desires; Living as a higher being; Accomplishing one's will perfectly; Being unimpeded in all actions.

Madame Blavatsky spoke guardedly in her writings of the Raj Yogins (see Chela and Helel), perfected in the siddhis, with whom she worked and studied. Even with the little information which surfaced about her days of training and few hints about the real range of her powers, it is apparent that she was guided into the development of the siddhis including that of tulku. "The true yogi can do that which the vulgar call miracles." Through her training in the mysterious Tibetan land, H.P.B. developed the sensitivity and powers to act as one of the most recent and most visible exponents of Tulku.

Madame B. journeyed far and wide, mostly in Asia, in her younger years. Many of her travels drew her to periods of intense study in the magical arts. She eventually assumed yogic powers in an increasing if not masterful degree. British writer A.P. Sinnett called her an "initiate" and the Vedantist T. Subba Row considered her "a great yogi."

Madame most particularly received training under the tutelage of Masters in Egypt, Syria and Tibet. She shrouded the details of that period of her life, but it is clear that for years she was under close supervision in order to become a tulku, a vehicle for transference of consciousness and transmission of knowledge.

Madame extended credit to her teachers for most of her writings as well as much of the phenomena that she exhibited. But, she also made it clear by using the pronoun "we" that many of her own experiences were chronicled in her famous volumes. Toward the end of her *Isis Unveiled*, H.P.B. recalled experiences of Tibetan holy places and an incident which pictured how the inner worlds blend with the outer.

Ever on the lookout for occult phenomena, hungering after sights, one of the most interesting that we have seen was produced by one of these poor travelling Bikshu (nun). It was years ago, and at a time when all such manifestations were new to the writer. We were taken to visit the pilgrims by a Buddhist friend, a mystical gentleman born at Kashmir, of Katchi parents, but a Buddha-Lamaist by conversion, and who generally resides at Lha-Ssa.

"Why carry about this bunch of dead plants?" inquired one of the Bikshuni, an emaciated, tall and elderly woman, pointing to a large nosegay of beautiful, fresh, and fragrant flowers in the writer's hands.

"Dead?" we asked, inquiringly. "Why they just have been gathered in the garden?"

"And yet, they are dead," she gravely answered. "To be born in this world, is this not death? See, how these herbs look when alive in the world of eternal light, in the gardens of our blessed Foh?"

Without moving from the place where she was sitting on the ground, the Ani (nun) took a flower from the bunch, laid it in her lap, and began to draw together, by large handfuls as it were, invisible material from the surrounding atmosphere. Presently a very, very faint nodule of vapor was seen, and this slowly took shape and color, until, poised in mid-air, appeared a copy of the bloom we had given her. Faithful to the last tint and the last petal it was, and lying on its side like the original, but a thousand-fold more gorgeous in hue and exquisite in beauty, as the glorified human spirit is more beauteous than its physical capsule. Flower after flower to the minutest herb was thus reproduced and made to vanish, reappearing at our desire, nay, at our simple thought. Having selected a full-blown rose we held it at arm's length, and in a few minutes our arm, hand, and the flower, perfect in every detail, appeared reflected in the vacant space, about two yards from where we sat. But while the flower seemed immeasurably beautified and as ethereal as the other spirit flowers, the arm and hand appeared like a mere reflection in a looking-glass, even to a large spot on the fore arm, left on it by a piece of damp earth which had stuck to one of the roots. Later we learned the reason why.

In Tibet and elsewhere, much of H.P. Blavatsky's work involved the development of her own latent powers which could be used for the betterment of all sentient creatures, most especially human ones. Her travels, her experiments in mediumship and spiritualism, even her illnesses were all part of her treading the path to become a yogi and thus a servant of the Masters and the world.

Madame Blavatsky appeared fragile in health much of her life. But, appearances can be deceiving. It seems likely that many of her supposed "nervous affections" actually involved partial or full abstractions from the body. So that she might roam and be free to do inner work. On her returns to the outer world, she was either unable or unwilling to share with the "profane" society around. H.P.B. often arose from her inner excursions with her body seeming to suffer with little continuing effects. Furthermore on those occasions, she usually was reported to move into a new stage of her life and work.

Abstraction from the body is common to all us. We fully or partially escape from our own flesh every time we sleep, are anesthetized or become intoxicated. Such occurrences hint at potentials we all possess to vacate the body for other purposes. H.P.B. wrote about other means to accomplish similar results in an early journal article. It is likely that her description leaves out key points on the operations she witnessed.

Have you read in the French papers the account of the recent great discovery in Australia, made by Professor Rotura? He plunges animals into a trance -- deathly to all appearance -- which lasts for about twenty days, two months, ten months, or more, as he wishes, and then he makes them revive at his will, perfectly well and happy; the whole thing is done by the manipulation of one of the arteries in the neck, in which he makes a tiny puncture with a needle dipped in the juice of a plant; it anaesthetises them. The paper which announces this 'Marvellous Discovery' which may revolutionize the marketing of cattle, shouts with triumph and delight because, it says, we shall now be able to send to London and elsewhere entire cargoes of living cattle at no cost for feeding; they will make the journey packed like dead carcasses. This paper, I say, published this matter on January the first.

The Brisham-Courier, the Pall Mall [Gazette], and other English papers have spoken of it to satiety; this discovery was made some six months before the publication, in May or June, 1878. Please look in La Revue Spirite *for July, 1878, and for October, 1878, where you have translated my interview with a reporter from the* New York World, *and compare it with what I told the reporter in regard to the liberation of the soul and of the astral body in animals by the Tibetan shepherds, who have possessed the secret for ages. And I added, 'I predict that, within a year, science will have discovered that method with the lower animals.' Exactly a year afterwards Rotura discovered it. Am I a medium? No. It was not a prophecy, for in a letter from India from one of our Brothers and Chiefs there, they directed me to announce it to the world and I did so. I contradicted the reporter in my article in October, because I never said I had myself helped in the operation done by the*

Tibetan shepherds, who live in the Himalayas at 28,000 feet above sea level, nor have I done it myself. But, as, until this day, it was one of the secrets of our Adepts I did not think I had the right to speak about it more than was necessary.

I have seen that operation done by our 'Brothers' fifty times, on human beings. They have operated on me, and I once slept for eleven weeks, believing myself to be awake the whole time, and walking around like a ghost of Pontoise, without being able to understand why no one appeared to see me and to answer me. I was entirely unaware that I was liberated from my old carcass which, at that time, however, was a little younger. That was at the beginning of my studies.

H.P.B. surely experienced a more extraordinary life than she ever told. Her training to become a tulku may have been its most amazing aspect. She gave few specifics about the process. However, In *H.P. Blavatsky, Tibet and Tulku*, Geoffrey Barborka used hundreds of pages of text to try to explain that fantastic part of Madame's life.

To be brief, but far from fully accurate, the idea of tulku brings together at least three trainable abilities: *Phowa, Trongjug* and *Avesa*. *Phowa* involves conscious projection of mind beyond the body. *Trongjug* transfers the consciousness to vitalize and animate another body. *Avesa* involves the entrance into and taking possession of the other vehicle. The latter, prepared or not, becomes the *Tulku*.

A story told of Sankaracharya, the sage of ancient India, adds light to the whole of the tulku phenomenon. So great were Sankara's powers in his earliest years that already at the age of twelve when living upon the banks of the Ganges River, he wrote commentaries on the *Sutras*, the *Upanishads*, and on the *Bhagavad-Gita*. There seemed few limits to his knowledge and wisdom. He was always victorious in discussion and debate of philosophy and religion with all opponents.

On one occasion preceded by seemingly miraculous circumstances, he suddenly appeared at the side of the renowned teacher, Mandana Misra, in a spacious hall in the latter's abode in Mahishmati. The astonished host and his unexpected guest entered into a lively discussion. When their debate continued into the evening hours, the wife of Mandana Misra entered the hall and acted as umpire between them. She placed garlands of fresh flowers around the neck of the two wise men and said, "Wear these as you talk, and he whose garland does not wither I shall deem victor." Before long, Mandana Misra's flowers were limp, but Sankara's remained fresh as when just picked.

But, the debate continued between Sankara and Misra's wife who was herself the embodiment of the Hindu goddess Sarasvati. The young sage could not be undone despite the depth of questioning until Sarasvati turned her questions to the science of love! Sankara was stumped and could make no answers. He left Mandana Misra and Sarasvati vowing to return.

Inevitably, he happened upon King Amaraka who lay dying with his friends mourning his imminent departure. When the soul of Amaraka took flight, Sankara left his own body, entrusting it to the care of his disciples. Then, he entered the body of the dead king. The king's retinue was overjoyed to see him return from "the forest of death back to the throne of royalty."

The new tenant took the opportunity to fill the shoes of Amaraka and learn all he desired about the science and art of love, and so be able to answer Sarasvati's questions. In the interlude, Amaraka's ministers recognized the difference between the old king and the new monarch. They endeavored to permanently capture Sankara by stealing away his original body and then burning it on a funeral pyre.

At the last moment, Sankara's disciples appeared at court and drew him back to his true form. He re-entered his own body before the flames could take him from life. Thence, they all traveled to the house of Mandana Misra, who became Sankara's disciple "after hearing the last question of Sarasvati answered with keen wit and wisdom."

Sankaracharya and Helena Blavatsky may not have been in the same league, but both were learned in the phenomenal talent of Tulku. In Madame's case, she became the occasional and temporary vehicle for more evolved Souls to work through her outer form. Her task was to withdraw - or at least make room for the Khechara (Skywalker) who could utilize her body for necessary work in the material world.

Her Masters frequently stepped into communicating roles after Madame's persona had been "overcome" and her consciousness set aside. H.P.B. told that she was aware of the process taking place, feeling a sense of freedom and liberation during the interlude. Surely, that manner of living was stressful and exacting on any body. Many tolls were taken on Madame's shell through such experiences as well as the other trials and tests of her unique life.

H.P.B. surely led a singular double life. (Pardon the expression.) She discussed this situation, at times, with her sister. On at least one occasion, Helena told her, "When his double, or the real Sahib leaves temporarily his vehicle, the body is left in a similar state to that we can observe in a calm idiot. He orders it either to sleep or it is guarded by his men. At first it seemed to me that he pushed me out of my body, but soon I seemed to become accustomed to it, and now during the moments of his presence in me, it only seems (to me) that I am living a double life....

"I am learning just now to leave my body; to do it alone I am afraid, but with him (Master) I am afraid of nothing. I shall try it with you. Only be kind enough not to resist and do not scream."

With this brief and incomplete sketch of H.P.B.'s tulku training, it may become clearer as to how she found herself "in company" on many occasions, how that company at times took residence in her very own body, and how the undereducated Russian woman was able to speak and write eruditely on almost any topic. "Several times a day I feel that besides me there is someone else, quite separable from me, present in my body. I never lose the consciousness of my own personality; what I feel is as if I were keeping silent and the other one -- the lodger who is in me -- were speaking with my tongue. For instance, I know that I have never been in the places which are described by my 'other me,' but this other one -- the second me -- does not lie when he tells about places and things unknown to me, because he has actually seen them and knows them well."

"Do not be afraid that I am off my head. All that I can say is that someone positively inspires me ... more than this: someone enters me. It is not I who talk and write: it is something within me, my higher and luminous Self, that thinks and write for me. Do not ask me, my friend (Sister Vera), what I experience because I could not explain it to you clearly. I do not know myself! The one thing I know is that now, when I am about to reach old age, I have become a sort of storehouse of somebody else's knowledge...."

Again, this very extraordinary phenomenon may seem alien, outrageous, inconceivable. But to those who have eyes to see, Jesus of Nazareth may be recognized as a Tulku for the Christ. This Gnostic and heretical idea has been broached by numbers of sources over the ages. Jesus is said to have been "overshadowed" by the Christ in the latter days of his ministry in Palestine. Furthermore, the whole concept of Avatars from Rama and Buddha to Chrishna and Christ can be viewed through the broader, living lens of Tulku.

There is no religion greater than

TRUTH

Chela
(Hindi for Agent)

"All that I was then permitted to reveal was,
that there existed somewhere such great men ...
also that I was a Chela ..."

"Somebody comes, winding around me like a misty cloud, and then, in one turn sends me out of my body, and I am no more Helen Petrovna, General Blavatsky's faithful spouse, but somebody else, born in a different part of the world, strong and mighty; as to me, it seems as if I were sleeping meanwhile, or at least dozed; not in my body, but beside it, as if there was some kind of thread only binding me to my body, and not letting me go more than paces from it. At other times, I see clearly everything done by my body and I understand and remember what it says: I see awe, devotion, and fear in the faces of Olcott and others, and observe how the Master looks condescendingly at them of my eyes and speaks to them with my physical tongue, yet not with my brain but his own, which enwraps my brain like a cloud."

The tests and trials laid down for a would-be tulku must be indeed weighty. H.P.B. gave out few details on her own path while offering some general hints on the steep climb. She did say that to become a chela accepted by a Master required a difficult period of probation and that few are they who are prepared to go through the process. Her own passage caused her to go where "no European man, let alone a woman, could ever penetrate into the inner recesses of the pagodas. But I have had many friends among Buddhists and knew well two Brahmins at Travancore and learned a great deal from them. I belong to the secret sect of the Druzes of Mount Lebanon and passed a long life among dervishes, Persian mullahs, and mystics of all sorts."

Early in their association, Madame wrote to Henry Olcott to advise him of what lay ahead should he throw down the gauntlet: "I am an *initiated* wretch, and I know what a curse the word '*Try*' has proved in my life, and how often I trembled and feared to misunderstand their orders and bring on myself punishment for carrying them *too far* or not far enough. You seem to take the whole concern for a child's play. Beware Henry, before you pitch headlong into it.... There is time yet, and you can decline the connexion as yet. But if you *keep* the letter I send you and *agree* to the word *Neophyte* you are cooked my boy and there is no return from it. Trials and temptations to your faith will shower on you first of all. (Remember *my* 7 years preliminary initiation, trials, dangers and fighting with all the Incarnated Evils and legions of Devils and think before you accept.) There are mysterious dreadful invocations in the letter sent you *human* and *made up* as it may appear [to] you perhaps. On the other hand if you are *decided*, remember my advice if you want to come out victorious of the affray. *Patience, faith, no questioning*, thorough *obedience* and *Silence*."

Her Masters and associates called Helena chela and initiate and yogi. Her history, talents and phenomenal life support those titles. As a chela, H.P.B. was one of a number who were in training to serve as intermediaries between the inner world of causes and the outer world of effects. She was student and disciple as well as laborer and agent in a great hierarchy of workers. That line stretches from mere novices to far-advanced adepts including the Buddha and the Christ. The Christ Himself, although the Teacher of Men and of Angels, is also said to be a student on the Higher Way.

It is fascinating to consider the fact that the hidden Masters sent out a European woman as their "agent in the field." She was in actuality an *agent of secrets*. Eventually, suspicious minds mistook her on many occasions for a Russian *secret agent*. This situation first developed when Helena and Colonel Olcott moved their Theosophical Society to India in 1879.

Although Helena had taken American citizenship (the first Russian woman ever naturalized) during her several years in the USA, she was known by her name and reputation as Russian born. And, Russia was at the time feared for its supposed designs on the Indian subcontinent and the British colony. So, Madame was followed for many months of her early residence in India by a government detective. The British minion was either not very careful about his own spying or maybe Madame's antennae were just sensitive enough to pick up his trail.

A.P. Sinnett wrote that, "Mme. Blavatsky fretted under the sense of insult this espionage inflicted on her, with the intensity of feeling she carries into everything. For my own part, I used often to tell her, when we laughed over the narrative of her adventures afterwards, I pitied the unhappy police officer, her spy, a great deal more than herself. She pursued this officer with sarcasms all the while that he, in the performance of his irksome duty, pursued her in her vague and erratic wanderings. She would offer him bags or letters to examine, and address him condolences on the miserable fate that condemned him to play the part of a *mouchard*. I suspect from what I heard at Simla at the time, that the Bombay Government must have been treated by the superior authorities to remarks that were anything but complimentary on the manner in which they conducted this business. At any rate, the mistake concerning the objects of the Theosophists was speedily seen through, and the local government instructed to trouble itself no more about them."

The official tail was lifted after Madame sent complaints to the American Consul. But, the damage was done. When representing the newly-formed Society for Psychical Research, Richard Hodgson appeared in Adyar in 1884 to investigate the Coulomb Affair (see Khan), he picked up the thread and resurrected the Russian espionage theory in regard to the motives for the unusual work she was about. At the time at Headquarters, Cooper-Oakley reported on Hodgson's investigating manner, "He is gone mad, behaved like one crazy. He fulminated against HPB insisting she was a Russian spy ... capable of every and any crime."

It is really laughable to imagine middle-aging and broadening, bold and boisterous, hobbling and chain-smoking Madame Blavatsky as an agent of mundane intrigue, even for one involving her beloved Russian homeland. Her devotion was placed elsewhere and to those who were so much greater than any of her countrymen or their loftiest leaders.

A chela implies teacher. Know one, you know the other.

Helena Blavatsky's teacher/s seemed to have been with or near H.P.B. from her earliest days. It can be inferred from the extraordinary events of her youth, from being saved from mishap and mayhem, from her protected path, from intersection in time and place with adepts and magicians, from her mysterious healings, and from the scope of her entirely unique life, that Helena Petrovna Blavatsky had guardians and masters watching over her. She returned their persistent care with her industry and loyalty, power and persistence.

Traveling wide swaths of the known and sometimes unknown world, H.P.B. made her way to teachers and initiates in Syria and Lebanon, Egypt and India, and even Europe. But, Tibet was clearly the major focus of her interest and training. Her Master resided there and so she seemed to circle around and back to Tibet - and northern India - as often as possible.

Tibet, the Forbidden Land, had its allure for many 19th-century adventurers. It still does despite being absorbed into the People's Republic of China in the 1950s. Madame entered that land on a number of occasions. Only once did H.P.B. describe the area where she lived and studied. And that occurred through the instigation of Dr. Franz Hartmann. He presented a German peasant woman with reported psychometric powers an unopened letter "purporting to come from an Adept, and bearing neither postmark, nor other indication regarding the place where it was written." With misgivings and forebodings as to his experiment, he handed the "occult letter" to the woman and asked her to put it to her forehead. She was taken back by the idea of such an unusual experiment. But, the woman assented and soon exclaimed in surprise, wonder and joy.

Ah! What is this? I never saw anything so beautiful in my life! I see before me a high but artificially made elevation or hill, and upon that hill a building which looks like a temple, with a high Chinese roof. The temple is of a splendid white, as if it were made of pure white marble, and the roof is resting upon three pillars. On the top of a roof there is a shining sun; --- but no! --- it only looks like a sun; it seems to be some kind of an animal. I do not know how to describe it; I never saw such a thing before; but it shines like a sun.

There is a beautiful walk of smooth stones and some steps leading up to that temple, and I am going up to it. Now I am there, and lo! the floor is like a lake, in which the light of that sun on the top of the roof is reflected! But no --- I am mistaken; it is no water at all; it is a kind of a yellowish marble, which shines like a mirror. Now I see it plainly! It is a square marble floor, and in the centre there is a dark round spot. This is all so very beautiful. It looks to a certain extent like the Walhalla near Regensburg.

Now I am in that temple, and I see two gentlemen looking at something on the wall. One is a very fine-looking gentleman, but he is dressed quite differently from the people in this country. He is dressed in a loose flowing robe of pure white, and the forepart of his shoes is pointed upwards. The other one is smaller and bald-headed; he wears a black coat and silver buckles on his shoes.

They are looking at a picture on the wall. The picture represents a vase with some tropical plants; something like prickly-pear leaves; but very different from all the prickly-pears I ever saw. The vase is not a painting, but a real vase. I first thought it was painted. It stands in a corner, and there are ornamental paintings on it.

There are some paintings and drawings on the wall. Below the ceiling, where the roof begins, there is a field, or panel, on which there are some curious figures. Some look like a 15 and one like a V, and others like squares and ciphers, with all sorts of garnishes between them. They look as if they were numbers; but I do not think they are. They may be some strange letters or characters.

Above that field or panel there is another one, on which there are some square pictures or plates, with some very queer things painted upon them. They are movable; at least I think that they are; but I am not quite certain.

Now these two gentlemen are going out, and I am following them. There are a great many trees looking like pine-trees. I think they are pines. There are others with big fleshy leaves and spikes something like prickly-pears. There are mountains and hills and a lake. They are taking me away from that temple. I am afraid I cannot find my way back to it. There is a big ravine, and there are some trees which I take to be olive-trees; but I am not sure of it, for I never saw any olive-trees. Now I have arrived at a place, where I can see over a wide expanse of country. The two gentlemen have gone away. Here there is some antiquity looking like an old ruined wall, and something like what I saw on that paper you showed me. I believe you call it a Sphinx. There is a sort of a pillar, and on the top of it is a statue, whose upper part looks like a woman, while the lower part of her body seems to be a fish. She seems to be holding some moss in her hands, or resting them upon it.

What a funny sight! There are lots of queer people! They are little women and children. They wear such funny dresses, and have fur caps on their heads. They have soles tied to their feet! They are collecting something from the shore and putting it into baskets. Now the whole scene dissolves into a cloud.

Dr. Hartmann sent the psychometrist's description on to Madame Blavatsky. She, in turn, wrote back with her reflections.

I am happy you got such an independent corroboration; astral light, at any rate, cannot lie for my benefit.... This looks like the private temple of the Teschu Lama, near Tchigadze -- made of the 'Madras cement'-like material; it does shine like marble and is called the snowy 'Shakang' (temple) -- as far as I remember. It has no 'sun or cross' on the top, but a kind of algiorna dagoba, *triangular, on three pillars, with a dragon of gold and a globe. But the dragon has a* swastica *on it and this may have appeared a 'cross.' I don't remember any 'gravel walk' -- nor is there one, but it stands on an elevation (artificial) and a stone* path leading to it, and it has steps -- how many I do not remember (I was never allowed inside); saw from the outside, and the interior was described to me. The floors of nearly all Buddha's (Songyas) temples are made of a yellow polished stone, found in those mountains of Oural and in northern Tibet toward Russian territory. I do not know the name, but it looks like yellow marble. The 'gentleman' in white may be Master, and the 'bald-headed' gentleman I take to be some old 'shaven-headed' priest. The cloak is black or very dark generally -- (I brought one to Olcott from Darjeeling), but where the silver buckles and knee-breeches come from I am at a loss. They wear, as you know, long boots -- up high on the calves, made of felt and embroidered often with silver -- like that devil of a Babajee had. Perhaps it is a freak of astral vision mixed with a flash of memory (by association of ideas) about some picture she saw previously. In those temples there are always movable 'pictures,' on which various geometrical and mathematical problems are placed for the disciples who study astrology and symbolism. The 'vase' must be one of many Chinese queer vases about in temples, for various objects. In the corners of the temples there are numerous statues of various deities (Dhyanis). The roofs are always (almost always) supported by rows of wooden pillars dividing the roof into three parallelograms, and the mirror 'Melong' of burnished steel (round like the sun) is often placed on the top of the Kiosque on the roof. I myself took it once for the sun. Also on the cupolas of the [dagoba] there is sometimes a graduated pinnacle, and over it a disk of gold placed vertically, and a pear-shaped point and often a crescent supporting a globe and the svastica upon it. Ask her whether it is this she saw, Om tram ah hri hum, which figures are roughly drawn sometimes on the Melong 'mirrors' -- (a disk of brass) against evil spirits -- for the mob. Or perhaps what she saw was a row of slips of wood (little cubes), on which such things are seen.

If so, then I will know what she saw. 'Pine woods' all round such temples, the latter built expressly where there are such woods, and wild prickly pear, and trees with Chinese fruit on that the priests use for making inks. A lake is there, surely, and mountains plenty -- if where Master is; if near Tchigadze -- only little hillocks. The statues of Meilha Gualpo, the androgyne Lord of the Salamanders or the Genii of Air, look like this 'sphinx;' but her lower body is lost in clouds, not fish, and she is not beautiful, only symbolical. Fisherwomen do use soles alone, like the sandals, and they all wear fur caps. That's all; will this do? But do write it out.

H.P.B.'s pathway to her Master's retreat was long and tortuous. While the description above may sound idyllic and ethereal, Helena undoubtedly paid the price for admission over and over again. "All chelas have terrible trials." And even during her dedicated training with the Master in some proximity, she must have taxed her "lazy ways" to get Master's approval and her own Soul's reward.

Young Helena had hints of things to come, subtle communications from hidden sources, and astral guardians from early years. But, she did not meet her Master in body until her twentieth birthday in London: August 12, 1851 (Gregorian - New Style Calendar). "When she was in London, in 1851, with her father, Colonel Hahn, she was one day out walking when, to her astonishment, she saw a tall Hindu in the street with some Indian princes. She immediately recognised him as the same person that she had seen in the Astral. Her first impulse was to rush forward to speak to him, but he made her a sign not to move, and she stood as if spellbound while he passed on. The next day she went into Hyde Park for a stroll, that she might be alone and free to think over her extraordinary adventure. Looking up, she saw the same form approaching her, and then her Master told her that he had come to London with the Indian princes on an important mission, and he was desirous of meeting her personally, as he required her co-operation in a work which he was about to undertake. He then told her how the Theosophical Society was to be formed, and that he wished her to be the founder. He gave her a slight sketch of all the troubles she would have to undergo, and also told her that she would have to spend three years in Tibet to prepare her for the important task."

Blavatsky zealously guarded her relationship with the Great Ones and their followers, but she did pass on tangential references to Them when the need or opportunity appeared. H.P.B.'s earliest experiences as a chela in Tibet were suggested in *Isis Unveiled* when she wrote.

The Upasakas and Upasakis, or male and female semi-monastics and semi-laymen, have equally with the lama-monks themselves, to strictly abstain from violating any of Buddha's rules, and must study Meipo [magic] and every psychological phenomenon as much. Those who become guilty of any of the 'five sins' lose all right to congregate with the pious community. The most important of these is not to curse upon any consideration, for the curse returns upon the one that utters it, and often upon his innocent relatives who breathe the same atmosphere with him. To love each other, and even our bitterest enemies; to offer our lives even for animals, to the extent of abstaining from defensive arms; to gain the greatest of victories by conquering one's self; to avoid all vices; to practice all virtues, especially humility and mildness; to be obedient to superiors, to cherish and respect parents, old age, learning, virtuous and holy men; to provide food, shelter, and comfort for men and animals; to plant trees on the roads and dig wells for the comfort of travellers; such are the moral duties of Buddhists. Every Ani or Bikshuni (nun) is subjected to these laws.

Numerous are the Buddhist and Lamaic saints who have been renowned for the unsurpassed sanctity of their lives and their 'miracles.' So Tissu, the Emperor's spiritual teacher, who consecrated Kublai-Khan, the Nadir Shah, was known far and wide as much for the extreme holiness of his life as for the many wonders he wrought. But he did not stop at fruitless miracles, but did better than that. Tissu purified completely his religion; and from one single province of Southern Mongolia is said to have forced Kublai to expel from convents 500,000 monkish impostors, who made a pretext of their profession, to live in vice and idleness. Then the Lamaists had their great reformer, the Shaberon Son-Ka-po, who is claimed to have been immaculately conceived by his mother, a virgin from Koko-nor (fourteenth century), who is another wonder-worker. The sacred tree of Kounboum, the tree of the 10,000 images, which, in consequence of the degeneration of the true faith had ceased budding for several centuries, now shot forth new sprouts and bloomed more vigorously than ever from the hair of this avatar of Buddha, says the legend. The same tradition makes him (Son-Ka-po) ascend to heaven in 1419. Contrary to the prevailing idea, few of these saints are Khubilhans, or Shaberons — reincarnations.

Many of the lamaseries contain schools of magic, but the most celebrated is the collegiate monastery of the Shu-tukt, where there are over 30,000 monks attached to it, the lamasery forming quite a little city. Some of the female nuns possess marvellous psychological powers. We have met some of these women on their way from Lha-Ssa to Candi, the Rome of Buddhism, with its miraculous shrines and Gautama's relics. To avoid encounters with Mussulmans and other sects they travel by night alone, unarmed, and without the least fear of wild animals, for these will not touch them. At the first glimpses of dawn, they take refuge in caves and viharas prepared for them by their co-religionists at calculated distances; for notwithstanding the fact that Buddhism has taken refuge in Ceylon, and nominally there are but *few of the denomination in British India, yet the secret Byauds (Brotherhoods) and Buddhist viharas are numerous, and every Jain feels himself obliged to help, indiscriminately, Buddhist or Lamaist.*

The secrets of schools and monasteries were treated much like the other mysteries surrounding the Arhats and Adepts, Masters and Mahatmas. Madame was just as protective of the Honor of the Masters as the Sanctity of the Truths that she was allowed to dole out piecemeal during her writing and teaching career. But giving out specific information on her Teachers was totally anathema to H.P.B. She would do anything to shield and protect them. "This I swear 'BY MASTER'S BLESSING OR CURSE' -- I will give a 1000 lives for Their honour in the people's minds. I will not see THEM desecrated."

Madame B.'s relationship to the Masters is key to understanding H.P.B. and her work. That story has been quite inapparent to many, including several biographers who tried to make the Masters into either mythic or mundane figures. They dared not open their eyes to realize that the Masters are beyond fabrication and illusion. It is we in the "civilized" world who live the life of illusion. The Masters are passing progressively into the Real world and ever so slowly trying to help us follow them. H.P.B. was one of the few in her day to dare to take larger steps to follow them along the Path.

That Pathway into which they drew her was one called Raj Yoga. Madame repeatedly made references to the Raj Yogins: workers in the Occult Sciences, Guardians of the Secret Doctrine, and the Knowers on Planet Earth. Sister Vera made it quite clear, "She asserts now as then that quite another power influenced her then as it does now, namely the power acquired by the Hindu sages -- the Raj-Yogis." Simply put, H.P.B. was in training to become a yogi.

Vera Zhelihovsky wrote to her sister that she was not comfortable with the idea that certain people in Tibet monopolized all the wisdom in the universe. H.P.B. responded that was hardly the case. She knew Masters in Tibet as her personal Teachers but was aware that others lived in various parts of the world who were equally advanced and wise. "In every country and in every age there were and there will be people, pure of heart, who, conquering their earthly thoughts and the passions of the flesh, raise their spiritual faculties to such a pitch that the mysteries of being and the laws governing Nature and hidden from the uninitiated, are revealed to them. Let blind men persecute them; let them be burned and hunted from 'societies acknowledged by law;' let them be called Magi, Wise Men, Raj Yogis or saints -- they have lived and they still live everywhere, recognized or unrecognized. For these people who have illumined themselves during their lifetime, there are no obstacles, there are no bodily ties. They do not know either distance or time. They are alive and active in the body as well as out of it. They are, wherever their thought and their will carries them. They are not tied down by anything, either by a place, or by their temporary mortal covering."

H.P.B.'s *From the Caves and Jungles of Hindustan* offers many intimations about the masters of Raj Yoga (and herself, their chela) especially through the one called the Thakur Gulab-Lal-Singh. The Thakur is clearly identified as a Raj Yogin and "an initiate of the mysteries of magic, alchemy, and various other occult sciences of India. He was rich and independent, and rumour did not dare to suspect him of deception, the more so because, though quite full of these sciences, he never uttered a word about them in public, and carefully concealed his knowledge from all except a few friends. He was an independent Thakur from Rajistan, a province the name of which means the land of kings. Thakurs are, almost without exception, descended from the Surya (sun), and are accordingly called Surya-vansa. They are prouder than any other nation in the world. They have a proverb, 'The dirt of the earth cannot stick to the rays of the sun.'"

The Thakur appeared in many key moments in H.P.B.'s narrative coming to the aid and rescue of Madame's small party of Indians, Americans and British as it traveled remote parts of India. At one juncture, he killed a Bengal tiger with only a word. Later, the Yogin single-handedly and to the amazement of bystanders extricated the swooning Madame from a dark, deep and breathless cavern. Gulab-Lal-Singh appeared unexpectedly, and in a miraculous manner, transported her to the surface before any others could navigate the underground channel for themselves.

H.P.B.'s story continued on with another tale of the Thakur's magical abilities. The impress of his being appeared slowly and subtly to influence the group and especially Mr. Y. during a rest stop.

"You have guessed rightly," absently answered Mr. Y., busy over his drawing apparatus (and landscape painting). "Narayan sees in you (the Thakur) something like his late deity Shiva; something just a little less than Parabrahm. Would you believe it? He seriously assured us ... that the Raj-Yogis, and amongst them yourself -- though I must own I

still fail to understand what a Raj-Yogi is, precisely -- can force any one to see, not what is before his eyes at the given moment, but what is only in the imagination of the Raj-Yogi. If I remember rightly he called it Maya.... Now, this seemed to me going a little too far!"

"Well! You did not believe, of course, and laughed at Narayan?" asked the Thakur as he fathomed with his eyes the dark green deeps of the lake.

"Not precisely.... Though, I dare say, I did just a little bit," went on Mr. Y., absently, being fully engrossed by the view, and trying to fix his eyes on the most effective part of it. "I dare say I am too sceptical on this kind of question."

"And knowing Mr. Y. as I do," said the Colonel, "I can add, for my part, that even were any of these phenomena to happen to himself personally, he, like Dr. Carpenter [British skeptic], would doubt his own eyes rather than believe."

"What you say is a little bit exaggerated, but there is some truth in it. Maybe I would not trust myself in such an occurrence; and I tell you why. If I saw something that does not exist, or rather exists only for me, logic would interfere. However objective my vision may be, before believing in the materiality of a hallucination, I feel I am bound to doubt my own senses and sanity.... Besides, what bosh all this is! As if I ever will allow myself to believe in the reality of a thing that I alone saw; which belief implies also the admission of somebody else governing and dominating, for the time being, my optical nerves, as well as my brains."

"However, there are any number of people, who do not doubt, because they have had proof that this phenomenon really occurs," remarked the Thakur, in a careless tone which showed he had not the slightest desire to insist upon this topic.

However, this remark only increased Mr. Y.'s excitement.

"No doubt there are," he exclaimed. "But what does that prove? Besides them, there are equal numbers of people who believe in the materialization of spirits. But do me the kindness of not including me among them!"

"Don't you believe in animal magnetism?"

"To a certain extent, I do. If a person suffering from some contagious illness can influence a person in good health, and make him ill, in his turn, I suppose another's overflow of health can also affect the sick person, and, perhaps cure him. But between physiological contagion and mesmeric influence there is a great gulf, and I don't feel inclined to cross this gulf on the grounds of blind faith. It is perfectly possible that there are instances of thought-transference in cases of somnambulism, epilepsy, trance. I do not positively deny it, though I am very doubtful. Mediums and clairvoyants are a sickly lot, as a rule. But I bet you anything, a healthy man in perfectly normal conditions is not to be influenced by the tricks of mesmerists. I should like to see a magnetizer, or even a Raj-Yogi, inducing me to obey his will."

"Now, my dear fellow, you really ought not to speak so rashly," said the Colonel, who, till then, had not taken any part in the discussion.

"Ought I not? Don't take it into your head that it is mere boastfulness on my part. I guarantee failure in my case, simply because every renowned European mesmerist has tried his luck with me, without any result; and that is why I defy the whole lot of them to try again, and feel perfectly safe about it. And why a Hindu Raj-Yogi should succeed where the strongest of European mesmerists failed, I do not quite see ..."

Mr. Y was growing altogether too excited, and the Thakur dropped the subject, and talked of something else.

The Babu and Mulji left us to help the servants to transport our luggage to the ferry boat. The remainder of the party had grown very quiet and silent. Miss X. dozed peacefully in the carriage, forgetting her recent fright. The colonel, stretched on the sand, amused himself by throwing stones into the water. Narayan sat motionless, with his hands round his knees, plunged as usual in the mute contemplation of Gulab-Lal-Singh. Mr. Y. sketched hurriedly and diligently, only raising his head from time to time to glance at the opposite shore, and knitting his brow in a preoccupied way. The Thakur went on smoking, and as for me, I sat on my folding chair, looking lazily at everything round me, till my eyes rested on Gulab-Singh, and were fixed, as if by a spell.

"Who and what is this mysterious Hindu?" I wondered in my uncertain thoughts. "Who is this man, who unites in himself two such distinct personalities: the one exterior, kept up for strangers, for the world in general; the other interior, moral and spiritual, shown only to a few intimate friends? But even these intimate friends -- do they know much beyond what is generally known? And what do they know? They see in him a Hindu who differs very little from the rest of educated natives, perhaps only in his perfect contempt for the social conventions of India and the demands of Western civilization.... And that is all -- unless I add that he is known in Central India as a sufficiently wealthy man, and a Thakur, a feudal chieftain of a Raj, one of the hundreds of similar Rajs. Besides, he is a true friend of ours, who offered us his protection in our travels and volunteered to play the mediator between us and the suspicious, uncommunicative Hindus. Beyond all this, we know absolutely nothing about him. It is true, though, that I know a little more than the others; but I have promised silence, and silent I shall be. But the little I know is so strange, so unusual, that it is more like a dream than a reality."

A good while ago, more than twenty-seven years, I met him in the house of a stranger in England, whither he came in the company of a certain dethroned Indian prince. Then our acquaintance was limited to two conversations; their unexpectedness, their gravity, and even severity, produced a strong impression on me then; but, in the course of time, like many other things, they sank into oblivion and Lethe. About seven years ago he wrote to me to America, reminding me of our conversation and of a certain promise I had made. Now we saw each other once more in India, his own country, and I failed to see any change wrought in his appearance by all these long years. I was, and looked, quite young, when I first saw him; but the passage of years had not failed to change me into an old woman. As to him, he appeared to me twenty-seven years ago a man of about thirty, and still looked no older, as if time were powerless against him. In England, his striking beauty, especially his extraordinary height and stature, together with his eccentric refusal to be presented to the Queen -- an honour many a high-born Hindu has sought, coming over on purpose -- excited the public notice and the attention of the newspapers. The newspaper-men of those days, when the influence of Byron was still great, discussed the "wild Rajput" with untiring pens, calling him "Raja-Misanthrope" and "Prince Jalma-Samson," and inventing fables about him all the time he stayed in England.

All this taken together was well calculated to fill me with consuming curiosity, and to absorb my thoughts till I forgot every exterior circumstance, sitting and staring at him ...

I gazed at the remarkable face of Gulab-Lal-Singh with a mixed feeling of indescribable fear and enthusiastic admiration; recalling the mysterious death of the Karli tiger, my own miraculous escape a few hours ago in Bagh, and many other incidents too many to relate. It was only a few hours since he appeared to us in the morning, and yet what a number of strange ideas, of puzzling occurrences, how many enigmas his presence stirred in our minds! The magic circle of my revolving thought grew too much for me. "What does all this mean!" I exclaimed to myself, trying to shake off my torpor, and struggling to find words for my meditation. "Who is this being whom I saw so many years ago, jubilant with manhood and life, and now see again, as young and as full of life, only still more austere, still more incomprehensible. After all, maybe it is his brother, or even his son?" thought I, trying to calm myself, but with no result. "No! there is no use doubting; it is he himself, it is the same face, the same little scar on the left temple. But, as a quarter of a century ago, so now: no wrinkles on those beautiful classic features; not a white hair in this thick jet-black mane; and, in moments of silence, the same expression of perfect rest on that face, calm as a statue of living bronze. What a strange expression, and what a wonderful Sphinx-like face!"

"Not a very brilliant comparison, my old friend!" suddenly spoke the Thakur, and a good-natured laughing note rung in his voice, whilst I shuddered and grew red like a naughty schoolgirl. "This comparison is so inaccurate that it decidedly sins against history in two important points. Primo, the Sphinx is a lion; so am I, as indicates the word Singh in my name; but the Sphinx is winged, and I am not. Secundo, the Sphinx is a woman as well as a winged lion, but the Rajput Singhs never had anything effeminate in their characters. Besides, the Sphinx is the daughter of Chimera, or Echidna, who were neither beautiful nor good; and so you might have chosen a more flattering and a less inaccurate comparison!"

I simply gasped in my utter confusion, and he gave vent to his merriment, which by no means relieved me.

"Shall I give you some good advice?" continued Gulab-Singh, changing his tone for a more serious one. '"Don't trouble your head with such vain speculations. The day when this riddle yields its solution, the Rajput Sphinx will not seek destruction in the waves of the sea; but, believe me, it won't bring any profit to the Russian Oedipus either. You already know every detail you ever will learn. So leave the rest to our respective fates."

And he rose because the Babu and Mulji had informed us that the ferry boat was ready to start, and were shouting and making signs to us to hasten.

"Just let me finish," said Mr. Y., "I have nearly done. Just an additional touch or two."

"Let us see your work. Hand it round!" insisted the Colonel and Miss X., who had just left her haven of refuge in the carriage, and joined us still half asleep.

Mr. Y. hurriedly added a few more touches to his drawing and rose to collect his brushes and pencils. We glanced at his fresh wet picture and opened our eyes in astonishment. There was no lake on it, no woody shores, and no evening mists that covered the distant island at this moment. Instead we saw a charming sea view; thick clusters of palm-trees scattered over the chalky cliffs of the littoral; a fortress-like bungalow with balconies and a flat roof, an elephant standing at its entrance, and a native boat on the crest of a foaming billow.

"Now what is this view, sir?" wondered the Colonel. "As if it was worth your while to sit in the sun, and detain us all, to draw fancy pictures out of your own head."

"What on earth are you talking about?" exclaimed Mr. Y. "Do you mean to say you do not recognize the lake?"

"Listen to him -- the lake! Where is the lake, if you please? Were you asleep, or what?"

By this time all our party gathered round the Colonel, who held the drawing. Narayan uttered an exclamation, and stood still, the very image of bewilderment past description.

"I know the place!" said he, at last. "This is Dayri-Bol, the country house of the Thakur-Sahib. I know it. Last year during the famine I lived there for two months."

I was the first to grasp the meaning of it all, but something prevented me from speaking at once.

At last Mr. Y. finished arranging and packing his things, and approached us in his usual lazy, careless way, but his face showed traces of vexation. He was evidently bored by our persistency in seeing a sea, where there was nothing but the corner of a lake. But, at the first sight of his unlucky sketch, his countenance suddenly changed. He grew so pale, and the expression of his face became so piteously distraught that it was painful to see. He turned and re-turned the piece of Bristol board, then rushed like a madman to his drawing portfolio and turned the whole contents out, ransacking and scattering over the sand hundreds of sketches and of loose papers. Evidently failing to find what he was looking for, he glanced again at his seaview, and suddenly covering his face with his hands totally collapsed.

We all remained silent, exchanging glances of wonder and pity, and heedless of the Thakur, who stood on the ferry boat, vainly calling to us to join him.

"Look here, Y.!" timidly spoke the kind-hearted Colonel, as if addressing a sick child.

"Are you sure you remember drawing this view?"
Mr. Y did not give any answer, as if gathering strength and thinking it over. After a few moments he answered in hoarse and tremulous tones: "Yes, I do remember. Of course I made this sketch, but I made it from nature. I painted only what I saw. And it is that very certainty that upsets me so."

Gulab-Lal-Singh was certainly modeled after Madame Blavatsky's personal Teacher, about whom the Hindu chela Damodar Mavalankar passed on more extraordinary information. In a letter to W.Q. Judge, Damodar told of an intimate meeting between Madame Blavatsky and a Hindu ascetic called Maji. During the conversation, Maji indicated that Madame and she had the same Master. H.P.B. asked for proofs which were readily given. Among other statements noted, Maji said that their "Guru was born in Punjab but generally lives in the Southern part of India, and especially in Ceylon. He is about *300 years old* and has a companion of about the same age, though both do not appear even forty."

H.P.B. told Countess Wachtmeister that her Mahatmas were different in character and lifestyle. Koot Humi was a Punjabi with family in Kashmir. He was more accessible and generally lived with close kin in the Kuen Lun Mountains. Morya, who was serious and stern, was not so tied down to a residence and was constantly traveling to be where needed.

While the names Koot Humi and Morya were used for theosophists to address the Mahatmas, it was made clear along the way that their true names and those of other Masters were never given out. This surely was done to protect them from more meddling energies of the outer world than they were willing to subject themselves.

The Masters generally live far from the beaten path, deal not with mundane concerns of the outer world, and relate to the clock much differently than common mortals. Thus, they are "... content to live as we do -- unknown and undisturbed by a civilization which rests so exclusively upon the intellect. Nor do we feel in any way concerned about the revival of our ancient arts and high civilization, for these are as sure to come back in their time, and in a higher form as the Plesiosaurus and the Megatherium in theirs. We have the weakness to believe in ever-recurrent cycles and hope to quicken the resurrection of what is past and gone. We could not impede it even if we would. The 'new civilization' will be but the child of the old one, and we have but to leave the eternal law to take its own course to have our dead ones come out of their graves; yet, we are certainly anxious to hasten the welcome event."

Other clues about the Masters appeared from time to time, especially through the communication between K.H. and A.P. Sinnett which resulted in the latter writing *The Occult World* and *Esoteric Buddhism*, and the eventual compilation of *The Mahatma Letters to A.P. Sinnett* after his death. Even more information which came out through correspondence between Sinnett and Blavatsky helped to explain Madame's writing and broader teaching work.

Large hints about the Masters and their chela appeared in an 1886 letter to Mr. Sinnett from H.P.B. in which she detailed a recent vision/dream. "I had vainly called upon the Masters -- who came not during my waking state, but now in my sleep I saw them both, I was again (a scene of years back) in Mahatma K.H.'s house. I was sitting in a corner on a mat and he walking about the room in his riding dress, and Master was talking to someone behind the door. 'I remind can't -- I pronounced in answer to a question of His about a dead aunt. -- He smiled and said 'Funny English you use.' Then I felt ashamed, hurt in my vanity, and began thinking (mind you, in my dream or vision which was the exact reproduction of what had taken place word for word 16 years ago) 'now I am here and speaking nothing but English in verbal phonetic language I can perhaps learn to speak better with Him.' (To make it clear with Master I also used English, which whether bad or good was the same for Him as he does not speak it but understands every word I say out of my head; and I am made to understand Him -- how I could never tell or explain if I were killed but I do. With D.K. [chela] I also spoke English, he speaking it better even than Mahatma K.H.) Then, in my dream still, three months after as I was made to feel in that vision -- I was standing before Mahatma K.H. near the old building taken down he was looking at, and as Master was not at home, I took to him a few sentences I was studying in Senzar in his sister's room and asked him to tell me if I translated them correctly -- and gave him a slip of paper with these sentences written in English. He took and read them and correcting the interpretation read them over and said 'Now your English is becoming better -- try to pick out of my head even the little I know of It.' And he put his hand on my forehead in the region of memory and squeezed his fingers on it (and I felt even the same trifling pain in it, as then, and the cold shiver I had experienced) and since that day He did so with my head daily, for about two months. Again, the scene changes and I am going away with Master who is sending me off, back to Europe. I am bidding good-bye to his sister and her child and all the chelas. I listen to what the Masters tell me. And then come the parting words of Mahatma K.H. laughing at me as He always did and saying 'Well, if you have not learned much of the Sacred Sciences and practical Occultism -- and who could expect a WOMAN to -- you have learned, at any rate, a little English. You speak it now only a little worse than I do!' and he laughed."

During her seven years of directed training as a chela, in Tibet-India and in scattered lands, Madame was taught the details of how to act as a receiver of thought, to be a ready channel of communication, and to accept precipitated messages. She also was quite capable of sending, directing and precipitating on her own. Yet, her abilities were far beyond receiving and transmitting messages Succinctly put, H.P.B. learned to manipulate energy just as we moderns do fairly well at exploiting and changing seemingly solid matter. Madame B. merely took the next steps to work with the subtle ethers, creating as nature does while living in the unnatural world of the "orphan humanity."

Thus, there are many clues about the wonder which was Madame Blavatsky. Still, no ordinary mortal, past or present, really knew H.P.B. Not even the likes of A.P. Sinnett who came so close to her work and person. "No one could understand Mme. Blavatsky without studying her by the light of the hypothesis -- even if it were only regarded as such -- that she was the visible agent of unknown occult superiors. There was much in her character on the surface as I have described it, which repelled the idea that she was an exalted moralist trying to lead people upward towards a higher spiritual life. The internal excitement, superinduced by the effort to accomplish any of her occult feats, would, moreover, render her too passionate in repudiating suspicions which could not but be stimulated by such protests on her part. Conscious of her failure very often to do more than leave people about her puzzled and vaguely wondering how she did her 'tricks,' she would constantly abjure the whole attempt, profess violent resolutions to produce no more phenomena under any circumstances for a sneering, undiscerning, materialistic generation; and as often be impelled by her love of wielding the strange forces at her command to fall into her old mistakes, to hurriedly rush into the performance of some new feat as she felt the power upon her, without stopping to think of the careful conditions by which it ought to be surrounded, if she meant to do more than aggravate the mistrust which drove her into frenzies of suffering and wrath. Once, however, recognize her as the flighty and defective, though loyal and brilliantly-gifted representative of occult superiors in the background, making through her an experiment on the spiritual intuitions of the world in which she moved, and the whole situation was solved, the apparent incoherence of her character and acts explained, and the best attributes of her own nature properly appreciated."

After her training, Madame was sent back to Europe and thence to America armed with many yogic powers. At the same time, she was tethered to her Teachers and handicapped as well. Still, H.P.B. was enabled to do the most extraordinary things and to try to convince "thick-headed materialists ... that immense powers reside in man."

For all her sacrifices, Helena Blavatsky surely received as she gave. The masters were apt to remind all that "ingratitude is not one of our vices." So within the range of her karma, H.P.B. was well cared for by her mentors. She was also given the singular honor of watching history pass before her eyes as she transcribed it into books like *Isis* and *SD*. Furthermore, her efforts on the Path must have emulated those of her adept Brothers. She was only a few steps behind them. "Believe me, there comes a moment in the life of an adept, when the hardships he has passed through are a thousandfold rewarded."

Hierophant
(Greek for Apostle)

"In their eyes ... I am the chief priestess and Pythia."

During her traveling days in Egypt, Helena Blavatsky encountered Albert Leigh Rawson who was an art student at the time. Versatile like H.P.B., Rawson eventually took divinity, law and medical degrees before becoming an archeologist and writer. He remembered from a meeting in Cairo circa 1853, "Her face was full, moon-shaped -- the outline so prized in the Orient; she had bright, clear eyes, mild as a gazelle's in repose, but flashing like a serpent's in anger or excitement. Her youthful figure, until she was thirty, was supple, muscular and well rounded, fit to delight an artist. Her hands and feet were so small and delicately molded as to suggest the fullness and softness of youth, and they never lost entirely those qualities."

Rawson saw her as tirelessly working and never satisfied. Always searching, probing boundaries, breaching barriers. H.P.B. told Rawson that she was engaged in a work to one day free humanity from mental bondage. Despite the grandeur of her aspiration, the young Blavatsky remained detached and at a distance, reciting ancient words from the New Testament: "This work is not mine, but his that sent me."

H.P.B. was aware that she had a calling even before she met her Master face to face in London in 1851. Still, she only gradually discovered the details of her mission, and passed on hints of what was to come to only a selected few.

If ever she was praised or someone tried to give her credit, Madame turned towards her Teachers. "I thank you, dear Sir, for the compliments you have paid me, but I hardly deserve them. I am only doing my duty, and I am but the humble disciple of our great Masters."

Koot Humi eventually tried to put Madame's phenomena and work in proper perspective: "Her impulsive nature ... is always ready to carry her beyond the boundaries of truth, into the regions of exaggeration; nevertheless without a shadow of suspicion that she is thereby deceiving her friends or abusing of their great trust in her. The stereotyped phrase: 'It is not I; I can do nothing by myself ... it is all they -- the Brothers.... I am but their humble and devoted slave and instrument' is a downright fib."

On the other hand, H.P.B. took on much of the blame for problems in the work assigned her and often let the buck stop on her own desk.

Still, she would laugh at conjectures that she was an independent agent, created the Theosophical Society, and did the Work under her own impetus. "I had always maintained that it was no spirit power that moved and helped me, but our Masters and their chelas."

Helena Blavatsky repeatedly declared she was sent out into the world to do her Masters' bidding. She was "ordered to do so." They were appreciative of her endless and dedicated works. Yet, they knew that she was far from a perfect vessel for the very difficult tasks laid upon her. Henry Olcott remarked that, "To get herself into the frame of mind when she could have open intercourse with them had -- as she had pathetically assured me -- cost her years of the most desperate self-restraint. I doubt if any person had ever entered the Path against greater obstacles or with more self-suppression.

"Of course, a brain so liable to disturbance was not the best adapted to the supremely delicate business of the mission she had taken upon herself; but the Masters told me it was far and away the best now available, and they must get all they could out of it. She was to them loyalty and devotion personified, and ready to dare and suffer all for the sake of the Cause. Gifted beyond all other persons of her generation with innate psychical powers, and fired with an enthusiasm that ran into fanaticism, she supplied the element of fixity of purpose, which, conjoined with a phenomenal degree of bodily endurance, made her a most powerful, if not a very docile and equable agent. With less turbulence of spirit she would, probably, have turned out less faulty literary work, but instead of lasting seventeen years under the strain, she would, doubtless, have faded out of the body ten years earlier and her later writings have been lost to the world."

Further, H.S.O. knew her, "living like other people when awake, but going into another world and dealing with nobler people, when asleep or in waking clairvoyance; a personality inhabiting an enfeebled female body, in which ... 'a vital cyclone is raging most of the time' - to quote the words of a Master."

She had returned from the intimate direction and protection of her Masters to live amongst a human race "composed of knaves and congenital idiots." Madame took on gargantuan tasks, the breadth of which only she and her Teachers understood. And, the Masters probably didn't anticipate all the effects of the unprecedented work H.P.B. attempted in the midst of that skeptical, materialistic era.

Madame wrote to Professor Hiram Corson early in 1875 about her mission: "I am here, in this country sent by my Lodge, on behalf of

Truth in modern Spiritualism, and it is my most sacred duty to unveil what is, and expose what is not. Perhaps, did I arrive here 100 years too soon. Maybe, (and I am afraid it is so) that in this present state of mental confusion, of doubt, of the endless and fruitless conflicts between the Tyndals and Wallaces [19th century scientists], the issue of which are arrested by the almighty power of the dollar, for people seem to care every day less for truth and every hour more for gold, -- my feeble protest and endeavors will be of no avail -- nevertheless, I am ever ready for the grand battle and perfectly prepared to bear any consequinces that may fall to my lot."

H.P. Blavatsky became the oracle of the 19th century, the priestess of a dark era, and the lone messenger for Great Ones who exposed themselves little to the Western world. And so, she was also the conduit for those distant mahatmas, received and transmitted a treasury of information, and shared a grand impulse for the millennium.

The reader will have noted by now that Madame Blavatsky "tuned into" all manner of human, political, and social conditions in her extended environment. At times, her tentacles reached to extremes not just for akashic information and directives of her Teachers but they also extended into the depths of her very own Soul.

She gave repeated warnings that the planet in the latter part of the 19th century was entering into a period where human choices would contribute to the fate of the world in the next. On the one hand, her writings suggested the hope that her fellows would make percipient decisions and live for the betterment of all nations and peoples.

Still, H.P.B. knew that the physical planet and astral worlds were spread with taints of the distant past. Leaders and nations harbored ancient spores which could germinate into catastrophic disorder. Helena, the sybil, used her "Karmic Visions" in 1888, "a dark combination of numbers," to predict a dire fate for Germany and the western world. H.P.B. wrote that the "Empire reached, virtually, the 18th year of its unification. It was during the fatal combination of the four numbers 8 that it lost two of its Emperors, [Frederick III and Wilhelm I] and planted the seed of many dire Karmic results."

Helena Blavatsky proceeded to unroll a panoramic vision of the Soul-Ego once known as Clovis (466-511) and latterly as Frederick III (1831-1888). Apparently over the intervening centuries, the Crown Prince had transformed himself from his former violent self as Clovis. He gradually became more and more abhorrent of war. Yet even as he inevitably became Emperor of Germany, he could not turn the rising tides of militarism and materialism which would sweep Europe and the whole world into the two Great Wars of the 20th century.

H.P.B. began by recounting her vision of an aged seeress (one cannot but wonder what Soul-Ego played that part in the drama) being brought before Clovis who demanded to be told the location of the heathen enemies' treasure. She replied,

"The gods say, Clovis, thou art accursed!... Clovis, thou shalt be reborn among thy present enemies, and suffer the tortures thou hast inflicted upon thy victims. All the combined power and glory thou hast deprived them of shall be thine in prospect, yet thou shalt never reach it!... Thou shalt ..."

The King leaped out with a roar and knocked the hag to the ground. Before Clovis could finish his deed, the Holy One of the Sun-worshippers let loose her last oath. *"I curse thee, enemy of Nerthus! May my agony be tenfold thine!... May the Great Law avenge ..."*

Clovis unleashed his heavy spear into the woman's throat, pinning her to the ground. The priestess expired quickly as her blood gushed from her terrible wound.

The effects of her death and curse were not fulfilled until over a millennium had passed. Frederick was about to become Emperor as his father Wilhelm I passed the age of 90. At the same time, Frederick neared death's door, burdened with a cancer on his throat. Physicians battled around him about his treatment which eventually produced the loss of his voice and necessitated a tracheotomy.

His days were numbered as was his reign as emperor. In his fitful sleeps and restless agonies, Frederick foresaw the carnage to come. *"What he now sees is a throng of bayonets clashing against each other in mist of smoke and blood; thousands of mangled corpses covering the ground, torn and cut to shreds by the murderous weapons devised by science and civilization, blessed to success by the servants of his God. What he now dreams of are bleeding, wounded and dying men, with missing limbs and matted locks, wet and soaked through with gore.... Every pang in his own wasting body brings to him in dream the recollection of pangs still worse, of pangs suffered through and for him. He sees and feels the torture of the fallen millions, who die after long hours of terrible mental and physical agony ..."*

Tortured in his bed of death, he was brought to recall times gloating over dead warriors at his feet and sending praise to the Almighty in thanks for victory. In his reverie, he heard his own Soul-Ego speak *forth: "Fame and victory are vain-glorious words.... Thanksgiving and prayers for lives destroyed -- wicked lies and blasphemy!"*

"What have they brought thee and thy fatherland, those bloody victories!"

"A population clad in iron armour."

"Two score millions of men dead now to all spiritual aspiration and Soul-life. A people, henceforth deaf to the peaceful voice of the honest citizen's duty, averse to a life of peace, blind to the arts and literature, indifferent to all but lucre and ambition. What is thy future Kingdom, now? A legion of war-puppets as units, a great wild beast in their collectivity."

Friedrich Wilhelm Nikolaus Karl is now known as the German Emperor and King of Prussia of 99 days in the 1888, the Year of the Three Emperors.

Such visions and prophecy were not typical of Helena Blavatsky's abilities. But, her "Karmic Visions" do show another of her extraordinary talents. Most of H.P.B.'s apostolic work was much more mundane: writing one article or book at a time, meeting with students and inquirers, presenting her gifts to those who would take the time to listen. She came forth to walk and talk, teach and write, and do battle as needed in her jaded environs. This even though H.P.B. was not temperamentally suited for all the tasks laid upon her. A.P. Sinnett remarked, "She certainly had none of the superficial attributes one might have expected in a spiritual teacher; and how she could at the same time be philosopher enough to have given up the world for the sake of spiritual advancement, and yet be capable of going into frenzies of passion about trivial annoyances, was a profound mystery to us for a long while, and is only now partially explainable, indeed, within my own mind, by some information I have received relating to curious psychological laws under which initiates in occult mysteries, circumstanced as she is, inevitably come. By slow degrees only, and in spite of herself -- in spite of injudicious proceedings on her part that long kept alive suspicions she might easily have allayed, if she could have kept calm enough to understand them, -- did we come to appreciate the reality of the occult forces and unseen agencies behind her." (See Aenigma.)

A.P. Sinnett and many contemporaries never fully *got* HPB: the extraordinary teacher, the "occult mother-in-law," the grand curiosity, and phenomenal carrier pigeon. Others came to recognize her as "our sphinx, our mystery, our dearly loved Old Lady. She was not a teacher in any ordinary sense, for she had no idea of teaching in any orderly or systematic fashion; indeed she detested the very idea of being considered a spiritual or ethical teacher, cried out loudly against it, protested she was the least fitted of all to be called to such an office. No, she was better than that, better than any formal instructor, for she was as it were a natural fire at which to light up enthusiasm for the greater life of the world, a marvellous incentive to make one grip on to the problems of self-knowing, a wonderful inspirer of longings for return, a true singer of the songs of home; all this she was at times, while at times she intensified confusion." (GRS Mead)

Countess Wachtmeister said much the same but in different words: "H.P.B. herself was constitutionally and by the innate turn of her mind, unfitted for the task of orderly and patient exposition of her teachings. I have before me a letter of hers, undated, but written about this time from Elberfeld, whither she went after Wurzburg, which gives a vivid picture of her droll despair at having such a burden imposed upon her. I give the extracts from her correspondence verbatim, for the quaintness of her phraseology was a peculiar characteristic of her own, and it is well known that as yet her English was very imperfect.

"'If you are distressed,' she writes to me, 'I am at an utter loss to understand what is expected of me. I have never promised to play guru, schoolmaster, or professor for Y., or any one else. Master told him to go to Elberfeld, and Master told me that he, was to come and that I would have to answer his questions. I have done so, and can do no more. I have read to him from the *S.D.* and found I could not proceed, for he interrupted me at every line, and not only with questions, but generally made a dissertation as an answer to his own question, which answer lasted twenty minutes. As for Y., he will answer you for himself, as I made him write to you. I told you repeatedly that I have never taught anyone but in my own usual way. Olcott and Judge have learnt all they know by associating with me. If I had to be inflicted the punishment of giving regular instructions in a professor-like way for one hour, let alone two in a day, I would rather run away to the North Pole or die any day, severing my connection with Theosophy entirely, I am incapable of it, as everyone ought to know who knows me. To this day I could not make out what Y. wants to know.'"

Despite her frustrated complaint above, Madame B. inevitably rose to the occasion and blossomed in extraordinary ways into a teacher sought after by many. And her teaching, from whatever source and through whatever media, spread out to the world and through generations continuing on long after her death. Her compatriot of many years, Henry Olcott, pronounced in his *Old Diary Leaves*. "I have known a Jewish Rabbi pass hours and whole evenings in her company, discussing the Kabballa, and have him say to her that, although he had studied the secret science of his religion for thirty years, she had taught him things he had not ever dreamed of, and thrown a clear light upon passages which not even his best teachers had understood.... and in her moments of inspiration -- if the term be admissible -- she astonished the most erudite by her learning quite as much as she dazzled all present by her eloquence and delighted them by her wit and humorous raillery."

Anthropologist, paleontologist, and comparative anatomist, Carter Blake, laid gasping praise on Madame and her grand writing: "On ordinary lines it is strange that an old, sickly woman, not consulting a library and having no books of her own of consequence, should possess the unusual knowledge that Madame Blavatsky undoubtedly did. Indeed, it is incomprehensible, unless she were of an extraordinary mental capacity, and had spent her whole life in study. On the contrary, from many sources we gain undoubted evidence that Madame Blavatsky's education had not even been carried as far as that of a High School student of the present day.

"But it is a fact that she knew more than I did on my own particular lines ... For instance, her information was superior to my own on the subject of the Naulette Jaw.... I remember in conversation with her in 1888, in Lansdowne Road, at the time she was engaged on *The Secret Doctrine*, how Madame Blavatsky, to my great astonishment, sprung upon me the fact that the raised beaches of Tarija were pliocene. I had always thought them pleistocene -- following the line of reasoning of Darwin and Spotswood Wilson. The fact that these beaches are pliocene has been proven to me since from the works of Gay ... Madame Blavatsky certainly had original sources of information ... transcending the knowledge of experts on their own lines."

H.P.B. dealt with practically any subject which came before her, if she was in the mood. In 1882, Madame encountered a secularist named R. Jagannathia who wrote for the *Philosophic Inquirer* in Madras. H.P.B. recognized his earnest interest in truth, even as he "questioned her on some points to all outward appearance difficult, each of which had been very carefully formulated by me overnight. As a member of the National Secular Society of England, I consoled myself with the idea that the problems I proposed were insoluble, and that they would tax her fine and philosophic intellect.

"To my great astonishment she took up question after question, and answered each most elaborately and satisfactorily. She occupied nearly three hours [that day] in solving my questions. The array of facts she cited in support of her forcible and incontrovertible arguments, historical, philosophical and scientific, confused my poor intellect. The whole audience was spellbound. And one peculiar point in her answering I cannot afford to omit. Her mastery of the various subjects was such that in her answer all the side-questions were anticipated and disposed of once for all. On the second and third day we were thus occupied for hours in the presence of the same audience; as the interest daily increased in proportion to my more and more difficult questions and her most able and satisfactory answer....

"On the third day, after answering the questions, on which I spent much thought and care, mustering all the force of my atheistic knowledge and learning, she cheerfully asked me if I had anything more to say. Readily and unreservedly I answered that 'my stock was exhausted,' and this afforded food for laughter for a few minutes to the whole company."

Madame B. was called to serve many masters. Some were living distantly, communicating telepathically or appearing in astral bodies. Others were those in physical bodies close at hand, whom she was intended to teach. Some were yet unborn, like this writer and yourself.

Her life was one of many and strenuous trials. Yet, she surely was comforted in so many ways through her continuous contact with her Master and the unseen (to us) worlds. Still, how confusing it must have been at times for H.P.B. and those around her. Visitors and assistants could hardly imagine what she might do or say next. Madame would receive calls via the astral bells and remove herself to an adjoining room to communicate with "the Chiefs." Or she would simply make space for one of them to enter her outer form. When writing *Isis Unveiled* and *The Secret Doctrine*, she would be transformed in front of people like Olcott who began to recognize her varied guises.

Now it was a curious fact that each change in the H.P.B. manuscript would be preceded, either by her leaving the room for a moment or two, or by her going off into the trance or abstracted state, when her lifeless eyes would be looking beyond me into space, as it were, and returning to the normal waking state almost immediately. And there would also be a distinct change of personality, or rather personal peculiarities, in gait, vocal expression, vivacity of manner, and, above all, in temper.

The reader of her Caves and Jungles of Hindustan *remembers how the whirling pythoness would rush out from time to time and return under the control, as alleged, of a different goddess? It was just like that -- bar the sorcery and the vertiginous dancing -- with H.P.B.: she would leave the room one person and anon return to it another. Not another as to visible change of physical body, but another as to tricks of motion, speech, and manners; with different mental brightness, different views of things, different command of English orthography, idiom, and grammar, and different -- very, very different command over her temper; which, as its sunniest, was almost angelic, at its worst, the opposite.*

... the H.P.B. manuscript varied at times, and that there were several variants of the one prevailing script; also that each change in the writing was accompanied by a marked alteration in the manner, motions, expression, and literary capacity of H.P.B. When she was left to her own devices, it was often not difficult to know it, for then the untrained literary apprentice became manifest and the cutting and pasting began; then the copy that was turned over to me for revision was terribly faulty, and having been converted into a great smudge of interlineations, erasures, orthographic corrections and substitutions, would end in being dictated by me to her to re-write....

Now often things were, after a while, said to me that would be more than hints that other intelligences than H.P.B.'s were at times using her body as a writing machine: it was never expressly said, for example, 'I am so and so,' or 'Now this is A or B.' It did not need that after we 'twins' had been working together long enough for me to become familiar with her every peculiarity of speech, moods, and impulses. The change was as plain as day, and by and by after she had been out of the room and returned, a brief study of her features and actions enabled me to say to myself, 'This is ___, or ___, or ___,' and presently my suspicion would be confirmed by what happened.

One of these Alter Egos of hers, one whom I have since personally met, wears a full beard and long moustache that are twisted, Rajput fashion, into his side whiskers. He has the habit of constantly pulling at his moustache when deeply pondering: he does it mechanically and unconsciously. Well, there were times when H.P.B.'s personality had melted away and she was 'Somebody else,' when I would sit and watch her hand as if pulling at and twisting a moustache that certainly was not growing visibly on H.P.B.'s upper lip, and the far-away look would be in the eyes, until presently resuming attention of passing things, the moustached Somebody would look up, catch me watching him, hastily remove the hand from the face, and go on with the work of writing.

Then there was another Somebody, who disliked English so much that he never willingly talked with me in anything but French: he had a fine artistic talent and a passionate fondness for mechanical invention. Another one would now and then sit there, scrawling something with a pencil and reeling off for me dozens of poetical stanzas which embodied, now sublime, now humorous ideas.

So each of the several Somebodies had his peculiarities distinctly marked, as recognisable as those of any of our ordinary acquaintances or friends. One was jovial, fond of good stories and witty to a degree; another, all dignity, reserve, and erudition. One would be calm, patient, and benevolently helpful, another testy and sometimes exasperating. One Somebody would always be willing to emphasise his philosophical or scientific explanations of the subjects I was to write upon, by doing phenomena for my edification, while to another Somebody I dared not even mention them.

I got an awful rebuke one evening. I had brought home a while before two nice, soft pencils, just the thing for our desk work, and had given one to H.P.B. and kept one myself. She had the very bad habit of borrowing pen-knives, pencils, rubber, and other articles of stationery and forgetting to return them: once put into her drawer or writing-desk, there they would stay, no matter how much of a protest you might make over it.

On this particular evening, the artistic Somebody was sketching a navvy's face on a sheet of common paper and chatting with me about something, when he asked me to lend him another pencil. The thought flashed into my mind, 'If I once lend this nice pencil it will go into her drawer and I shall have none for my own use.' I did not say this, I only thought it, but the Somebody gave me a mildly sarcastic look, reached out to the pen-tray between us laid his pencil in it, handled it with his fingers of that hand for a moment, and lo! a dozen pencils of the identical make and quality! He said not a word, did not even give me a look, but the blood rushed to my temples and I felt more humble than I ever did in my life. All the same, I scarcely think I deserved the rebuke, considering what a stationery-annexer H.P.B. was!

Now when either of these Somebodies was 'on guard,' as I used to term it, the H.P.B. manuscript would present the identical peculiarities that it had on the last occasion when he had taken his turn at the literary work. He would, by preference, write about the class of subjects that were to his taste, and instead of H.P.B. playing the part of an amanuensis, she would then have become for the time being that other person.... If you had given me in those days any page of Isis *manuscript, I could almost certainly have told you by which Somebody it had been written.*

Where, then, was H.P.B.'s self at those times of replacement? Ah, that is the question; and that is one of the mysteries which are not given to the first comer. As I understood it, she herself had loaned her body as one might one's type-writer, and had gone off on other occult business that she could transact in her astral body; a certain group of Adepts occupying and manoeuvring the body by turns.

When they knew that I could distinguish between them, so as to even have invented a name for each by which H.P.B. and I might designate them in our conversation in their absence, they would frequently give me a grave bow or a friendly farewell nod when about to leave the room and give place to the next relief-guard. And they would sometimes talk to me of each other as friends do about absent third parties, by which means I came to know bits of their several personal histories; and would also speak about the absent H.P.B., distinguishing her from the physical body they had borrowed from her.

Like unto the dioramas which before her own eyes when writing her *Isis* and *SD,* H.P.B. presented more and more amazing pictures to Colonel Olcott. "She and I were in our literary workroom in New York one summer day after dinner. It was early twilight, and the gas had not been lighted. She sat over by the South front window, I stood on the rung before the mantle-piece, thinking. I heard her say 'Look and learn'; and glancing that way, saw a mist rising from her head and shoulders. Presently it defined itself into the likeness of one of the Mahatmas, the one who, latter, gave me the historical turban, but the astral double of which he now wore on his mist-born head. Absorbed in watching the phenomenon, I stood silent and motionless. The shadowy shape only formed for itself the upper half of the torso, and then faded away and was gone; whether re-absorbed into H.P.B.'s body or not, I do not know. She sat statue-like for two or three minutes, after which she sighed, came to herself, and asked me if I had seen anything. When I asked her to explain the phenomenon she refused, saying that it was for me to develop my intuition so as to understand the phenomena of the world I lived in."

It is hard for anyone to understand H.P.B.'s phenomenal life and work. And, it is even harder to explain them. Thus, the numerous failed attempts by many interviewers and biographers to give sound portraits of the one called Helena Blavatsky.

Even her Teachers and Masters were stretched in many ways having Madame Blavatsky as their major representative on the world stage in the 19th century. "... we employ agents -- the best available. Of these, for the last thirty years, the chief has been the personality known as H.P.B. to the world (but otherwise to us). Imperfect and very 'troublesome,' no doubt, she proves to some; nevertheless, there is no likelihood of our finding a better one for years to come, and your Theosophists should be made to understand it ... Her fidelity to our work being constant, and her sufferings having come upon her through it, neither I nor either of my Brother Associates will desert or supplant her. As I once before remarked, ingratitude is not among our vices.... To help you in your present perplexity, H.P.B. has next to no concern with administrative details, and should be kept clear of them so far as her strong nature can be controlled. But this you must tell to all; with occult matters she has everything to do.... We have not abandoned her; she is not 'given over to chelas.' She is our direct agent."

Acting as amanuensis and agent, teacher and priestess, Madame B. challenged herself, her followers and her adversaries. Sometimes willingly and sometimes quite oppositely. In her direct involvement with the press and professors, and especially students and seekers, H.P.B. seemed to have been able to get to the heart of matters.

Her unfailing acceptance of "all comers" made her a veritable magnet for the "new" teachings. This benevolent attitude became a major force in the expansion of Theosophy in India, and later on the British Isles and the European continent. The Blavatsky Lodge was eventually formed on her move to London and Helena made good use of her "bully pulpit." Students were drawn from far and wide to sit at the feet of the Russian woman who had seemingly been everywhere and done everything: A teacher who also was quite able to discourse and write about those experiences and continue on to elucidate whatever was left. But much more than that, was the woman who could enter into another's very heart, mind and soul. The Countess Wachtmeister made it known, "I have never seen her treat two persons alike.

The weak traits in everyone's character were known to her at once, and the extraordinary way in which she would probe them was surprising. By those who lived in daily contact with her the knowledge of Self was gradually acquired, and by those who chose to benefit by her practical way of teaching progress could be made. But to many of her pupils the process was unpalatable, for it is never pleasant to be brought face to face with one's own weaknesses; and so many turned from her, but those who could stand the test, and remain true to her, would recognise within themselves the inner development which alone leads to Occultism."

H.P.B. warned her pupils in early instructions to the Esoteric Section of the Theosophical Society: "There is a strange law in Occultism which has been ascertained and proven by thousands of years of experience; nor has it failed to demonstrate itself, almost in every case, during the thirteen years that the T.S. has been in existence. As soon as anyone pledges himself as a 'Probationer' certain occult effects ensue. Of these the first is the throwing outward of everything latent in the nature of the man: his faults, habits, qualities or subdued desires, whether good, bad or indifferent. This is an immutable law in the domain of the occult."

Regardless of the price or problem, with or without immutable occult law, Helena met people as they came to her. The reader will encounter many in the next chapter whose faults rose prominently and painfully to the surface when they had chanced (or been fated) to pass into Helena Blavatsky's sphere of occult influence.

Then, who but H.P.B. bore the brunt of those faults which came frothing to the surface in the lives of her probationers? She may well have been speaking of herself when she wrote, "... those western Hierophants being often themselves ignorant of the danger they incur -- one and all of these 'Teachers' are subject to the same inviolable law. From the moment they begin really to teach, from the instant they confer any power -- whether psychic, mental or physical -- on their pupils, they take upon themselves all the sins of that pupil, in connection with the Occult Sciences, whether of omission or commission, until the moment when initiation makes the pupil a Master and responsible in his turn."

Regardless, H.P.B. proceeded on with iron will and forgiving heart. Her methods were hardly those of the typical teacher as she reached deep within her own and other Selves to bring forth Light and Truth. Henry Edge found her teaching to go far beyond speech and writing to relationship and revelation. "Then there is the responsiveness of the Teacher to one's secret aspirations and other feelings ... What I do mean can be illustrated by an instance. Having on one occasion, while far away from London, chanced to be thinking of H.P.B., and to have achieved some kind of realization for her real character and work, I had felt a glow of the true Love go forth from my heart. The next time I saw the Teacher, she had something for me, something which only a Teacher can give, something which not even a Teacher can give except to one who has asked, 'Knock, and it shall be opened to you.'

"She turned one's aspirations into the right channel and inculcated the Heart-Doctrine, which supersedes all personal motives by the power of universal Love -- the life of the Spiritual Man. The Teacher can appeal directly to the real Self of the pupil ..."

Henry Edge, Jasper Niemand, and others became aware by degrees of Madame's work in the inner worlds and dimensions. Jasper sensed the "sound-combinations of the Adept," the higher vibrations, and the subtle hidden meanings with which H.P.B. surely always worked.

Jasper (aka Julia Ver Planck) was an American who never saw H.P.B. in physical form. Still she was moved merely by reading one of the several sophomoric prosecutions made against Madame and then came to know her and learn from her across the broad Atlantic Ocean. "Evidently here was a power, whether for good, or for evil. Either she was an adventuress far surpassing all the world had ever known, an original adventuress who slaved for intellectual progress and rule as others slave for nothing, not even for gold -- or she was a martyr. I could see no mean between....

"I never met her, I never looked into her eyes. Words cannot picture regret. But after a time she wrote to me, of her own precedent and motion, as one who responds from afar to the longing of a friend. Prompt to reply if I asked help for another, silent only to the personal call; full of pity and anguish for the mistaken, the deserter, the suffering; solicitous only for the Cause, the Work, so I found her always. Although she had a lion heart, it bled; but it never broke. The subtle aroma of her courage spread over seas, invigorated and rejoiced every synchronous heart, set us to doing and to daring. Knowing thus her effect upon our lives, in its daily incentive to altruistic endeavour, truth and virtue, we can smile at all alien testimony. Only from kindred virtues do these virtues spring. She could never have strengthened us in these things if she had not been possessed them in abundant measure."

Jasper Niemand put the whole of H.P.B.'s teaching into perspective. "Madame Blavatsky was to be found in the philosophy taught by her. Message and messenger are one and the same thing in the laws of the supra-natural ... A person may teach a truth and yet may not be that truth, by virtue of living it. But he cannot impart a truth in its vitality, so that it fructifies -- an energetic impulse of power -- in other lives, unless he possesses that life-impulse by reason of his living; become it. He cannot give what he has not."

H.P.B. was truly about the task of pointing her brethren to the Light of the Soul in as many ways as she could in her sixty brief years. Thus, Madame Blavatsky was much like the apostles of old East and West: fearless, taking the high road at all costs and giving until it hurts. Had either psychic investigators or modern biographers ever peered really deeply enough into H.P.B.'s life and work, they would have discovered the real secret she was carrying. H.P. Blavatsky was "the greatest Soul of our times ... whose grandeur of purpose escapes lesser mortals, and who are consequently almost invariably misunderstood, and but too often hated."

Khan
(Mongolian for Potentate)

"Those wishing to destroy me cannot do so. I am in no danger. Others ... have tried to bend me to their ideas, or to break me. But I have the epidermis of a Tartar ..."

"An immense feeling of power surrounded her; it was like being in a room with a tremendously active volcano, though eruptions -- and there were eruptions -- had less to do with that impression of power than had the steadily maintained force that was present in everything she did, -- was present equally when she seemed to be doing nothing....

"In talking to her, one had always the sense of power, wisdom, integrity, humour. But at rare intervals there was a notable change. It was as though a door had opened within her, a door into the infinite worlds. One had a sense of a greater than H.P.B. speaking, a tremendous authority and force."

So remembered Charles Johnston on his introduction to Helena Blavatsky. "The Tartarian termagant" nearly bowled him and others over on first meeting. "She turned to greet me, the powerful face lit up by a smile in the great blue eyes, her hair light golden brown, naturally waved or rippled, and parted and drawn back."

The extraordinary potency of her being left its indelible marks on Johnston from his very first experiences of Helena Petrovna Blavatsky. "I never saw anything so overwhelming. She rose up in her wrath like the whole Russian army of five millions on a war footing and descended on the poor Briton's devoted head, with terrific weight. When she was roused, H.P.B. was like a torrent; she simply dominated everyone who came near her; and her immense personal force made itself felt always, even when she was sick and suffering, and with every reason to be cast down. I have never seen anything like her tremendous individual power. She was the justification of her own teaching of the divinity of the will."

Madame Blavatsky took on the role of leader in her latter years as a pure matter of necessity. But, she was not one who merely assumed power. H.P.B. was power personified. Her appearance, manner, and whole being all conveyed the sense of power. People who came into her presence felt a suppressed excitement tinged with awe. She ever emanated fearlessness, unconventionality, wisdom, vast experience, hearty good will, and especial sympathy for the underdog.

In a letter to her sister Vera, H.P.B. told of the unusual leadership role which befell her once the TS was formed. "The only thing I know is that I have called forth an unknown power which ties the destinies of other people to my destiny, to my life.... I know also to my great relief, that many amongst those devoted to me look up to me as to their rescuer. Many were heartless egotists, faithless materialists, worldly, lightheaded sensualists, and many have become serious people, working indefatigably, sacrificing everything to the work: position, time, money, and thinking but of one thing: their spiritual and intellectual development. They have become in a way the victims of self-sacrifice, and live only for the good of others, seeing their salvation and light in me. And what am I? I am what I always was. At least so far as they are concerned, seriously. I am ready to give the last drop of my blood for Theosophy, but as for Theosophists I hardly love anyone amongst them personally. I cannot love anyone personally, but you of my own blood.... What a blind tool I am, I must own, in the hands of the one whom I call my Master!"

Madame Helena Blavatsky was the chosen vessel of the Masters and their Teachings for the 19th century. The last quarter of every century is said to bring one or more such harbingers of hidden things to the fore. Their names are subject to debate, but Bacon-Shakespeare and the Enlightenment, Isaac Newton and the Dawn of Science, and St. Germain and the Era of Great Revolutions were the most noteworthy of those preceding H.P.B. in recent centuries. It also was more than coincidental that H.P. Blavatsky appeared ahead of scientific works in atoms and radiation: Crookes inventing the cathode ray tube, Rontgen discovering x-rays, the Curies unveiling radio-activity, and Thomson, Planck and Einstein positing laws involving electrons, quantum mechanics and relativity.

Helena Blavatsky seemingly arose from nowhere, a lone woman in foreign lands. Yet, she eventually drew around her a large following while giving forth those "secrets" permitted to be passed on to posterity. The reactive media and walls of expanding materialism, entrenched Christian churchianity and Darwinian scientism stood to thwart her at most every turn.

But, H.P.B. held to the task as she took on labors which might have required small armies in other circumstances. She accomplished a tremendous amount of work in less than a score of years due to her phenomenal talents, her incredible industry, her undaunted loyalty, and her grand world experience and knowledge. Above all, it was her will and power which kept her "in the body" and producing long after most anyone else would have thrown in the towel.

H.P.B.'s middle name Petrovna derives from the Greek word for Peter and means "rock." Like her own phenomenal nature, genuine adamantine power defined H.P.B. in many ways. It was clear to most everyone that Madame was a woman of force and strength. Jasper Niemand thought H.P.B. "... had the sturdiness and dignity of the druidic oak, and she was well expressed by the druidic motto: 'The Truth against the World.'"

Personal magnetism, huge intellect, and forceful language were the first things that strangers recognized on coming into her presence. And yet, H.P.B. managed to submerge that potency into extraordinarily positive and productive efforts. "I never had either personal ambition or love of power, and had ever shown myself to people in my worst light. Had I been an actress or a hypocrite, no enemy could have crushed me. It is my actual position that can alone defend me, if not now then after death. I am a beggar in the full sense of the word -- and I am proud of it: I am a wanderer on the Earth without roof or home -- or any prospect of returning to India, and I feel ready even for this sacrifice provided I can do good to our Society by my physical and mental suffering.

"All this will 'defend' and JUSTIFY me when I am gone. From Christ to Gladstone, from Buddha to the poor President of the T.S. ... no one who has worked unselfishly (mistakes are in human nature) escaped being spat upon."

H.P.B.'s works became often quite visible in her latter years. But, she was hardly a grandstander. She did her work publicly through her pen and by opening her door to practically all who would dare to enter. She did "write, write, write, and teach whoever wants to learn."

Typical leaders in most any time stand in the limelight. Madame B. certainly could have filled that role, but she knew better and acted otherwise. She also deprecated many of her own abilities, yet kept on working. "There's the difference I cannot pretend to explain in English the situation; nor would I perhaps in any language since I never had the gift of the gab nor could I write unless dictated to."

Many people would have disagreed with her on both counts. But, what Helena may have been trying to say was that she was not a chatterbox and preferred to deal with issues of substance. The Old Lady certainly could hold an audience whenever she spoke, and did so with authority. She also wrote of her own volition on a variety of subjects.

Not just when dictated to. Still, the latter was to her of much greater import. Her own writing efforts never being good enough or weighty enough compared to those which passed through her from the Masters.

While much of Madame's work was ordered, directed and dictated, other aspects surely sprang from her own unique, expansive being. Many times during her public years, H.P.B.'s flat, apartment or home became like unto a forum. The first such magnetic place which drew many early students was called the *Lamasery*. H.P.B. and H.S.O. occupied half a floor in a building located at 47th Street and 8th Avenue in New York City. The structure and the furnishings seemed commonplace for the time -- until one entered a large dining room which also served as workspace, library and reception area. One wall was covered with a picture made of dried forest leaves to appear as a tropical jungle scene showing a tiger about to attack an elephant with a serpent coiled around a tree trunk in the background. Elsewhere in the large room, the head of an angry lioness was strategically placed. "It was one of our jokes," said Colonel Olcott, "to have newcomers seated in an easy chair that faced the door, and enjoy their start when their eyes wandered from H.P.B. to glance around the room. If the visitor chanced to be a hysterical old maid who screamed on seeing the trophy, H.P.B. would laugh heartily."

Palm fronds reaching to the ceiling stood in two corners of the room. Stuffed monkeys peered over curtains. An embalmed snake lay atop the mantel mirror, head over one corner. Another stuffed ape, a baboon, dressed up with a collar, cravat and spectacles, stood in another corner. He carried in one arm a lecture manuscript entitled "Descent of Species."

And there was more. A large grey owl on a bookcase, lizards climbing the wall, carved images of the Lord Buddha and Siamese monkeys, a Swiss cuckoo clock, Japanese cabinets. Curios of all sorts dotted the room. The center of the room was occupied by a long writing table; book shelves took up part of one wall; chairs and couch took up floor space. Most of the room was thus filled, so that visitors had to pick their way through the chamber. A four-light gas chandelier with a drop-light hung over the table.

The room was colorful and pleasing to guests and occupants, and became the theme of many newspaper descriptions. The setting quite suited the bizarre personality of its mysterious occupant, Madame Blavatsky. Colonel Olcott seemed happy with the arrangement. A correspondent for a Hartford newspaper wrote thusly after a visit with

H.P.B. at the Lamasery: "Madame was seated in her little work-room and parlor, all in one, and we may add her curiosity-shop as well, for never was apartment more crammed with odd, elegant, old, beautiful, costly, and apparently worthless things, than this. She had cigarette in mouth, and scissors in hand, and was hard at work clipping paragraphs, articles, items, criticisms, and other matter, from heaps of journals from all parts of the world, relating to herself, to her book, to the Theosophical Society, to any and everything connected with her life-work and aims. She waved us to a seat, and while she intently read some article we had a chance to observe the walls and furniture of this NEW YORK LAMASERY. Directly in the centre stood a stuffed ape, with a white 'dickey' and necktie around his throat, manuscript in paw, and spectacles on nose. Could it be a mute satire on the clergy? Over the door was the stuffed head of a lioness, with open jaws and threatening aspect; the eyes glaring with an almost natural ferocity. A god in gold occupied the centre of the mantelpiece; Chinese and Japanese cabinets, fans, pipes, implements, and rugs, low divans and couches, a large desk, a mechanical bird which sang as mechanically, albums, scrap-books, and the inevitable cigarette-holders, papers, and ash-pots, made the loose rich robe in which the Madame was apparelled seem in perfect harmony with her surroundings. A rare, strange countenance is hers. A combination of moods seems to constantly play over her features. She never seems quite absorbed by one subject. There is a keen, alert, subtle undercurrent of feeling and perception perceivable in the expression of her eyes. It impressed us then, and has invariably, with the idea of a double personality: as if she were here, and not here; talking and yet thinking, or acting far away. Her hair, light, very thick, and naturally waved, has not a grey thread in it. Her skin, evidently somewhat browned by exposure to sea and sun, has no wrinkles; her hands and arms are as delicate as a girl's. Her whole personality is expressive of self-possession, command, and a certain *sangfroid* which borders on masculine indifference, without for a moment overstepping the bounds of womanly delicacy."

The Colonel told how the two hired a maid-of-all-work to do a variety of chores for them. Housekeeping was simple, food was plain, and no spirits were kept in their apartment. Their young maid returned to her home in the evening and they were left to their own devices even when they had numerous callers many nights of the week.

While Madame was aristocratic in some ways, she answered the door and made visitors feel at home. Her other domestic abilities and interests were minimal. She was not above entering the kitchen, but she knew little more than how to boil water for tea. H.S.O. once caught her laying "raw eggs on the live coals" in lieu of boiling them. Visitors were eventually invited to be members of the "Kitchen Cabinet." Col. Olcott hung a prominent sign: "Guests will find boiling water and tea in the kitchen, perhaps milk and sugar, and will kindly help themselves." Scholars and professors, doctors and lawyers, artists and journalists, lords and ladies got used to the Bohemian environ of the Lamasery. At first amusing, the said practices became an accepted part of visiting the Old Lady and the Colonel.

In that time, Henry Olcott was lawyering during the day and stationed at the Lamasery in the evening with Madame and visitors. Or helping her in writing *Isis*. As time marched on, H.P.B. was occupied morning until night. Company appeared often, but work and writing took precedence.

In later years, Archibald Keightley told of his being drawn into the work of bringing forth *The Secret Doctrine* when H.P.B. was for a time settled at Ostend. "... there I found her living with the Countess Wachtmeister, hard at work writing from six a.m. till six p.m., only omitting very short intervals for meals. She wrote and slept in one room, emerging to meals in the next room...."

Archibald's nephew Bertram recalled Madame's disciplined qualities, "I have seen her after a day's work so tired that she looked positively ill and quite unfit for any further exertion, but if need arose, if fresh work was to be done, or some theosophical question came up for discussion, she seemed to renew her strength with the desire, and would plunge into whatever offered with a resistless energy as if she had never known weariness."

Css. Wachtmeister also recounted H.P.B.'s routine during the many months of her composing *The Secret Doctrine*. The description of a single day serves to picture the work routine of her life at that time.

At six o'clock I was awakened by the servant coming with a cup of coffee for Madame Blavatsky, who, after this slight refreshment, rose and dressed, and by seven o'clock was at her desk in the sitting room.

She told me that this was her invariable habit, and that breakfast would be served at eight. After breakfast she settled herself at her writing desk and the day's work began in earnest. At one o'clock dinner was served, whereupon I rang a small hand-bell to call H.P.B. Sometimes she would come in at once, but at other times her door would remain closed hour after hour, until our Swiss maid would come to me, almost with tears in her eyes, to ask what was to be done about Madame's dinner, which was either getting cold or dried up, burnt, and utterly spoiled. At last H.P.B. would come in weary with so many hours of exhausting labour and fasting; then another dinner would be cooked, or I would send to the Hotel to get her some nourishing food.

At seven o'clock she laid aside her writing, and after tea we would spend a pleasant evening together. Comfortably seated in her big armchair, H.P.B. used to arrange her cards for a game of Patience, as she said to rest her mind. It seems as if the mechanical process of laying her cards enabled her mind to free itself from the pressure of concentrated labour during the day's work. She never cared to talk of Theosophy in the evenings.

"The mental tension during the day was so severe that she needed above all things rest, and so I procured as many journals and magazines as I could, and from these I would read the articles and passages that I thought most likely to interest and amuse her. At nine o'clock she went to bed, where she would surround herself with her Russian newspapers and read them until a late hour.

In some ways, H.P.B. was constrained almost like a machine, an aging one at that, to churn out work persistently as long as the "electricity was in service." While she was a multi-talented savant, Madame Blavatsky accomplished many of her tasks by dint of unrepentant effort rather than perfect understanding and abilities.

One day at this time, when I walked into H.P.B.'s writing room, I found the floor strewn with sheets of discarded manuscript. I asked the meaning of this scene of confusion, and she replied: 'Yes, I have tried twelve times to write this one page correctly, and each time Master says it is wrong. I think I shall go mad, writing it so often; but leave me alone; I will not pause until I have conquered it, even if I have to go on all night.'

I brought a cup of coffee to refresh and sustain her, and then left her to prosecute her weary task. An hour later I heard her voice calling me, and on entering found that, at last, the passage was completed to satisfaction, but the labour had been terrible, and the results were often at this time small and uncertain. How often, then, did I grieve over reams of manuscript, carefully prepared and copied, and, at a word, an intimation from the Masters, consigned to the flames ...

Madame persisted. Even when bowled over by the report of the Psychical Research Society (see below), whelmed by worries and put to bed with one of her recurring ailments, she "toiled away" endlessly.

To say she did so with never a whimper, however, would be short of the truth. Her letters to A.P. Sinnett were peppered with fussing and fuming. "DAMN MY FATE, I tell you death is preferable. Work, work, work and no thanks." "I am now ordered to hold my tongue, hence I have more time to hold my pen."

H.P.B. was not only the stolid Sphinx and the lion-hearted one in the eyes of many, but she also took on the "lion's share" of work and responsibility. As chela and agent, teacher and leader all wrapped in one she was fated to have all manner of slanders and lies, suspicions and intrigues land at her footsteps. And naturally enough "... it becomes more and more my duty to sacrifice myself for the good of others and to my own detriment. Such is the law." "I have sacrificed my individuality long ago."

Madame B. continued on regardless of circumstance. She gave no quarter and expected no concessions from her teachers, associates or adversaries. Compromise regarding Truth was not part of her vocabulary in any of the many languages she spoke, read or transcribed. H.P.B. came into the world to stand for Truth and to take on any challenge to its exposition in her writings and journals, organization and influence. "... war to death of every unproven human dogma, superstition, bigotry, and intolerance."

In a letter from the last months of her life to William Judge in the USA, Blavatsky quipped about her work log: "'... what am I busy with?' I, is it? I tell you, if there ever was in the world an overworked victim it is your long-suffering sister. Do take the trouble to count my occupations, you heartless Zoilas. Every month I write from forty to fifty pages of 'Esoteric Instructions,' instructions in secret sciences, which must not be printed. Five or six wretched voluntary martyrs among my esotericists have to draw, write and lithograph during the nights, some 320 copies of them, which I have to superintend, to rectify, to compare and to correct, so that there may be no mistakes and my occult information may not be put to shame.

"Well, my only friend, you ought to know better. Look into my life and try to realize it -- in its outer course at least, as the rest is hidden. I am under the curse of ever writing, as the wandering Jew was under that of being ever on the move, never stopping one moment to rest. Three ordinary healthy persons could hardly do what I have to do. I live an artificial life; I am an automaton running full steam until the power of generating steam stops, and then -- good-bye."

That steamy stance was sure to bring forth challengers as well as enemies. Most came from within the ranks of her own Theosophical Society. And, there in fact lay the rub. Even from a grand distance in time and space, one can sense the envy which sometimes grew into jealousy and spite for an eccentric like Madame Helena Blavatsky.

Early on in her public life, H.P.B. met with quite obvious opponents through the press. Various factions took exception often vociferously on the one hand to her defense of the phenomena of spiritualism and on the other to her continual attempts to undermine its basic premise that "spirits of the dead" speak through mediums and give important information about the other side. Many berated her for her anti-church polemics or her sneers at the postures of the science of the times. Indeed, Madame did do battle with dogma of most any kind. And quite regardless of the results. She was a fearless leader on many issues of the day. Neither khan nor king, emperor nor potentate did more battles with more diverse and serpentine enemies.

But, her obvious adversaries were much easier to deal with than the ones who acted or posed as friends for periods of time. Eventually, numbers of people who were close to her fell away and several of them determined to get back at "the one who had fed them."

It is fascinating to see the names of H.P.B.'s most tenacious foes: Emma (Cutting) and Alexis Coulomb, Mabel Collins (Cook) and Elliott Coues, William Emmette Coleman, Vsevelod Solovyov.

The reader should be able to detect a clear pattern. Almost all of her nemeses had names beginning with C, and not just with C but Co. Solovyov is an exception, but not entirely. Because Solovyov reads as Соловьев when written in the Russian Cyrillic alphabet. At one point in history, H.P.B. was cautioned that her major challenges would come from people with names beginning with the letter *C*. Madame seems to inconveniently have forgotten the warning until there was little but to ponder on the wonder of such a thing.

All of those people - with the exception of Coleman - at one time or another were fellow theosophists or close associates of Madame. Some did her good deeds. Most certainly, Madame repaid them. Yet, they turned viciously against the original Theosophist. Fate and Karma and Occult Law played major roles in those proceedings. Madame knew that, but her temperament made it difficult for her to adjust to unprovoked and unexpected attacks from one-time friends and co-workers.

One layer of Madame's work, which few understood, entailed teaching and working with questionable students. Many had problems written very large in their karmic histories and in the auras of their inner bodies, both of which H.P.B. could read quite easily. Under normal world circumstances, she might have turned them back on their heals and told them, "You are soiled, unworthy, not prepared to enter into this work."

Colonel Olcott remembered his comrade after her passing as one "who overflowed with exuberant spirits and enjoyed nothing more than a comic song or story, [but] was not the H.P.B. of India or London, nor recognisable in the mental colossus of latter days. She changed in many things, yet in one thing she never improved, viz., the choice of friends and confidants. It almost seems as though she were always dealing with inner selves of men and women, and had been blind to the weakness or corruption of their visible, bodily shells. Just as she flung her money to every specious wretch who came and lied to her, so she made close friends of the passing hour with people the most unworthy. She trusted one after another, and, for the time being, there seemed nobody like them in her eyes; but usually the morrow brought disillusion and disgust ..."

Most of us know little enough about dealing with personalities. How can we understand another who meets humans as Souls and endeavors to support them to rise into the fullness of their Beings? H.P.B. did just that and so told Countess Wachtmeister, "What right have I to refuse to any one the chance of profiting by the truths I can teach him, and thereby entering upon the Path? I tell you that I have no choice. I am pledged by the strictest rules and laws of occultism to a renunciation of selfish considerations, and how can I dare to assume the existence of faults in a candidate and act upon my assumption even though a cloudy forbidding aura may fill me with misgivings?"

To A.P. Sinnett, she wrote, "Has not Master left it to my choice, to either follow the dictates of Lord Buddha, who enjoins us not to fail to feed even a starving serpent, scorning all fear lest it should turn round and bite the hand that feeds it -- or to face Karma which is sure to punish him, who turns away from the sight of sin and misery, or fails to relieve the sinner and the sufferer. I knew her and tried my best not to hate her, and since I always failed in the latter, I tried to make it up by sheltering and feeding the vile snake. I have what I deserve, not for the sins I am charged with but for those which no one -- save Master and myself know of."

The preceding words refer to Emma Coulomb who became the centerpiece of what was to be called the Coulomb Affair. Madame Coulomb's supposed revelations and obvious collusion with Christian missionaries in India precipitated the Hodgson Report of the Society for Psychical Research. The unusual story spawned numerous newspaper articles, reports, and books written even into recent times more than a century after the incident.

The Coulomb Affair evolved over years and continents. Madame B. first met Emma Cutting in Egypt after she survived the explosion of the SS Eunomia. At that point, Emma took H.P.B. in and helped her on her way. Eventually, the tables turned and Emma and her husband Alexis Coulomb appeared destitute in Ceylon in 1879. Helena returned the favor and absorbed them into the household of the Theosophical Society as it eventually moved from Bombay to the Adyar suburb of Madras where H.P.B. imagined spending her final years in the tranquil spot close to the ocean. Emma became housekeeper and Alexis was handyman and carpenter for the compound.

The arrangement held for some years even though the Coulombs became possessive of their jobs and their supposed rapport with the Founder of the Theosophical Society. At the same time, the Coulombs were confirmed Christians and looked more and more askance at Madame's involvement with Masters none of whom they dared call their own. Eventually, Madame and the TS Council told them "No" too many times in response to Emma's demands for household control and to her attempts to extort money from wealthy friends of the founders.

While Madame was traveling to Europe in 1884, the Coulombs were discharged. Thence, they put themselves into the hands of Christian missionaries. With their backing, the Coulombs made charges of fraud upon Madame and her Masters. In the near time, the developing Society for Psychical Research in England initiated an investigation into the claims.

Richard Hodgson, a not-yet-30-year-old Australian, became the SPR's lone investigator. Hodgson had spent practically his whole life in school or university, taking one degree after another: B.A. (1874), LL.B. (1875), M.A. (1876) and LL.D. (1878). He was a scholar at Saint Johns College, University of Cambridge, when tapped to go to India and study the accusations made against Madame Blavatsky and the Theosophical Society.

The charges made suggested that H.P. Blavatsky forged the letters of the Mahatmas, used the Coulombs to produce phenomena, and was a fraudulent medium for the Theosophical Society. Mr. Hodgson took to his work aggressively, was allowed full access to investigate problems, and conferred with involved parties. But, he spent the bulk of his time trying to prove the Coulomb's claims. Hodgson did not interview H.P.B. during his four-month stay although he dined with her. Mr. Hodgson seems to have had the same attitude in his dealings in India that he carried with him into America when he began in later years to investigate the medium Leonora Piper. He eventually admitted, "I had but one object, to discover fraud and trickery ... of unmasking her." Hodgson inevitably became convinced of the validity of Piper's meager mediumistic work after long hours of observation. Would that he had spent a similar amount of energy trying to study and understand Madame Blavatsky's vastly superior gifts.

Besides the Coulombs, Hodgson's main sources of information were native workers who did not know how to respond to an intrusive, intimidating *Sahib*. Neither Hodgson nor the Society paid heed to Colonel Olcott and western staffers who were made to be "dupes" of H.P.B.'s "tricks." Madame complained to A.P. Sinnett after the fact: "It is that ignorance of Occult transactions that gave such a hold to Hodgson and Massey and others. It is my obligatory absolute silence that now forces me to live under the shower of people's contempt."

Richard Hodgson acted as a one-man courtroom and eventually compiled a host of accusations from two disaffected employees paid by Christian missionaries to make their claims, many pages of secondhand information, and a thoroughly one-sided perspective before making his brief to the Society for Psychical Research in London. H.P.B. and the Theosophical Society were not given the opportunity to review or contest the report before it was made public. The 200-page Hodgson Report was hurriedly passed by SPR committee persons and given to the press. It concluded Madame Blavatsky to be "one of the most gifted, ingenious and interesting impostors in history." Mr. Hodgson continued on to settle on a motive behind her imposture. He ruled out financial gain or yearning for notoriety and decided that her theosophical work was a cover for her clandestine work as a Russian spy!

H.P.B. pressed on despite external enemies and intrigues, internal agitation and illnesses. In a letter to A.P. Sinnett, Madame tried to separate herself from the turmoil which raged all round her: "And now, dear Mr. Sinnett, my last decision. I shall have no more to do with anything coming from the S.P.R. I shall stoop to no explanations except to you and a few friends. I have with Masters' help even -- but a short time to live and the work I have on hand is enormous. I have to save the *Theosophist*, to write and finish *The Secret Doctrine*. What good shall I do the cause and any of you who believe in me, by convincing at the cost of superhuman efforts a dozen or two, and having the outsiders disbelieving in me as they ever have. The Coulombs and Missionaries have sworn to ruin the Society: they have failed to do so by ruining me -- why should I to save my reputation with the few -- help myself to ruin the Society by depriving it of the *S.D.* and its members of what I can teach them? And I will be doing so if I lose my time over the filthy lies, intrigues and ever and daily arising new complications. Those who believe in me, let them remain quiet, oppose a passive and negative resistance to the enemy and no more. The others if we pay no attention to them shall soon tire out, for it takes two to quarrel. Write in this spirit simply and tell them in your cultured quiet and clear English to go to their grandfather -- Old Nick. I told you I had become callous -- so do not mind me. If you believe, if a few dozen devoted students believe in the Masters and that I am only their humble factotum -- and ALL India does -- then what does it matter. If nothing can take out of their heads the expert's opinion that the letters are genuine -- let them go. Master said last night only -- 'By showing them that you are as firm as a rock; by showing contempt or even indifference to their opinions -- proceeding with your work and duty harder than before -- you shall kill and silence them more surely than anything you may say and do to disabuse their minds. The cycle is not over yet -- the Karma not expended --.' And I shall do so."

Every leader, great and not-so-great, carries the burden of Karma for nation, clan or organization. The law is inexorable and Madame, as founder and focal point of relatively alien teachings which she most vociferously promoted, bore the brunt of attacks which came in all manners and from every direction. To Constance Wachmeister, she cried, "This is the Karma of the Theosophical Society, and it falls upon me. I am the scapegoat. I am made to bear all the sins of the Society, and now that I am dubbed the greatest impostor of the age, and a Russian spy into the bargain, who will listen to me or read *The Secret Doctrine*? How can I carry on Master's work? O cursed phenomena, which I only produced to please private friends and instruct those around me. What an awful Karma to bear! How shall I live through it? If I die Master's work will be wasted, and the Society will be ruined!"

Following on the Hodgson Report, Madame wanted for a time to sue the offenders. But, she was deflected from her intentions by Colonel Olcott and a committee of the Theosophical Society. They imagined and rightly so that had H.P.B.'s case gone to court, the issue of the existence of the Masters would have come to center stage. That was the last thing that Madame wanted to happen. So, the issue was allowed to fade over time. Still, "Occultism will remain forever, no matter how assailed, and Occult Phenomena can never be proved in a Court of Law during this century."

Eventually on different occasions and at varied venues, she made her very penetrating case about the Masters and her subservient relationship to them. "The really important fact to ascertain is simply whether H.P. Blavatsky is, or is not, possessed of the occult knowledge, whose source was hitherto attributed to the teaching of the MASTERS. The answer is easy and self-evident. If the TEACHERS whom she claims to know, do not exist, then every bit of philosophy from the earliest Esoteric Buddhism, down to the latest Secret Doctrine, in short, every tenet of the Occult Sciences taught and learnt in the T.S., comes from her; this, whether she has invented it all, or acquired the knowledge by some mysterious means. Turn it whichever way you will, the fact remains the same for the Theosophists -- she is the origin, the fountainhead, of all the esoteric knowledge they have learned or may learn. Whether she be the source, or only the modest channel, as claimed by her, H.P. Blavatsky has the means and the necessary knowledge to teach.

"Reverend satirists! Don't you think that for the family honour of your caste you should invent something new, some fresh slander and accusation a little less stale and improbable? The famous Report, upon the willows of which you hang your Aeolian harps, made to groan by every passing wind -- cannot be all true on strictly logical grounds. For, the wicked 'Jezebel' of the T.S. has either invented the 'Mahatmas,' in which case she had also to invent their supposed handwritings, and thus committed no forgery, or she has not, and in the latter case the Report falls to pieces. If she has fabricated these 'Beings,' and written letters in their names, then she did not forge 'other people's handwriting.' As you have to catch a hare before you can make a soup of it, so a 'handwriting' has to exist as well as the hand to which it belongs before it can be imitated. One may fabricate a bogus letter, but then it is not the handwriting of 'other people.'"

It was possible that H.P.B.'s attackers could have come to far different conclusions and even made some recognition of her potent and advanced state of being. But, "it takes one to know one." Such thinking is quite beyond the yet-to-be-evolved qualities of most of our kin. That was a large step for all but a very few to imagine. "In fact, the powers of psychology attributed to me by my enemies, whenever a fact or a 'phenomenon' could not be explained away, are so great that they alone would have made of me a most remarkable Adept -- independent of any Masters or Mahatmas."

Clear and direct shots were taken at the Report over the years by A.P. Sinnett, William Kingsland, and others. Numbers who studied the brief made by Hodgson were able to read between the lines and then see through his appallingly weak presentation. Annie Besant, Julia Ver Planck, and other report readers became followers and faithful contributors to Theosophical thought, in part, because of Hodgson's shoddy work which highlighted rather than submerged the real H.P.B.

Over the years, the Society for Psychical Research slowly distanced itself from the Report. In 1960 Walter Carrithers, a member of the SPR, published an analysis on the report questioning its reliability. By 1968 in a letter to *Time* magazine, the Secretary of the SPR wrote of Hodgson's report that "Any accusations therein are the responsibility of the author and not this organization." Finally in 1986, the *Journal of the Society for Psychical Research* published a critical examination of the handwriting portion Hodgson's report by Vernon Harrison, another member. Harrison, an expert in authenticity, forgeries and counterfeiting of documents, thoroughly studied all available papers regarding the Hodgson Report.

Dr. Harrison's own conclusion reads, "BE IT KNOWN THEREFORE that it is my professional OPINION derived from a study of this case extending over a period of more than fifteen years, that future historians and biographers of the said Helena Petrovna Blavatsky, the compilers of reference books, encyclopaedias and dictionaries, as well as the general public, should come to realise that The Report of the Committee Appointed to Investigate Phenomena Connected with The Theosophical Society, published in 1885 by the Society for Psychical Research, should be read with great caution, if not disregarded. Far from being a model of impartial investigation so often claimed for it over more than a century, it is badly flawed and untrustworthy."

It may be worth noting that Madame herself admitted that she was not beyond forging documents or lying, yet only under extraordinary circumstances. "I know one thing, that if it came to the worst and Master's truthfulness and notions of honour were to be impeached -- then I would go to a desperate expedient. I would proclaim publicly that I alone was a liar, a forger, all that Hodgson wants me to appear that I had indeed INVENTED the Masters and thus would by that 'myth' of Master K.H. and M. screen the real K.H. and M. from opprobrium. What saved the situation in the Report was that the Masters are absolutely denied. Had Hodgson attempted to throw deception and the idea that They were helping, or encouraging or even countenancing a deception by Their silence -- I would have already come forward and proclaimed myself before the whole world all that was said of me and disappeared for ever. This I swear 'BY MASTER'S BLESSING OR CURSE' -- I will give a 1000 lives for Their honour in the people's minds. I will not see THEM desecrated."

Madame dealt with numerous other detractors in the likes of William Emmette Coleman, who took her to task in a pamphlet for supposed plagiarism in her voluminous writings. Coleman was and is easily dispensed with. His charge was ludicrous because H.P.B.'s major works are filled with footnotes and backed by dozens of pages of indexes. She readily and repeatedly made it clear that her ideas and information were not original, that the keys and essence of her fundamental teachings were drawn from ancient times, and that she was guided in all her major works by her Teachers.

The Ballad of Mabel Collins and Elliott Coues is not so simple. Mabel had been a close associate of Madame, opened her house to H.P.B. for a time, and co-edited *Lucifer* with Helena for some months. Mrs. Collins was gifted as a writer in usual and unusual ways. She was at times impressed by a Teacher and produced beautiful, challenging, classic pieces including *Light on the Path* and *The Idyll of White Lotus*.

Collins also was for a time a member of Madame's inner circle. Friction and fallout were inevitable as Mabel took certain oaths and did not live up to them. Madame confronted her, "Repent, or else."

Enter Elliott Coues. The highly educated and esteemed American ornithologist became deeply involved in theosophy on the western side of the Atlantic. Coues had ambitions to be the leader of Theosophy in America and believed H.P.B. would help him move to the top. When he was rebuked, Coues started his own American Theosophical Society without approval from the parent TS. He then tried to join forces with Mrs. Collins against Madame Blavatsky.

The two took H.P.B. to court in England. Prior to the court date, a letter arrived from Madame's hand with incriminating information (never made public) which Mabel Collins definitely did not want brought to light. The case was withdrawn.

Coues persisted in the USA and wrote a vile and scurrilous article which appeared in the *New York Sun* newspaper in July 1890. Through William Judge, H.P.B. filed suit against Coues and the paper for libel. Before the case could be tried, Helena died. Coues never retracted his piece (supposed interview), but the newspaper eventually produced a full-page piece apologizing for its errors in judgment on ever printing Coues's article.

It is interesting to recall the prequel to Coues's battles with the Theosophical Society and Madame, the press and the courts. A few years prior to his venomous attacks, Coues had declared in a letter to H.P.B.: "You are a grand and wonderful woman, whom I admire as much as I appreciate.... I admire your fortitude and endurance in bearing burdens enough to kill anybody but the Blavatsky whose like has not before been seen, nor will be ever.... *Never mind your enemies! They will get a spurious and vicarious reputation by attacking you* [this author's italics], which you can afford to let them have, though you don't want to confer upon them the immortality they would get by your condescending to fight them. When History comes to be written they will appear, if at all, hanging on to your skirts. Shake them off, and let them go!" (Nov. 1885)

"I think you are the greatest woman in the world, controlling today more destiny than any queen upon her throne." (Mar. 1886) One might wonder about the destiny of Elliott Coues.

The saddest and strangest tale of all Madame Blavatsky's adversaries involved Vsevelod Solovyov. It was particularly sad because Solovyov was a fellow Russian whom Madame befriended and took under her wing. (H.P.B. relished contact, especially face-to-face, with anyone from her homeland.) Solovyov imagined that he was going to be Madame's savior, writing partner and agent, and fellow initiate along the expanding way.

Solovyov was given glimpses and gifts, even from Madame's master, which might have induced many others to "join the club." But, his impatience and pride were much too strong. Solovyov would not allow time and training, trials and testing to unfold entry into proximity with the Teachers.

After Madame Blavatsky's death, Solovyov published in Russia an infamous attack on her. Then, the Society for Psychical Research sponsored its translation and publication as *A Modern Priestess of Isis*. Early in the book, Vsevelod wrote about his encounter - dream, or hallucination - of the Master M. after an evening at the Gebhards in Germany. Solovyov's own detailed stories shine much light on the occult path. At the same time, they give plentiful insights regarding H.P.B.'s last, most persistent and saddest adversary.

The curtains were suddenly drawn back, and two wonderful figures, illuminated with a brilliant, bluish light, concentrated and strengthened by mirrors, rose before us. At the first moment I thought I was looking on living men, so skilfully was the whole thing conceived. But it turned out that they were two great draped portraits of the Mahatmas Morya and Koot Hoomi, painted in oils by Schmiechen, an artist related to the Gebhards.

Subsequently, when I had thoroughly examined these portraits, I found in them much that was unsatisfactory from an artistic point of view; but their life-likeness was remarkable, and the eyes of the two mysterious strangers gazed straight at the spectator, their lips could almost have been said to move.

The artist, of course, had never seen the originals of these two portraits. Madame Blavatsky and Olcott assured us all that he had painted by inspiration, that 'they' had themselves guided his pencil, and that 'the likeness was extraordinary.' However that might be, Schmiechen had painted two beautiful young men. Mahatma Koot Hoomi, clad in a graceful sort of robe, trimmed with fur, had a tender, almost feminine face, and gazed with a pair of charming light eyes.

But as soon as one looked at the master, Koot Hoomi, for all his tender beauty, was at once forgotten. The fiery black eyes of the tall Morya fixed themselves sternly and piercingly upon one, and it was impossible to tear oneself away from them. The 'master' was represented as in the miniature in Madame Blavatsky's locket, crowned with a white turban and in a white garment. All the power of the reflectors was turned upon this sombrely beautiful face, and the whiteness of the turban and dress completed the brilliance and life-likeness of the effect.

Madame Blavatsky asked for still more light upon her 'master' so Rudolf Gebhard and Keightley altered the mirrors, arranged the drapery round the portrait, and placed Koot Hoomi aside. The effect was surprising. One had to force oneself to remember that it was not a living man. I could not turn my eyes away.

Olcott and Madame Blavatsky kept me more than an hour before this portrait. At last my head began to ache with the excessively bright light, and I felt all the symptoms of severe fatigue; the journey and the two almost sleepless nights had begun to tell upon me. I told Miss A that I was not capable of staying any longer, and that it was high time for us to return to our Hotel Victoria and go to bed at once. She also complained of extreme fatigue. Madame Blavatsky bade us good-bye, after making us promise that we would come back as early as possible in the morning.

On the way to the hotel we could talk only of the wonderful portrait of the 'master,' and in the darkness he seemed to stand before me. I tried to shut my eyes, but I still saw him clearly in every detail. When I reached my room, I locked the door, undressed, and went to sleep.

Suddenly I woke up, or, what is more probable, I dreamt, I imagined, that I was awoke by a warm breath. I found myself in the same room, and before me, in the half-darkness, there stood a tall human figure in white. I felt a voice, without knowing how or in what language, bidding me light the candle. I was not in the least alarmed, and was not surprised. I lighted the candle, and it appeared to me that it was two o'clock, by my watch. The vision did not vanish. There was a living man before me, and this man was clearly none other than the original of the wonderful portrait, an exact repetition of it. He placed himself on a chair beside me, and told me in 'an unknown but intelligible language' various matters of interest to myself. Among other things he told me that in order to see him in his astral body I had had to go through much preparation, and that the last lesson had been given me that morning, when I saw with closed eyes the landscapes through which I was to pass on the way to Elberfeld; and that I possessed a great and growing magnetic force. I asked how I was to employ it; but he vanished in silence. I thought that I sprang after him; but the door was closed. The idea came upon me that it was an hallucination, and that I was going out of my mind. But there was Mahatma Morya back again in his place, without movement, with his gaze fixed upon me, the same, exactly the same, as he was imprinted on my brain. He began to shake his head, smiled, and said, still in the voiceless, imaginary language of dreams: 'Be assured that I am not an hallucination and that your reason is not deserting you. Madame Blavatsky will show you to-morrow in the presence of all that my visit was real.' He vanished; I looked at my watch, and saw that it was about three o'clock; I put out the candle, and went to sleep at once.

I woke at ten o'clock and remembered everything quite clearly. The door was locked; it was impossible to tell from the candle if it had been lighted during the night, and if it had been long burning, as I had lighted it on my first arrival before the visit to Madame Blavatsky.

In the coffee-room of the hotel I found Miss A at breakfast. "Have you had a good night?" I asked her.

"Not very, I have seen the Mahatma Morya."

"Really? And I have seen him too."

"How did you see him?"

I had committed myself, and it was too late to withdraw. I described to her my vivid dream, or hallucination, and learnt from her that while she was thinking whether she should formally turn theosophist, or if there was not something 'dark' in it, Mahatma Morya had appeared to her and said: "We have great need of a 'little beetle' like you."

"That is exactly what he said, a 'little beetle,' and he said it in Russian," Miss A assured me, extremely delighted, for some reason or other, that the Mahatma had called her a 'little beetle.'

She then went on: "So let us go to Madame Blavatsky. What will she say? If it was Morya, and not our own fancy, she must know."

We set off to the Gebhard's. Madame Blavatsky met us, as I thought, with an enigmatical smile, and asked: "Well, what sort of a night have you had?"

"Very good," I replied, and thoughtlessly added: "Have you nothing to tell me?"

"Nothing particular," she said; "I only know that the 'master' has been to see you with one of his chelas."

In these words there was no evidential value whatever. She had more than once, both by word of mouth and by letter, assured me that the master visited me. But Miss A considered her words wonderful, and began to narrate our visions. Madame Blavatsky could not conceal the delight which came upon her. She forgot all her sufferings, and her eyes flashed sparks.

"There, there, you are done for, Mr. Sceptic and Suspecter!" she kept on repeating. "What will you say now?"

"I shall say that I had a very clear, vivid dream, or hallucination, produced by my nervous state, my great fatigue in consequence of the journey, after two sleepless nights, and the powerful impression which had been produced on me by the brilliantly lighted portrait on which I gazed for more than an hour. If it had been in the day-time, or in the evening before I went to sleep, or if, on the other hand, I had not gone to sleep again when the Mahatma disappeared, I should have been inclined to believe in the reality of what happened to me. But you see this came between two sleeps and he did not talk to me with a voice, or in words, or in any language that I know; and finally, he did not leave me any material proof of his visit, or take the turban off his head, as he did with Olcott. These are three important considerations which point to its having been only a dream or a subjective delusion."

"Well now, really, God knows what this means!"

Helena Petrovna grew warm. "You will drive me out of my mind with your incredulity. But you say he told you some very interesting things?"

"Yes, he told me just what I was busy with, and what was to be found in my brain."

"But he himself assured you that he was not an hallucination?"

"Yes, but he said you would prove this to me in the presence of all."

"And have I not proved it by knowing about his visit?"

"I do not consider this a valid proof."

"Very well, I will prove it in another way. Meanwhile, you surely do not mean to deny that you have seen him and talked to him?"

"How can I possibly deny what Miss A has heard from my own mouth, and you have heard from hers? I ought not to have committed myself, but now you know yourself it is too late; as they say, a word is not a sparrow; once off, there is no enticing it back again."

Madame Blavatsky rang an electric bell, collected all her theosophists, and began, with the irritating loudness which was natural to her, to tell about the great phenomenon which had taken place.

It is easy to imagine my position, when all these ladies and gentlemen began to congratulate me on the high honour, happiness, and glory which I had won, in the visit which I had received from Mahatma Morya. I declared that I was much inclined to regard the manifestation as a dream or delusion, produced by the state of my nerves and by fatigue. At this they began to regard me with horror as a blasphemer.

The day passed in nothing but talk about the 'great phenomenon.'

In the evening we were all assembled in the pretty 'Oriental' room, all but Olcott who was on the second floor. Suddenly Madame Blavatsky, who had been brought to us in her arm-chair, announced: "The master was upstairs just now; he passed by Olcott's side and put something in his pocket. Keightley, run upstairs and bring the colonel."

Olcott appeared. "Have you just seen the master?" asked Madame. The 'old cat's' eye got loose, and began to stray.

"I felt his presence and his touch," he replied.

"On which side?"

"On the right."

"Show us all you have got in your right-hand pocket. Turn it out."
Olcott obediently began to carry out her order slowly and methodically. He brought out first a small key, then a button, then a match-box, and a tooth-pick, and lastly a small piece of paper folded up.
"What is that" exclaimed Madame Blavatsky.
"I do not know; I had no piece of paper," said the 'old cat,' in a tone of the most innocent surprise. So Madame Blavatsky used to call Colonel Olcott in his absence.
Madame Blavatsky seized the piece of paper, and solemnly proclaimed: "The letter of the master. Yes, it is so, the master's letter."
She opened and read it. There was written on the paper, in the 'unmistakable' hand of the master, in English: "Certainly I was there; but who can open the eyes of him who will not see? — M."

This episode warrant repetition of Mahatma K.H.'s statement made anent H.P.B.'s authorship of *The Secret Doctrine*: "the more proof given the less believed."

Vsevelod became progressively more disturbed by his failure to receive special attention and entry into Madame's secret dealings. He joined forces with the SPR and eventually and conveniently wrote his own version of Isis after her death in 1891 (1892 in Russian - 1895 in English). *A Modern Priestess of Isis* is a fascinating, though troubling read. Solovyov's narrative made him appear as a jilted lover, like a pupil rejected for tuition, akin to the sadly tortured Salieri next to the genius Mozart (*Amadeus*), and acting the part of Judas, the betrayer of Jesus. By the end of the book, Madame persists as the substantial Sphinx and Vsevelod plays the weak Weasel.

Aenigma
(Latin for Enigma)

"This is an impenetrable mystery!
I - a psychological enigma, a puzzle for future generations, a Sphinx!"

Throughout *A Modern Priestess of Isis*, Vsevelod Solovyov exposed his delicate state of nerves, his fragile ego, and his obvious envy of the gifts of Helena Petrovna, as he always called her. Despite his animosity to the original Theosophist, Mr. Solovyov made it clear that he had no choice but to see her as an "unequaled phenomenon."

Like many others over the years, the Weasel couldn't grasp what "the Sphinx of the nineteenth century" was really about. Still, he did marvel at her talent as a storyteller and writer, her immense memory and grasp of diverse subjects, and her ability to write on them at will. Solovyov had sure suggestions of her station between two worlds and coveted a role in her life. Even "... if all these phenomena, absolutely all, were one great fraud, what sort of woman could this Helena Petrovna be? She had need of me; no doubt, in a matter like this, she had need of a man who writes a great deal, and whom people read. I had marked and divined a soul not yet wholly lost."

Years after they parted ways, Vsevolod wrote about his fantasized mission: "Perhaps it was still possible, by one means or another, to stop her and save her, as much for her own sake as for those whom she might ruin with her falsehood and fraud. And besides all this, might she not be herself the most interesting phenomenon of all, with her intellect and talents, with her funny simplicity and naivete, wither her lies and her sincerity? It was tempting to see through and read such a phenomenon, such a living 'human document.'"

How very strange that one could practically worship the work of another and yet try to destroy the reputation of that person gone to the grave. Solovyov freely admitted during HPB's life, "It seems to me that *Isis Unveiled* is the most interesting of Helena Petrovna's phenomena, and, perhaps, the most inexplicable." He continued to hold that opinion after her death. No mention can be found regarding Solovyov's opinion of later and greater works.

Repeatedly, the Weasel projected wondrous contradictions on HPB: "Most probably she was genuine, and was playing a part at the same time; in her the irreconcilable was reconciled." He only viewed her for a few months, yet saw more than he could begin to understand. During a serious illness, a famous specialist appeared to consult and told Solovyov, "She has several mortal diseases -- an ordinary person would have been dead long ago from any one of them. But hers is a phenomenal nature.... Her life has been in danger for years, but you see she is alive. A wonderful, wonderful phenomenon."

In the midst of her ills, he watched her "working double tides." "I again found Helena Petrovna all swollen up and almost without movement. But a day passed, and she managed to crawl out of her bed to her writing-table, and wrote for several hours, gnashing her teeth with anguish. She told me that she used to work the whole night, but that, at all events, I could not verify. However that may be, pages and sheets were pouring from her pen at an astonishing rate."

While Helena Petrovna appeared to him as a "true talent" and "inspired prophetess," her fellow Russian dared not accept the obvious wonders poured out before his eyes. Solovyov remained "waiting for the promised 'phenomena.'" Unfortunately for Mr. Solovyov and the rest of us, we stand in the midst of the other world with its hidden powers and mysterious phenomena, yet we see them not or dismiss them as misperceptions. Solovyov was one of many who cannot or dare not see even when standing face-to-face.

Many parted from H.P.B. simply because they could not deal with the strong light that passed through her quite freely. Publisher-writer A.P. Sinnett, who received so much from Madame and her Masters, fell away in latter years. This occurred in part because of his inability to comprehend the teacher and friend he knew for so long: "Now, do you really think that you know ME my dear Mr. Sinnett? Do you believe that, because you have fathomed -- as you think -- my physical crust and brain; that shrewd analyst of human nature though you be -- you have ever penetrated even beneath the first cuticles of my Real Self? You would gravely err, if you did. I am held by all of you as untruthful because hitherto I have shown the world only the true exterior Mme. Blavatsky. It is just as if you complained of the falseness of a moss and weed covered, and mud-covered, stony and rugged rock for writing outside 'I am not moss covered and mud-plastered; your eyes deceive you for you are unable to see beneath the crust,' etc. You must understand the allegory. It is not boasting for I do not say whether inside that unprepossessing rock there is a palatial residence or an humble hut. What I say is this: you do not know me; for whatever there is inside it, is not what you think it is; and -- to judge of me therefore, as of one untruthful is the greatest mistake in the world besides being a flagrant injustice. I, (the inner real 'I') am in prison and cannot show myself as I am with all the desire I may have to. Why then, should I, because speaking for myself as I am and feel myself to be, why should I be held responsible for the outward jail-door and its appearance, when I have neither built nor yet decorated it?"

H.P.B. repeated similar words, "you do not know me, nor have you ever known me as I really am," to more than a few associates over the years. Some got glimpses and others managed to catch whole swatches of the real Being called Blavatsky. Louisa Andrews, who was briefly acquainted with Madame during her early years in the USA, may have had H.P.B. pegged right when she wrote, "She is a 'double natural woman.'" But then, the observer must come to terms with what a double natural woman might be.

Alice Cleather "got" the Teacher and Initiate Blavatsky. "Her mere presence conveyed an overwhelming impression of power and knowledge, despite the apparently irascible temper, and the general puzzle which her personality presented to the ordinary mind.

"All I realised was that 'she' or something behind 'her,' was entirely different from all those who surrounded her; that she belonged in fact to a totally different world, a world of which ordinary mortals have no conception. A much more real world than that cognisable by our senses ... To this (inner) world H.P.B. really belonged. She once told us -- 'I work all the twenty-four hours; in this body all day, in another [more ethereal] one, all night. But I remember all I do [in the latter], you do not.'"

Scotsman Dr. George Wyld viewed H.P.B. from a decidedly Christian angle. Eventually, he parted with Madame's Theosophy because of her pronouncements on the nature of a personal God. Still, he wrote that she "is not so easily understood (compared to Colonel Olcott), for she is *sui generis* and unique, a mystery and an enigma."

Swarthy, and of Tartar aspect, she is tall, strong, vigorous, and in perfect bodily health [in 1879]. She resembles a very powerful woman, about fifty-five years of age, but she asserts that she is eighty-two years of age. Her jaws are large, and furnished with perfectly regular and strong teeth; and her eyes, though almost without colour, yet can read without glasses the smallest print, and can look you through and through, and can read your character and thoughts at will. She is highly accomplished in languages and music, but is totally indifferent to the exhibition of these accomplishments, and to personal appear-

ances, although she is possessed of a form and bearing of queenly dignity, if she only condescended to assume the garments and the mien. With irresistible powers of fascination, she seems only to despise the use of these powers. Enjoying enormous fits of laughter, she is yet for ever restless and sad. She possesses that powerful dramatic force which proceeds from the intense convictions of a powerfully emotional nature. She declaims on all subjects, rapidly passing from one to another, yet ever returning to her central idea; the spiritual wisdom and power of the East, from which must appear the coming man to rule the spiritual world.

Of truly a great nature, but with, to my mind, one extravagant defect, shown in her book and in her talk, an unreasoning and intolerant hatred of the doctrines and works of all Christian teachers. If you explain to her that your form of Christianity is spiritual and esoteric, and show that the essence of esoteric Brahmanism, Buddhism, and Christianity are one and identical, namely, to find your hidden spiritual light, and unite this with the fountain and centre of all light, she at once accepts you as a spiritual brother; but she cannot rest in this, but noisily and for ever persists in confusing the essence with the external garments of Christianity. You may criticise herself freely as you like, but if you whisper a word of treachery against her revered chiefs, you convert her into an implacable enemy, and from this characteristic it will be seen that she is very far from having reached that dignified and calm repose and sublime toleration which all who attain to the wisdom of the soul possess.

Beyond all doubt she is a magician controlling movements of matter and countering the action of poisons, as I experienced in my own person. She is wonderful and unique, and to have known her as I have, is always to remember her with affection, admiration, and respect.

Wyld read Madame Blavatsky as one of a kind, a kind that all but unknown in Europe and America in her century - or any century. Some who claimed to "know" her stood in awe or even fear of her stature, power and ability. Others were confused and intimidated. Still others proud and immoveable. All were difficult places in which to stand.

Even her sister Vera and long-standing comrade Colonel Olcott never claimed to understand H.P.B. They tried to explain Madame by narrating their experiences of her. But, they really knew not whence she came nor what she had gone through in trials and training and challenges in her so extraordinary life. Olcott wrote, "Just because I did know her so much better than most others, she was a greater mystery to me than to them. It was easy for those who only saw her speaking oracles, writing profound aphorisms, or giving clue after clue to the hidden wisdom in the ancient Scriptures, to regard her as an Earth-visiting *angelos* and to worship at her feet; she was no mystery to them. But to me, her most intimate colleague, who had to deal with the vulgar details of her common daily life, and see her in all her aspects, she was from the first and continued to the end an insoluble riddle. How much of her waking life was that of a responsible personality, how much that of a body worked by an overshadowing entity? I do not know. On the hypothesis that she was a medium for the Great Teachers, only that and nothing more, then the riddle is easy to read; for then one can account for the alterations in mind, character, tastes, and predilections...."

Only a Mahatma who could begin to make sense of H.P.B. "Of course, she is utterly unfit for a true adept: her nature is too passionately affectionate and we have no right to indulge in personal attachments and feelings. You can never know her as we do, therefore -- none of you will ever be able to judge her impartially or correctly. You see the surface of things; and what you would term 'virtue,' holding but to appearances, we judge but after having fathomed the object of its profoundest depth, and generally leave the appearances to take care of themselves. In your opinion H.P.B. is, at best, for those who like her despite herself -- a quaint, strange woman, a psychological riddle: impulsive and kindhearted, yet not free from the vice of untruth. We, on the other hand, under the garb of eccentricity and folly -- we find a profounder wisdom in her inner Self than you will ever find yourselves able to perceive. In the superficial details of her homely, hard-working common-place daily life and affairs, you discern but unpracticality, womanly impulses, often absurdity and folly; we, on the contrary, light daily upon traits of her inner nature the most delicate and refined, and which would cost an uninitiated psychologist years of constant and keen observation, and many an hour of close analysis and efforts to draw out of the depth of that most subtle of mysteries -- human mind -- one of her most complicated machines, -- 'H.P.B.'s mind' -- and thus learn to know her true inner Self."

Madame was not simply a medium nor even a mere mediator for the Great Ones. She was much more. Like you and I, we are far more than we appear. We all have many layers, parts, personas, principles. How many of us are able to unravel our own being?

Still, trying to peel back layers of H.P.B. may help us see parts of her self as well as of our own. Helena was born in a Russian body on the edge of Asia. A nominal Christian by birth, she was exposed to numerous religions and traditions from youth. Madame remembered fondly and spoke affectionately of the Kalmuck Buddhists, passing months near them and their priest when a girl. Helena often made light of her appearance remarking about her Kalmuck face.

From birth, she had East and West built in her form, her family traditions, and world environment. She swam in the superstitions of serfs and nannies as well as the massive libraries of her grandmother. Then, there were the wonders of the natural and *unnatural* worlds. Madame once wrote, "Space is filled with spirits and life."

Besides her penetrating eyes and Kalmuck grin, her wavy hair and supple white hands stood out when people first met Madame Blavatsky. Her features became points of wonder to people like Olcott who noticed sometimes subtle changes and at other times dramatic, incredible changes in his colleague. "H.P.B. explained to ourselves and two visitors the duality of her personality and the law which it illustrated. She admitted without qualification that it was a fact that she was one person at one moment and another the next. She gave us an astounding bit of proof in support of her assertion. As we sat chatting in the gloaming, she silent near the window with her two hands resting on her knees, she presently called us and looked down at her hands. One of them was as white, as sculpturesque as usual; but the other was the longer hand of a man, covered with the brown skin of the Hindu; and, on looking wonderingly into her face, we saw that her hair and eyebrows had also changed color, and from fair brown had become jetty black!

"On five different occasions ... she gathered up a lock of her fine, wavy auburn hair, and either pulled it out by the roots or cut it off with scissors, and gave it to one of us. But the lock would be coarse, jet black, straight and without the least curliness or waviness in it; in other words, Hindu or other Asiatic human hair, and not in the least like her own flossy, baby-like, light-brown locks.... I have two locks taken from her head, both black as jet and far coarser than hers, but one distinctly coarser than the other. The former is Egyptian, and the latter Hindu hair. What better explanation of this phenomenon is there than that of supposing that the men to whom these black locks had belonged were actually occupying the *mayavic* H.P.B. body when they were removed from the head?"

Questions only began with her appearance and form. Sometimes, Madame's sex came into question. H.P.B. had an obvious female frame. Yet, numbers considered her "sexless." Others spoke of "him" on occasion: the yogi in the body, the brother, the vagabond in man's clothes, the masters' chosen middle man. "Dr. Pike, looking at H.P.B. several times, started and said that no one in the world impressed him so much. Once he sees in H.P.B. a girl of 16, at another an old woman of 100, and again a man with a beard!"

"One Mahatma, writing me (Olcott) about some occult business, speaks of it -- the H.P.B. body -- as 'the old appearance'; again, in 1876, he writes about 'it and the Brother inside it'; another Master asks me -- *a propos* of a terrific fit of anger to which I had (unintentionally) provoked H.P.B. -- 'Do you want to kill the body?'; and the same one, in a note of 1875, speaks of 'those who represent us in the shell' -- the underscoring of the word being his. Can any one understand my feelings upon discovering on a certain evening that I had unsuspiciously greeted the staid philosopher described in the next few sentences of the main text, with an hilarious levity that quite upset his usual calm? Fancying that I was addressing only my 'chum' H.P.B., I said: 'Well, Old Horse, let us get to work!' The next minute I was blushing for shame, for the blended expression of surprise and startled dignity that came into the face, showed me with whom I had to deal."

It is quite certain that Helena Petrovna Hahn Blavatsky was born in 1831 in the Ukraine (Russia), but her age was commonly disputed even by herself. Damodar wrote that, "'Maji' then came for the second time [when H.P.B. and H.S.O. traveled near Benares] and on this occasion all of us were present except Swamiji and Madam who came afterwards. Col. Olcott then asked 'Maji' some questions about Madam. And 'Maji' said that Madam was not what she seems to be. Her interior man had already been twice in a Hindu body and was now in his third. She also said that until that time she had never seen a European but, having got the information from her Guru, about Madam, she had come to see her. I then asked her if the real H.P.B. was still in the body, but she refused to answer that question, and only added that she herself -- 'Maji' -- was inferior to Madam."

Maji also made the claim that Madame's body harbored a 130-year-old yogi. Adding to the quandary, H.P.B. herself was wont to remark from time to time that she didn't know whether she was 40 or 80 or 120. Helena was likely making fun, but there were probably grains of truth in her words.

Helena's volatile state of health was just as curious and of more immediate concern to friends and family. She had many close calls with violent injury. But, there were even more confrontations with death via illness, some detailed already. H.P.B. was attended by physicians in several countries who threw up their hands, either unable to diagnose her condition or fearing that they had nothing to offer when her life seemed to be ebbing quickly from her body. On other occasions, it appeared that Madame Blavatsky just vacated her body for periods of time. "Where did she go?"

Henry Olcott recounted several of Madame's many illnesses and close calls. In the midst of emotional stresses in 1876, H.P.B. had bruised her knee in a sidewalk fall in New York. That injury was said to eventually result in "violent inflammation of the periosteum and partial mortification of the leg." Physicians were consulted and later an eminent surgeon, Dr. Seth Pancoast, who declared "she would die unless the leg was instantly amputated." Her leg was apparently gangrenous and her case was hopeless, but according to Niece Vera Johnston, "she was successfully treated by a negro who was sent to her by the 'Sahib.'" Olcott said, "She got better in one night, by one of her quasi-miraculous cures."

Sister Vera wrote of another extraordinary challenge to H.P.B.'s health, one reminiscent of previous apparent illnesses (as in Mingrelia) which presaged great changes in her life. "In the spring of 1878 a strange thing happened to Madame Blavatsky. Having got up and set to work one morning as usual, she suddenly lost consciousness, and never regained it again until five days later. So deep was her state of lethargy that she would have been buried had not a telegram been received by Colonel Olcott and his sister, who were with her at the time, emanating from him she called her Master. The message ran, 'Fear nothing, she is neither dead nor ill, but she has need of repose; she has overworked herself.... She will recover.' As a matter of fact she recovered and found herself so well that she would not believe that she had slept for five days. Soon after this sleep, H.P. Blavatsky formed the project of going to India."

Early in her TS days in India (1881), Helena was again in difficult straits. Mahatma K.H. made note of Madame B.'s perilous condition. "Our hapless 'Old Lady' is sick. Liver, kidneys, head, brain, every organ and limb shows fight and snaps its fingers at her efforts to ignore them. One of us will have to '*fix*' her' as our worthy Mr. Olcott says, or it will fare bad with her."

In an 1882 letter to the Sinnetts, Madame gave a graphic picture of her then current ailment and its severity. "I am afraid you will have soon to bid me good-bye. This time I have it well and good. Bright's disease of the kidneys, and the whole blood turned into water, ulcers breaking out in the most unexpected spots, blood, or whatever it may be, forming into bags *a la* kangaroo, and other pretty extras and *et ceteras*. This all, *primo*, brought on by Bombay dampness and heat; and, *secundo*, by fretting and bothering. I have become so stupidly nervous that the unexpected tread of Babula's naked foot near me makes me start with the most violent palpitations of the heart. [Dr. D.E.] Dudley says -- I forced him to tell me this -- that I can last a year or two, and perhaps but a few days, for I can die at any time in consequence of an emotion...."

" ... I can hardly write, I am really too weak. Yesterday they drove me down to the Fort to the doctor. I got up with both my ears swollen thrice their natural size, and I met Mrs ____ and sister, her carriage crossing mine slowly. She did not salute nor make a sign of recognition, but looked very proud and disdainful. Well, I was fool enough to resent it. I tell you I am very sick."

Yet, she recovered again and again from some very frightening ailments. Helena seemed to emulate her feline younger brothers "like the cats I have nine lives in me it appears ..." While seeming as solid as stone and strong as steel, she was ever susceptible to sudden swings from health to illness, vigor to lethargy, vitality to near death. Still in India, H.P.B. wrote, "I carry two mortal diseases in me which are not cured in heart, and kidneys. At any moment the former may have a rupture, and the latter carry me away in a few days. I will not see another year. All this is due to five years of constant anguish, worry and repressed emotion."

Amazingly, her sensitive body was subject to instant refreshment sometimes by the slightest of touches via her deeper nature. While in Paris in 1884 and barely able to ambulate on her own, Madame Blavatsky traveled with her sister and aunt from Gare du Nord train station. Sister Vera wrote, "H.P.B. was very unwell, being hardly able to move her swollen feet which gave her awful pain. Most probably I was not the only one to nourish angry thoughts against her powerful Mahatmas -- if they actually were so kind as described -- thinking that they might help her, relieving her suffering, were it only in part, now that she had a long trip and the sorrow of parting with us before her. As usual she stood up for them, assuring us that though they do not think it a good thing to relieve people's suffering (the latter being the lawful reaction on each separate person), yet her own particular Master had often helped her, saving her from mortal illnesses. I walked, supporting her under the arm, to the platform, when suddenly she drew herself up, and glancing over her shoulder exclaimed: 'What is that? Who touched me on the shoulder? Did you see a hand?' No one had seen any hand, and we all started at each other in astonishment. But how great was our surprise when Helena Petrovna smiled, and, pushing my arm aside, walked ahead firmly and briskly as I had never lately seen her do. 'So now,' she said, 'this is an answer to you, Vera; you have been abusing them for their lack of desire to help me, and this moment I saw the hand of the Master. Look how I walk now.' And in fact she walked all the time on the platform, quickly and quite easily. Though she had to change the railway carriage twice, she got in and got out each time without visible effort, assuring us that her pain had entirely gone and that is was long since she had felt herself so well physically."

Early in 1885, Henry Olcott was doing duty with the Buddhists in Burma when called to return to India by a telegram saying, "Return at once, Upasika dangerously ill." Fearing that he might really be losing his chum and partner of many years, "I hurried home and found H.P.B. in a state between life and death, with congestion of the kidneys, rheumatic gout, and an alarming loss of vitality. Added to this, an enfeebled action of the heart had brought her to a crisis where her life trembled in the balance. She was so delighted to see me that she put her arms around my neck, as I came to her bedside, and wept on my breast. I was unspeakably glad to be there to, at least, bid her farewell and assure her of my steadfastness. Her attending physicians, Dr. Mary Scharlieb and Dr. Franz Hartmann, M.D., said it was simply a miracle that she was alive. Our Teacher had worked the wonder by coming one night when they were waiting for her last gasp, laying his hand on her, and snatching her back from death. Wonderful woman! This same thing happened with her at Philadelphia, when Dr. Pancoast told her that her leg must be cut off to save her life ..."

H.P.B. had recovered again, but the Coulomb Affair went through more chapters to disturb Madame's mind and body. "All this excitement told almost fatally upon my dear Chum's health. It was awful to see her, with her face empurpled by the blood that rushed to her head, her eyes almost standing out from their orbits and dead-looking, as she tramped up and down the floor, denouncing everybody and saying wild things. Her physicians said this could not last, she must have rest and quiet or she would drop down dead some day without giving us a moment's warning." In that case, as others, the Masters did not come to her direct aid. She was instead sent off to Europe in far from fulsome health, but away from the active and thunderous discord of her immediate environs.

Still on many occasions, the "call" eventually went out beyond the medical profession which had nothing of substance to offer Madame. Her Master or a high chela had to step in to bring H.P.B. back to life or at least offer her relief. A few moments in his presence, a touch and a dose of directed force, and Madame would rebound into full function for days or months. This state of affairs not only pointed to the many sides of H.P.B. but also to the singular potency of a Teacher's aura.

While in Belgium with Countess Wachmeister in 1887, Helena entered a "lethargic state." She was then in and mostly out of consciousness for hours. She could not be roused by any means. A Belgian doctor was unable to help. Dr. Ashton Ellis, an Englishman, crossed the Channel and tended her closely for days. Both physicians were at a loss to understand her condition. "The Belgian doctor said that he had never known a case of a person with the kidneys attacked as H.P.B.'s were, living as long as she had done, and that he was convinced that nothing could save her. He held out no hope of her recovery. Mr. Ellis replied that it was exceedingly rare for anyone to survive so long in such a state."

Watching and waiting for hours and days, the Countess remarked, "Even to me, who had been alone with her for so many months, she was an enigma, with her strange powers, her marvellous knowledge, her extraordinary insight into human nature, and her mysterious life, spent in regions unknown to ordinary mortals, so that though her body might be near, her soul was often away in commune with others. Many a time have I observed her thus and known that only the shell of her body was present."

Wachtmeister began to sense the "faint odour of death" and feared that H.P.B. would not live through the night. The Countess kept guard until fatigue also put her to sleep. "When I opened my eyes, the early morning light was stealing in, and a dire apprehension came over me that I had slept, and that perhaps H.P.B. had died during my sleep -- died whilst I was untrue to my vigil. I turned round towards the bed in horror, and there I saw H.P.B. looking at me calmly with her clear grey eyes, as she said, 'Countess, come here.' I flew to her side. 'What has happened, H.P.B. -- you look so different to what you did last night.'

She replied, 'Yes, Master has been here; He gave me my choice, that I might die and be free if I would, or I might live and finish *The Secret Doctrine*, He told me how great would be my sufferings and what a terrible time I would have before me in England (for I am to go there); but when I thought of those students to whom I shall be permitted to teach a few things, and of the Theosophical Society in general, to which I have already given my heart's blood, I accepted the sacrifice, and now to make it complete, fetch me some coffee and something to eat, and give me my tobacco box.'"

The state of Madame Blavatsky's health generally correlated with her emotions and tempers. She was usually affable, friendly and even accommodating. But, many could attest that her world was liable to sudden and radical change in a number of directions. Typically, H.P.B. was easily swayed by her crusade for truth and just as readily disturbed by those who tried to thwart her endeavors.

Illnesses came and went, but the most dramatic ones were either related to some inner work with her Masters or to trials brought to her by adversaries in the outer arenas. Her physicians in India forced her into a ship leaving for Europe during the turmoil surrounding the Coulomb Affair. That thorn in the side persisted for some years and contributed to Madame's numerous heartaches and bodily setbacks.

Archibald Keightley, an English medical doctor and committed Theosophical worker, viewed H.P.B. from a number of angles in her last years and pronounced with some authority: "I may say as a physician and not simply upon my own authority, but as a fact known to some of the leading medical practitioners of London, that never before has a patient been known to live even a week under such conditions of renal disorder as have been chronic with her for many months past.... Very frequently she has attacks of cerebral apoplexy, but without any treatment known to medical science wards them off and goes on, firmly confident as ever that her present life will not end before its work is fully accomplished."

Problems in the material and bodily worlds are rarely straightforward, neither for the likes of Madame Blavatsky, nor for ourselves. Most particularly in H.P.B.'s case, the important details were often hidden and deliberately so. H.P.B., the teacher, revealed in one moment and re-veiled in the next. She withheld and avoided many issues while offering up reams of knowledge hidden for ages. Surely, this was the case in her medical and emotional life as well. Madame Blavatsky was forced to write and speak and *live* in blinds; an occult blind being meant to conceal secrets from those who might misuse information while giving hints and clues to the serious and worthy student. "I told you the truth, however much of it I concealed."

"I am a Thibetian Buddhist, you know, and pledged myself to keep certain things secret." H.P.B. had no choice but to work thus as decreed by her Masters and for the greater good. "I do not want to lie, and I am not permitted to tell the truth." "It is this perpetual balancing on a tight rope between the abyss of divulging that which is not lawful, and either telling what people call lies or being accused of having things to conceal -- that has ruined the whole situation, and given a handle to the enemy."

Nothing was ever simple - to outsiders - with Madame and her Masters. Countess Wachtmeister remarked to Sinnett about the imperfect instrument chosen for the Truth Mission of the 19th century.: "It seems to me incredible how one person can have so many bitter enemies, I suppose it is in a great measure because she lets her tongue run wild wounding people's susceptibilities without meaning it or thinking of the consequences."

Humble she may have been, but she also carried a veritable volcano of feelings with her, in her and around her. H.P.B. seemed capable of erupting on minor provocation. Still, as A.P. Sinnett noted, Madame was generally malleable and willing to forgive, forget and carry on with great benevolence. "And just as the history of Mme. Blavatsky's work is a party-colored page, so her personality, her external character, is equally variegated. I have said a good deal of her impetuosity and indiscretions of speech and manner and of the way in which she will rage for hours, if allowed, over trifles which a more phlegmatic, not to speak of a more philosophical temperament would barely care to notice. But it must be understood that, almost at any time, an appeal to her philosophical intellect will turn her right off into another channel of thinking, and then, equally for hours, may any appreciative companion draw forth the stores of her information concerning Eastern religions and mythology, the subtle metaphysics of Hindu and Buddhist symbolism, or the esoteric doctrine itself, so far as in later years some regions of this have been opened out for public treatment. Even in the midst of passionate lamentations -- appropriate in vehemence to a catastrophe that might have wrecked the fruits of a life-time -- over some offensive sneer in a newspaper article or letter, an allusion to some unsolved problem in esoteric cosmogony, or misinterpretation by a European orientalist of some Eastern doctrine, will divert the flow of her intense mental activity, and sweep all recollection of the current annoyance, for the moment, from her mind."

Still, H.P.B. was ever on guard against some enemy or wondering if she should be reconciling with a disaffected supporter, soothing someone in need. Her temperament seems to have nearly "done her in." The wear and tear to her nervous system and other body parts caused by her perpetual agitation was indeed drawn large.

Nonetheless while in India, Sinnett related, "... she would generally be up at an early hour writing at her Russian articles or translations, or at the endless letters she sent off in all directions in the interest of the Society, or at articles for The Theosophist; then during the day she would spend a large part of her time talking with native visitors in her verandah room, or hunting them away and getting back to her work with wild protests against the constant interruption she was subject to, and in the same breath calling for her faithful 'Babula,' her servant, in a voice that rang all over the house, and sending for some one or other of the visitors she knew to be waiting about below and wanting to see her. Then in the midst of some fiery argument with a pundit about a point of modern Hindu belief that she might protest against as inconsistent with the real meaning of the Vedas, or a passionate remonstrance with one of her aides of *The Theosophist* about something done amiss that would for the time overspread the whole sky of her imagination with a thundercloud, she would perhaps suddenly 'hear the voice they did not hear' -- the astral call of her distant Master, or one of the other 'Brothers,' as by that time we had all learned to call them, -- and forgetting everything else in an instant, she would hurry off to the seclusion of any room where she could be alone for a few moments, and hear whatever message or orders she had to receive.

"She never wanted to go to bed when night came. She would sit on smoking cigarettes and talking -- talking with a tireless energy that was wonderful to watch -- on Eastern philosophy of any sort, on the mistakes of theological writers, on questions raised (but not settled) in *Isis*, or, with just as much intensity and excitement, on some wretched matter connected with the administration of the Society, or some foolish sarcasm levelled against herself and the attributes imputed to her in one of the local newspapers. To say that she never would learn to estimate occurrences at their proper relative value is to express the truth so inadequately that the phrase does not seem to express it at all."

Regardless of her temperament, impetuosity, and other obvious shortcomings, Sinnett and others readily admitted, "The tree may not have assumed a shape that passing strangers would admire, but the fruit it has borne has been a stupendous harvest."

The temperament which made her the Messenger also made her the Sphinx. Like many of our own "tempers," Madame's had upsides to make up for her downsides. Her willfulness and potency made her productive, phenomenal and famous. The girl who held her foot in boiling water until family gave in to her demands was also the woman who could accomplish most anything she willed herself to do. "I don't know a will on earth that would not break like glass in contact or conflict with mine."

In a letter to Aunt Nadya, H.P.B. laid the whole conundrum down in simple words for all to see and ponder. "Now then, tell me: How could it have happened that I, a perfect ignoramus up to my mature years, as you know, have suddenly become a phenomenon of learning in the eyes of people who are really learned?

"This is an impenetrable mystery! I -- a psychological enigma, a puzzle for future generations, a Sphinx!... Just fancy that I, who never studied anything in life; I, who did not have the least idea, either about chemistry or physics, or about zoology, am now writing dissertations on all of these subjects. I enter into discussions with scholars and come out victorious."

Being known as the Sphinx ought to have been a clue writ so large that the person called Helena Blavatsky might remain undeciphered. The grand mythological creature, for whom she was nicknamed, stands guard at the gates of the great Egyptian pyramids as an almost eternal witness to vast wonders which may take equally long periods to be discerned. Like the Oracle of Delphi, the Sphinx confronted the explorer as well as seeker and said, "Man, Know Thy Self." To KNOW was Madame's personal mission. And one to which she invited her fellow humans. H.P. Blavatsky kept her own secrets while pointing her contemporaries to look within for their own.

Helena Blavatsky embodied the inscrutable Sphinx metaphorically if not otherwise. She was practically kin to that most formidable creature with the torso of a bull, the chest and paws of a lion, the wings of an eagle, and the face of a wo/man representing the four fixed signs of the zodiac: Taurus, Leo, Scorpio (Aquila), and Aquarius. H.P.B. was strong and immoveable as a bull. At the same time, she was lion-like in courage and compassion (born both a Leo and a Sedmitchka). She was also a high-flying aquiline spirit who carried the waters of Aquarius for coming generations.

Olcott reported on the many-sided Sphinx from his own keen observations during the early *Isis* years: "I noticed ... that at times when the physical H.P.B. was in a state of supreme irascibility, the body was rarely occupied save by the Master whose own pupil and spiritual ward she was, and whose iron will was even stronger than her own; the gentler philosophers keeping aloof. Naturally, I asked why a permanent control was not put upon her fiery temper, and why she should not always be modified into the quiet, self-centred sage that she became under certain obsessions. The answer was that such a course would inevitably lead to her death from apoplexy; the body was vitalised by a fiery and imperious spirit, one which had from childhood brooked no restraint, and if vent were not allowed for the excessive corporeal energy, the result must be fatal."

To complicate matters more, Colonel Olcott threw in some of his own conjectures: "I have sometimes been even tempted to suspect that none of us, her colleagues, ever knew the normal H.P.B. at all, but that we just dealt with an artificial animated body, a sort of perpetual psychical mystery, from which the proper *jiva* was killed out at the battle of Mentana, when she received those five wounds and was picked out of a ditch for dead. There is nothing intrinsically impossible in this theory ... She was such a bundle of contradictions, so utterly incapable of being classified like any of us common folk, that as a conscientious man I shrink from anything like dogmatic assertion. Whatever she may have said to myself or anybody else, counts with me for very, very little, for having lived and travelled with her so long, and been present at so very many of her interviews with third parties, I have heard her tell the most conflicting stories about herself. To have been open and communicative would have been to betray the residences and personalities of her Teachers to that multitude of self-seekers whose egotistic importunities have ever driven the would-be Yogi to the seclusion of the cave or forest. She chose as the easiest way out of the difficulty to contradict herself and throw the minds of her friends into confusion."

Others like Dr. Archibald Keightley made their own diagnosis of the grand Blavatsky phenomenon: "Some people have advanced as a theory to account for these changes, that Mme. Blavatsky was the scene of mediumistic oscillations or that, at least, she was the scene of action of not merely double but of multiple personality. These suggestions are really the wildest of hypotheses -- much less, working hypotheses. To those who know the laws which govern the relation of the physical instrument to the subtle astral and spiritual forces which dominate it, the explanation is simple. But I will put forward my own theory. For the purposes of the theosophical work that body was an instrument used by one of the Masters, known to us as H.P.B. When he had to attend to other business, the instrument was left in charge of one of his pupils or friends, who ran the body as an engineer directs his machine when taking duty for another. But the substitute engineer has not the same sympathy with his machine or instrument as the regular man and is 'outside the machine.' I conceive that, just as the engineer and his machine overcome the inertia of matter, so the body and its tendencies proved no light task to control in the absence of the real owner and head engineer. And a certain letting off of steam was the result. But the energy was not wasted but used up in the work."

The enigma and the Sphinx for the 19th century (and more to come) remains unsolved, yet there is one further looming hint to consider. It should trump all the rest. Letters sent between the Master K.H., A.P. Sinnett, and A.O. Hume -- considered in proper light -- do to a large degree explain the essence of H.P.B.'s extraordinary problem.

K.H.'s Confidential Memo about the Old Lady.
Received Simla, Autumn, 1881.

I am painfully aware of the fact that the habitual incoherence of her statements -- especially when excited -- and her strange ways make her in your opinion a very undesirable transmitter of our messages. Nevertheless, kind Brothers, once that you have learned the truth; once told, that this unbalanced mind, the seeming incongruity of her speeches and ideas, her nervous excitement, all that in short, which is so calculated to upset the feelings of sober minded people, whose notions of reserve and manners are shocked by such strange outbursts of what they regard as her temper, and which so revolt you, -- once that you know that nothing of it is due to any fault of hers, you may, perchance, be led to regard her in quite a different light. Notwithstanding that the time is not quite ripe to let you entirely into the secret; and that you are hardly yet prepared to understand the great Mystery, even if told of it, owing to the great injustice and wrong done, I am empowered to allow you a glimpse behind the veil. This state of hers is intimately connected with her occult training in Tibet, and due to her being sent out alone into the world to gradually prepare the way for others. After nearly a century of fruitless search, our chiefs had to avail themselves of the only opportunity to send out a European body upon European soil to serve as a connecting link between that country and our own. You do not understand? Of course not. Please then, remember, what she tried to explain, and what you gathered tolerably well from her, namely the fact of the seven principles in the complete human being. Now, no man or woman, unless he be an initiate of the 'fifth circle,' can leave the precincts of Bod-Las and return back into the world in his integral whole -- if I may use the expression. One, at least of his seven satellites (principles) has to remain behind for two reasons: the first to form the necessary connecting link, the wire of transmission -- the second as the safest warranter that certain things will never be divulged. She is no exception to the rule ... The bearing and status of the remaining six depend upon the inherent qualities, the psycho-physiological peculiarities of the person, especially upon the idiosyncracies transmitted by what modern science calls 'atavism.'

Mr. Hume was less than pleased and tried to refute the Master's elucidation of the riddle of H.P.B. in a letter to her. He dared or cared not to accept, "... that you are a psychological cripple, one of your seven principles being in pawn in Tibet ..."

According to ancient teaching from India to Greece, every human being is composed of seven principles or satellites, bodies or skins. The hidden energetic aspects which stand within and beyond the outer visible human form are the true substance of our nature. Some go to dust at death, others continue in the inner worlds between lives. It is they which create the next body commensurate with our recent and not so recent incarnations, making human beings ever the product of past actions and overriding karma. "Till heaven and earth pass, one jot or one tittle shall in no wise pass from the law, till all be fulfilled."

In the case of a chela who leaves the abode of the masters in Tibet (or elsewhere), a "deposit" is required to be left with them. Clearly it was one of great sacrifice and explains the handicap under which H.P. Blavatsky traveled back into the common world.

There are a number of hints as to this state of affairs in the writings of H.P.B. and others. The popular English novelist James Hilton seems to have understood the wonder and the gravity of a seeker passing into the inner circles of the Forbidden Land. So, either he had delved deeply into Helena Blavatsky's life or else he used a keen bit of intuition when writing *The Lost Horizon*. In his story, Westerners who left the land of Shangri-La were soon drawn back, subject to amnesia and hysteria, or prone to rapid aging and death. Thus, the secrets of Bod-Las were not allowed to escape control and be misused.

Likewise, Helena Petrovna Blavatsky is sure to remain another secret of the Bod-Las, a perpetual enigma and the "sphinx of the XIXth century." H.P.B.'s paradoxes distressed and disturbed many, but thankfully not all.

William Kingsland, one of Helena's students and early biographers, remembered that, "Yes, her stormy life was, on the surface, full of inconsistencies, puzzles, enigmas, contradictions, misunderstanding -- mistakes also, if you like -- but which of us can cast a stone at her in respect of any of these? On the surface, Yes. But underneath was a heart of gold, and iron will, an inflexible purpose, a steadfast devotion to the case of Truth and to the Master whom she served. Underneath was -- the real H.P. Blavatsky."

The Real H.P.B. made larger sacrifices than we can begin to imagine in our present limited awareness. Only when we stand in shoes like her own will we really KNOW.

Helel
(Hebrew for Light Bearer)

"She was a torch ..." Henry Edge
"She was a messenger of Light ..." Alice Cleather

The outer world was quite in the dark as the fresh light began to enter the world in the last quarter of the 19th century. But, a little known Indian yogi repeatedly predicted the eventual work of H.P.B. and the Theosophical Society. A pandit (scholar) at Madras Presidency College wrote A.O. Hume to inform him about his late guru. T.V. Mudaliar told Hume about Ramalinga Pillay Avergal. The devotee first reported that his guru was able to recite the contents of great Vedic writings (without prior exposure) at age nine. He was an alchemist, could turn a carnivore into a vegetarian at a glance, and could read other men's minds. "His habits were excessively abstemious. He was known to hardly ever take any rest. A strict vegetarian, he ate but once in two or three days, and was then satisfied with a few mouthfuls of rice. But when fasting for a period of two or three months at a time, he literally ate nothing, living merely on warm water with a little sugar dissolved in it."

Pandit Mudaliar went on to say that his guru taught that the esoteric meaning of sacred books of the East soon would be revealed by the Mahatmas, that the distinction between races and castes would be replaced by a Universal Brotherhood, that God would eventually be understood as the principle of Universal Love, and that men would discover the latent powers within them.

On the 30th of that month 1874, at Metucuppam, we saw our master for the last time. Selecting a small building, he entered its solitary room after taking an affectionate farewell of his Chelas, stretched himself on the carpet, and then, by his orders, the door was locked and the only opening walled up. But when, a year later, the place was opened and examined, there was nothing to be seen but a vacant room. He left with us a promise to reappear some day but would give us no intimation as to the time, place, or circumstances. Until then, however, he said that he would be working not in India alone, but also in Europe and America and all other countries, to influence the minds of the right men to assist in preparing for the regeneration of the world.

Such, in short, is the history of this great man. The facts I have referred to above are within the knowledge of thousands of people. His whole occupation was the preaching of the sublime moral doctrines contained in the Hindu Shastras, and the instilling into the masses of the principles of Universal Brotherhood, benevolence and charity. But to his great disappointment he found among his large congregations but few who could appreciate his lofty ethics. During the latter part of his visible earthly career, he often expressed his bitter sorrow for this sad state of things, and repeatedly exclaimed:

"You are not fit to become members of this Society of Universal Brotherhood. The real members of that Brotherhood are living far away, towards the North of India. You do not listen to me. You do not follow the principles of my teachings. You seem to be determined not to be convinced by me. YET THE TIME IS NOT FAR OFF, WHEN PERSONS FROM RUSSIA, AMERICA (these two countries were always named), and other foreign lands WILL COME TO INDIA AND PREACH TO YOU THIS SAME DOCTRINE OF UNIVERSAL BROTHERHOOD. Then only, will you know and appreciate the grand truths that I am now vainly trying to make you accept. You will soon find that THE BROTHERS WHO LIVE IN THE FAR NORTH will work a great many wonders in India, and thus confer incalculable benefits upon this our country."

Pandit Mudaliar went on to conclude, "This prophecy has, in my opinion, just been literally fulfilled. The fact, that the Mahatmas in the North exist, is no new idea to us, Hindus; and the strange fact that the advent of Madame Blavatsky and Colonel Olcott from Russia and America was foretold several years before they came to India, is an incontrovertible proof that my Guru was in communication with those Mahatmas under whose directions the Theosophical Society was subsequently founded."

Helena Petrovna Blavatsky has passed before the reader's eyes in ten major roles, thus far. Each has shown a larger-than-life, though flawed human being. Two or three of her life roles would have been more than enough for most humans to shoulder in any one lifetime.

But, there is more to be considered in this brief portrait of H.P.B. and her many lives. In her three other roles, Madame Blavatsky dutifully filled her major mission in founding the Theosophical Society and nursing it along for the latter sixteen years of her life.

That Society inaugurated in New York City on November 17, 1875, became the focal point of H.P.B.'s life, writing, and contributions to 19th, 20th, and 21st century thought. Helena was aware for decades that she had a large Work to do in the world, even though it took years to materialize. Henry Olcott only gradually recognized that the Theosophical Society had developed as a final step following progressive efforts to "enlighten" spiritualism in New York, to build a spiritualistic newspaper in Boston, and to create Olcott's "Miracle Club" in Philadelphia. "All things show me that the movement as such was planned out beforehand by the watching Sages, but all details were left for us to conquer as best we might."

The immensity of the task and the inevitable opposition portended an effort against overwhelming odds. Even the Sages were unsure of things to come when Helena and Henry volunteered as soldiers for a "Forlorn Hope." The Master Morya wrote to A.P. Sinnett saying, "One or two of us hoped that the world had so far advanced intellectually, if not intuitionally, that the Occult doctrine might gain an intellectual acceptance, and the impulse given for a new cycle of occult research. Others -- wiser as it would now seem -- held differently, but consent was given for the trial. It was stipulated, however, that the experiment should be made independently of our personal management; that there should be no abnormal interference by ourselves."

For many years, Madame Blavatsky and Colonel Henry Olcott shouldered the burdens of building the organization, vitalizing it and spreading its influence around three continents. Olcott managed the administration of the whole Society and especially of its Indian and Asian branches. He also took on the job of helping to revitalize Buddhism in southern Asia. Eventually, William Quan Judge manned practically the whole TS work in North America in teaching, writing and administration.

Henry Olcott was a key figure in the diverse works and interests of the Theosophical Society. But, Madame Blavatsky was ever the focal point, spearhead, and soul of the Society -- and still is. A web of forces always worked within and behind the early Society. Yet, things inevitably turned back to H.P.B. for inspiration and direction. While Olcott, Judge, and other later leaders did in fact "carry on," Madame was the visible light of the TS.

H.P.B., in fact, epitomized its major principles (per Henry Olcott):
1. The study of occultism;
2. The formation of a nucleus of universal brotherhood;
3. The revival of Oriental literature and philosophy.

Restating these purposes, the Theosophical Society may be seen to have been energized and organized to:

1. Resurrect the ancient and august Light of the East;
2. Demonstrate its reality in philosophy and phenomena;
3. And substantiate the innate Unity of Life and Brotherhood of Man.

H.P.B. appeared at a pivotal moment of history in which her specific work was meant to open or re-open a stream of light and knowledge, especially to the western world. She reminded us that the whole of the objective universe - macrocosm and microcosm - is forever passing through cycles. That the Kali Yuga (Dark Age) was completing its first five-thousand-year passage. Materialism was then and continues to be overwhelmingly powerful in the physical realm. Madame's work was meant to "pierce the (hardened) veil" and allow some modest amount of inner light to pass into the outer world.

The Piscean Age was trailing off into the Age of Aquarius. She was one of the latter's forerunners. H.P. Blavatsky has been considered the "Harbinger of the New Age" and the "Mother of Modern Spirituality."

Madame B. also dealt with lesser cycles as the 20th century neared. The Industrial Era was in full swing. The Electrical Revolution was at hand. The World War was on the horizon and predicted in her writings. The Atomic Age foreseen. While focused outwardly on the near times, Madame drew from the ancient past, the inscrutable East, and the inner worlds to share with those who were ready and willing.

Literally and symbolically, light enters into our lives from the East. The Sun ascends there and the Soul has also its rising. H.P.B. made her entrance from that direction in a number of ways. Helena was born and reared in Eurasia. She was trained with her Masters in the hidden reaches of Tibet and the Himalayas. Madame B. gathered their gifts and teachings and came to the West to pass them on.

These were but the first layers of a vast knowledge which waits patiently for receptive human hearts and minds. In her voluminous writings, Madame repeatedly stated that only a limited range of information could be given out in the late 19th century. More was and is sure to follow, but that depends on how what has been given is used.

The Star in the East is a wonderful image which undergirds many religions and traditions. H.P.B. pressed that issue in many ways in her writings. Time and time again, she stressed that "The Greatest Religion is Truth." The source of that Truth and Light is the East.

Even modest thinkers pay homage to the Wise Men of the Near East in the likes of Socrates, Plato, and Pythagoras. The list could be made quite long of true Greek sages, many of whom were more advanced and enlightened than the greatest of our modern era.

But, Madame Blavatsky retreated further and further into distant eras to discuss how the Greeks were beholden to the Egyptians, Persians, Chaldeans and others. And all of the above gathered their wisdom from the Aryans of ancient India and Tibet.

Greeks: Pythagoras learned his cosmological theory of numbers at Thebes, Orpheus studied at Memphis, and Plato at Heliopolis. Pythagoras was called Yavanacharya during his researches in India whence he brought the idea of the heliocentric system 2000 years before Copernicus developed his "revolutionary" teachings. The worship of Hercules (Baladeva) was borrowed by the Greeks from Egypt after it had been transplanted from India and Lanka.

Hebrews: Madame noted that all of the structures of the western bibles, like the Indian Vedas, fall back on God-in-Nature and Nature-in-God. Daniel was the last of the old school Jewish initiates and chief of the Magi-Astrologers of Chaldea. The kabala goes back to Chaldea.

Egyptians: Some of the arts and sciences of Egypt (as well as of Rome and Chaldea) continue to be far superior to those of the present. The ancient pyramids clearly attest to that fact. Madame B. quoted Ragon writing that, "Indian philosophy, without mysteries, ... penetrated into Chaldaea and ancient Persia, gave rise to the doctrine of Egyptian Mysteries." H.P.B. remarked repeatedly that Moses was initiated into the Egyptian secret priesthood. St. Peter, though not an initiate, had studied their mysteries as well.

Persians: Aryan allegories passed through Persian tradition before reaching the Egyptian Gnostics into the Genesis of the Hebrews. The Zoroastrians borrowed many of their conceptions from India, the Jews borrowed their angels from Persia, and the Christians borrowed from the Hebrews.

Chaldeans: Modern astronomy owes much to Chaldean astrolatry and the astronomical calculations of the Magi. The symbolical kabala of the Chaldeans is the most ancient system extant. The secret wisdom of heavenly mythology and of the cycles of time passed through the hands of the Chaldean initiates. The Chaldeo-Tibetan and Aryan doctrines of the seven-fold principles in man are identical.

"But the great cycle, the first one within the Kali-yuga, is at an end; the day of resurrection for all that is dead may not be too far off. The great Swedish Seer, Emmanuel Swedenborg, said: 'Seek the lost word among the hierophants, in great Tartary and Tibet.'"

Standing behind Tartary and Tibet were the Atlanteans of which Madame said relatively little. She recognized that it would be difficult for westerners to accept the hidden teachings of the ancient East even from verified historical places and periods. H.P.B. resisted delving deeply into Atlantis and its Fourth Race from which the Aryans drew all of their secrets and initiations. The ancient Egyptian priests and the Brahmins of old received their powers from the Sons of Will and Yoga who united to resist the Adepts of the left-hand path in Atlantis.

Aryans: H.P.B. spoke of the Aryans in at least two ways. The Aryan or Fifth Race rose in central Asia from the remnants of the previous Fourth as Atlantis passed under the waters and new lands were raised over a period of tens of thousands of years. The Aryan teachers took up residence in Aryavarta, the region of the Himalayas north of India. It was there that the initiates collected and maintained, protected and revealed (when timely) the secrets of time immemorial.

Knowledge really has neither beginning nor end. Thus, Madame remarked that, "There were no mysteries in the beginning, we are taught. Knowledge (*vidya*) was common property, and it reigned universally throughout the Satya Yuga (Golden Age)." With the Dark Ages which passed, the powers were guarded (within the bounds of Karmic Law) from those who would misuse them. Still, the esoteric doctrine -- the most profound of all philosophies -- was continuously taught through the Vedic Upanishads and by the likes of Gautama Buddha that ignorance might be destroyed leading to spiritual liberation. The Christ of the West taught the same principles to his disciples and to those who might hear as he said, "You shall know the truth and the truth shall set you free."

Referring to the Upanishads (Upanishad is another word for Secret Doctrine), H.P.B. wrote, "It is these very teachings of the oldest conceptions in the world, that we consider to be the chief witnesses to that which we call the Wisdom-Religion (the religion of reason), Theosophy -- and we call our teaching a religion only because (owing to the etymology of the word) these tenets once upon a time united the entire human race by means of their spiritual thought. He who understands the essence and the meaning of universal truth, will not be surprised therefore to find its rays fragmented here and there, not only in the ancient philosophical beliefs but even in the gross fetishism of the savage, where it is still possible to trace them in the dying sparks of that truth."

The world has become more and more materialistic over recent millennia (this is still the Kali Yuga) - and more especially in the past century since Madame B. departed the scene. A relative few have been seeking for the true light. Most have been satisfied with transient flares sent out by modern science and the dim bulbs of crystallized religions. Philosophers of recent times have generally added little to the mix.

"Ragon was right in saying in his *Maconnerie Occulte*, that 'Humanity only seems to progress in achieving one discovery after the other, whereas in truth it only finds that which it had lost. Most of our modern inventions for which we claim such glory, are, after all, things people were acquainted with three and four thousand years back. [The learned Belgian Mason would be nearer the mark by adding a few more ciphers to his four thousand years. HPB] Lost to us through wars, floods and fire, their very existence became obliterated from the memory of man. And now modern thinkers begin to rediscover them once more.'"

Leaving religion aside, many arts and sciences traveled East to West through the impetus and guidance of the Aryan Brothers. (Read the story of Marco Polo.) The art of writing came to the West specifically through the old Sanskrit language and Devangari characters.

"For thousands of years, one initiate after another, one great hierophant succeeded by other hierophants [from the East], has explored and re-explored the invisible Universe, the worlds of the interplanetary regions, during long periods when his conscious soul, united to the spiritual soul and to the ALL, free and almost omnipotent, left his body. It is not only the initiates belonging to the 'Great Brotherhood of the Himalayas,' who give us these doctrines; it is not only the Buddhist Arhats who teach them, but they are found in the secret writings of Sankaracharya, of Gautama Buddha, of Zoroaster, as well as in those of the Rishis."

Helena Blavatsky "merely" followed in the footsteps of the Great Ones. Henry Olcott paid H.P.B. repeated tribute yet always in respect to her Teachers and their guiding Light: "Where was there a human being of such a mixture as this mysterious, this fascinating, this light-bringing H.P.B.? Where can we find a personality so remarkable and so dramatic; one which so clearly presented at its opposite sides the divine and the human? Karma forbid that I should do her a featherweight of injustice, but if there ever existed a person in history who was a greater conglomeration of good and bad, light and shadow, wisdom and indiscretion, spiritual insight and lack of common sense, I cannot recall the name, the circumstances or the epoch. To have known her was a liberal education, to have worked with her and enjoyed her intimacy, an experience of the most precious kind. She was too great an occultist for us to measure her moral stature. She compelled us to love her, however much we might know her faults; to forgive her, however much she might have broken her promises and destroyed our first belief in her infallibility. And the secret of this potent spell was her undeniable spiritual powers, her evident devotion to the Masters whom she depicted as almost supernatural personages, and her zeal for the spiritual uplifting of humanity by the power of the Eastern Wisdom. Shall we ever see her like again? Shall we see herself again within our time under some other guise? Time will show."

H.P.B.'s great chore was to transport beams of light - spiritual and symbolic, phenomenal and mental - from the East into the West as guided by her Teachers. Many who caught a few rays may have been in awe of what passed before them. But, Madame would have wryly reminded them, "There is nothing new under the Sun." She humbly passed on what had been vouchsafed to her from those who themselves had received in an everlasting tradition, teacher to student. To her Aunt Nadya, Madame B. wrote, "... your learning is the sturdy progeny of your own brain and understanding, while mine is derived from my Superior. I am nothing but a reflector of someone else's bright light. However it may be, this light has little by little entered into me, has been filtered into me, has permeated me, as it were; thus I cannot help it; all these ideas have entered into my brain, into my very soul."

H.P.B.'s travels in the East brought her near the great torch bearers. She studied in their very light and carried that radiance to the West. "When, years ago, we first travelled over the East, exploring the penetralia of its deserted sanctuaries, two saddening and ever-recurring questions oppressed our thoughts: Where, WHO, WHAT is GOD? Who ever saw the IMMORTAL SPIRIT of man, so as to be able to assure himself of man's immortality?

"It was while most anxious to solve these perplexing problems that we came into contact with certain men, endowed with such mysterious powers and such profound knowledge that we may truly designate them as the sages of the Orient. To their instructions we lent a ready ear. They showed us that by combining science with religion, the existence of God and immortality of man's spirit may be demonstrated like a problem of Euclid. For the first time we received the assurance that the Oriental philosophy has room for no other faith than an absolute and immovable faith in the omnipotence of man's own immortal self. We were taught that this omnipotence comes from the kinship of man's spirit with the Universal Soul -- God! The latter, they said, can never be demonstrated but by the former. Man-spirit proves God-spirit, as the one drop of water proves a source from which it must have come. Tell one who had never seen water, that there is an ocean of water, and he must accept it on faith or reject it altogether. But let one drop fall upon his hand, and he then has the fact from which all the rest may be inferred. After that he could by degrees understand that a boundless and fathomless ocean of water existed. Blind faith would no longer be necessary; he would have supplanted it with KNOWLEDGE. When one sees mortal man displaying tremendous capabilities, controlling the forces of nature and opening up to view the world of spirit, the reflective mind is overwhelmed with the conviction that if one man's spiritual Ego can do this much, the capabilities of the FATHER SPIRIT must be relatively as much vaster as the whole ocean surpasses the single drop in volume and potency. *Ex nihilo nihil fit*; prove the soul of man by its wondrous powers -- you have proved God!"

H.P.B. never claimed to be a guru or yogi -- one fully (or nearly so) united with the higher Self. But, she surely accomplished the major work to become Hierophant and Helel for generations to come. Like her Masters, Madame B. was a Raj Yogin. Only a few big steps behind them, she carried their impress, their seal and their powers wherever she roamed.

"Truth is stranger than fiction. It may any day, and most unexpectedly, vindicate its wisdom and demonstrate the conceit of our age, by proving that the Secret Brotherhood did not, indeed, die out with the Philaletheians of the last Eclectic School, that the Gnosis flourishes still on earth, and its votaries are many, albeit unknown. All this may be done by one, or more, of the great Masters visiting Europe, and exposing in their turn the alleged exposers and traducers of Magic."

The Light H.P.B. passed on was drawn from the same sources which students of ALL six schools of Indian philosophy eventually must absorb. Those schools are the logical of Gautama, the atomism of Kanada, the pantheism of Kapila, the mystical yoga of Patanjali, the truths of Mimamsa, and the higher inquiry of Vedanta.

The Indian philosophy, Secret Doctrine, and Ageless Wisdom from which Helena Blavatsky drew were like fingers pointing to the Moon. HPB urged students and seekers along the Path to their own discovery of the Moon. "The study of these powers and the art of developing them by practice formed the science of the soul, which Madame Blavatsky taught. All the rest of her doctrines, regarding the constitution of man, the evolution of worlds, etc., etc., were merely accessories to facilitate self-knowledge; to destroy bigotry and superstition, and by freeing the mind from prejudices, to give it a wider range of ennobling thought, and enable it to form a grander and higher conception of God, Nature and Man." (Franz Hartmann)

Access to Truth only arises from the most subtle, diligent, and persistent mental investigation. The work is somewhat akin to our modern-day Albert Einstein who accomplished so much merely with pencil and paper, chalk and board, and focused mind and intuition. He required no laboratory or calculator or computer to complete his extraordinary investigations into the realms of relativity. Thomas Edison did similar *exploratory* work showing that "Ideas come from space." All true genii, like the Greatest Ones, draw their inspiration from the same Source and give out their gifts to a needy world.

To a greater or lesser degree, Madame matriculated into the same course of study that neophytes and eventual masters follow. H.P.B. was miles ahead of Edison and Einstein who were in some senses her students and followers. Edison became a member of the Theosophical Society in 1878 before the Twins went off to India. Einstein kept a copy of *The Secret Doctrine* on his desk and knew quite well the limits of the concrete mind.

Helena Blavatsky was trained as were Pythagoras and Plato, Siddhartha and Sankara, and her own teachers Morya and Koot Humi. The Buddha was most certainly a Raj Yogin who became the exponent of one of the great schools. Jesus Christ was a Yogin and Magician as well as Prophet. Many of his missing years from ages 12 to 30 were spent in the East where He continues to be remembered as Saint Issa.

It gradually becomes clear -- to those with eyes to see -- that all the Great Sons of Men inevitably follow much the same Path (at least towards its end) back to True Knowing and Direct Experience. They all become Raja Yogins and Magicians. These names are synonymous with Adept, Esotericist, Occultist, Theurgist -- in their truest senses. They all point to the grand potential for human beings to bring to awareness complete knowledge of the vast and the infinitesimal, the past and the future, the inner and the outer worlds.

Many moderns may denounce such ideas as "ridiculous," "foolish," "impossible," "bombastic," and "nonsense." But, the potential remains and has been factually shown by Great Ones of all times and traditions that IMMENSE POWERS do in fact lie within man. H.P.B. was the latest one to prove such in her own unique way.

To borrow a word that H.P.B. often used, *pygmies* of the modern western world limit themselves and their kin, are too often short on imagination, and prefer to focus on sin and the senses rather than the wonderful and the possible. The motto of the true Occultist and Yogin for thousands of years even into the midst of the Iron Age continues as: TO KNOW, TO WILL, TO DARE, AND TO KEEP SILENT.

Indian philosophy anciently received from the Atlantean adepts involves experimental psychology -- in the truest sense of the phrase -- to extract the student from the material world to the threshold of universal consciousness. To those who have the keys, the Indian Vedas and similar texts help to open the gates of the six great schools of Aryan philosophy which lead to the doorsteps of Magic.

Warning may be given, most obviously that the work has little or nothing to do with the physical training of Hatha Yoga. The real work begins with the mind and passes eventually into the realm of the ever-present spirit. "The kingdom of heaven is in your very midst."

As Patanjali wrote in his Sutras, Indian Yoga is the only true science. All other sciences are only reflections and approximations, subject to change, relative illusions based on the senses and apprehension of the outer world. Modern scientific investigation and technology have their places, but are only shadows of the real science which is played out in the realms of inner thought and gnosis.

Helena Blavatksy equated Theosophy and Indian Yoga when she wrote that, "Theosophy rejects the testimony of the physical senses entirely, if the latter be not based upon that afforded by the psychic and spiritual perceptions. Even in the case of the most highly developed clairvoyance and clairaudience, the final testimony of both must be rejected unless by those terms is signified the *photos* of Iamblichus, or the ecstatic illumination, the *agoge manteia* of Plotinus and Porphyry. The same holds good for the physical sciences; the evidence of reason upon the terrestrial plane, like that of our five senses, should receive the imprimatur of the sixth and seventh senses of the divine Ego, before a fact can be accepted by the true occultist."

"Knowledge comes in visions, first in dreams and then in pictures presented to the inner eye during meditation. Thus have I been taught the whole system of evolution, the laws of being and all else that I know -- the mysteries of life and death, the workings of karma. Not a word was spoken to me of all this in the ordinary way, except, perhaps, by way of confirmation of what was thus given me -- nothing taught me in writing. And knowledge so obtained is so clear, so convincing, so indelible in the impression it makes upon the mind, that all other sources of information, all other methods of teaching with which we are familiar dwindle into insignificance in comparison with this. One of the reasons why I hesitate to answer offhand some questions put to me is the difficulty of expressing in sufficiently accurate language things given to me in pictures, and comprehended by me by the pure Reason, as Kant would call it."

While the kingly science of Raja Yoga is imminently practical and philosophical, it can be apprehended by but a few in this round of spiritual evolution. It is as far beyond the student of calculus as s/he is beyond a child counting 1 to 10. Basic preparations through lifetimes of experience and simple character development are fundamental. Integration of a full personality and alignment with the Soul is basic. "By Yoga training, the body becomes pure as a crystal casket, the soul purged of all its grossness, and the spirit which, before the beginning of his course of self-purification and development, was to him but a dream, has now become a reality -- the man has become a demi-god."

Every soul slowly evolves from ignorance eventually to graduated levels of higher awareness. Every chela of the sublime science then awakens fully along the passageway from outer illusory knowledge into the light of truth. "May I be led from darkness into Light, from the unreal to the Real, and from death to Immortality."

Eventually, said K.H., "... there comes a moment in the life of an adept, when the hardships he has passed through are a thousandfold rewarded. In order to acquire further knowledge, he has no more to go through a minute and slow process of investigation and comparison of various objects, but is accorded an instantaneous, implicit insight into every first truth.... the adept sees -- and feels and lives in the very source of all fundamental truths the Universal Spiritual Essence of Nature, Shiva the Creator, the Destroyer, and the Regenerator."

When such is accomplished, the developing adept becomes "simply the custodian of the secrets of the hidden possibilities of nature; the master and guide of her undiscovered potentialities, one who awakens and arouses them into activity by abnormal yet natural powers, and by furnishing them with the requisite group of conditions which lie dormant and can, rarely, if ever, be brought together if left alone."

In sum, the Raja Yogin studies, practices and lives to unite the personal Soul with the Universal Soul. Man returns to the Godhead. Then arise the talents and gifts of Spirit: Prophetic Discernment through the Soul (Inner God), Ecstasy and Illumination, Action in Spirit through

Will, and Domination over the Elements and Elementals.

Helena Blavatsky, the Raj Yogin, continued on in her decrepit body long enough to give out a host of secrets never before revealed for public consumption. This was done in a variety of ways, but *The Secret Doctrine*, as her magnum opus, surely passed on some of the deepest and most important mysteries of the Ageless Wisdom held in trust by the Mahatmas.

H.P.B. made clear that she purveyed no revelation, but synthesized material "scattered throughout thousands of volumes embodying the scriptures of the great Asiatic and early European religions, hidden under glyph and symbol, and hitherto left unnoticed because of this veil.... The sole advantage which the writer has over her predecessors, is that she need not resort to personal speculations and theories. For this work is a partial statement of what she herself has been taught by more advanced students ..."

The Secret Doctrine is based on Stanzas from the Book of Dzyan, recorded by an unnamed ancient people, written in the sacred Senzar language, and guarded by Knowers in lands beyond the Himalayas. *The Secret Doctrine* draws on "the mysterious power of Occult symbolism, that the facts which have actually occupied countless generations of initiated seers and prophets to marshal, to set down and explain, in the bewildering series of evolutionary progress, are all recorded on a few pages of geometrical signs and glyphs. The flashing gaze of those seers has penetrated into the very kernel of matter, and recorded the soul of things there, where an ordinary profane, however learned, would have perceived but the external work of form.... That it is the uninterrupted record covering thousands of generations of Seers whose respective experiences were made to test and to verify the traditions passed orally by one early race to another, of the teachings of higher and exalted beings, who watched over the childhood of Humanity. That for long ages, the 'Wise Men' of the Fifth Race, of the stock saved and rescued from the last cataclysm and shifting of continents, had passed their lives in learning, not teaching. How did they do so? It is answered: by checking, testing, and verifying in every department of nature the traditions of old by the independent visions of great adepts; i.e., men who have developed and perfected their physical, mental, psychic, and spiritual organisations to the utmost possible degree. No vision of one adept was accepted till it was checked and confirmed by the visions -- so obtained as to stand as independent evidence -- of other adepts, and by centuries of experiences."

The two volumes of *The Secret Doctrine* elucidate the creation of the universe and explain humanity's place and evolution in the midst of the greater whole. *The Secret Doctrine* begins with three fundamental propositions (synopsized here) to unfold the Ageless Wisdom:

(a) An Omnipresent, Eternal, Boundless, and Immutable Principle which transcends the power of human conception.
(b) The Eternity of the Universe which exists as a boundless plane and periodically manifests and disappears during the Days and Nights of Brahma.
(c) The Identity of all Souls with the Universal Over-Soul (an aspect of the Unknown Root) and the obligatory pilgrimage for every Soul through the Cycle of Incarnation in accordance with Karmic law.

Madame Blavatsky transcribed major portions of the Sacred Doctrine of the East while manifesting its Ancient Light through her own being. Years earlier, H.P.B. had been able to proffer the tales of *Isis* even as she lived *her* story.

Phenomene
(French for Phenomenon)

"It was tempting to see through and read such a phenomenon, such a living 'human document.'"
Vsevelod Solovyov

That evening (in Benares) ... There were H.P.B., Mrs. Gordon, Dr. Thibaut, the Swami, Pramada Babu, Ram Rao, Damodar, and myself (Henry Olcott) present. The talk was on the subject of Yoga "Matam Plavatsky,'"said Dr. Thibaut, in his strong German accent, "dese Pandits tell me dat, untoutedly, in te ancient times dere vere Yogis who hat actually teveloped the Siddhis tescribed in the Shastras; tat dey could too vonterful tings; for instance, tey coult make fall in a room like dis, a shower of roses; put now nobody can do dat."

I ask my friend's pardon for transcribing his then accent and words, but the scene comes back to me so vividly that I can almost hear him speaking. He can get his revenge the first time he hears me speak German! I see him now; as he sat on a sofa to H.P.B.'s right, with his frockcoat buttoned to his chin, his intellectual, pale face as solemn as though he were pronouncing a funeral oration, and his hair cut as short as it could be, and standing up like spikes all over his head. He had no sooner pronounced the last word than H.P.B. started up in her chair, looked scornfully at him, and burst out: "Oh, they say that, do they? They say no one can do it now? Well, I'll show them; and you may tell them from me that if the modern Hindus were less sycophantic to their Western masters, less in love with their vices, and more like their ancestors in many ways they would not have to make such a humiliating confession, nor get an old Western hippopotamus of a woman to prove the truth of their Shastras!"

Then, setting her lips together and muttering something, she swept her right hand through the air with an imperious gesture, and bang! on the heads of the company fell about a dozen roses. As soon as the momentary shock of surprise was over, there was a scramble for the roses, but Thibaut sat as straight as a post and seemed to be casting it up, pro and con, in his mind. Then the discussion proceeded with renewed vivacity. The Sankhya was the topic and Thibaut put many searching questions to H.P.B., which she answered so satisfactorily that the Doctor said that neither Max Muller nor any other Orientalist had made so clear to him the real meaning of the Sankhya philosophy

as she had, and he thanked her very much.
  Towards the end of the evening, in a pause in the conversation, he turned to H.P.B. and -- always keeping his eyes fixed towards the floor according to his habit -- said that, as he had not been so fortunate as to get one of the roses that had so unexpectedly fallen, might he be favored with one "as a souvenir of this very delightful evening?" Those were his very words. His secret thought probably was, that if the first floral rain had been a trick she would not be ready for a second, if taken unawares! "Oh yes, certainly," she said, "as many as you like." And, making another of her sweeping gestures, down fell another shower of flowers; one rose actually hitting the Doctor on the top of his head and bounding into his lap as he sat bolt upright. I happened to be looking at him at that moment and saw the whole incident. Its effect was so funny as to set me off into a fit of laughter. He gave a little, very slight start, opened and shut his eyes twice, and then taking a rose and looking down at it, said with imperturbable solemnity: "De veight mooltiplied py te felosity, proves dat it moost haf come from a creat distance." There spoke the hard savant, the unimaginative scholar, who reduces all life to an equation, and expresses all emotions by algebraical signs!

Madame Blavatsky's materialization of roses for Dr. Georg Thibaut may be seen as a gift to the Sanskritist, a sign of her fantastic work, and a symbol of the flower of her being. For keen students, there seems no end to Mme. Blavatsky's unique and phenomenal abilities.
  Helena Blavatsky was clearly the chief exponent and symbol for the second mission of the Theosophical Society, intended to be the elucidation of the occult sciences. Occultism was meant to bridge the chasm between the aspiration for a Brotherhood of Man and the ever Wonderful Gnosis of the East. In *The Occult World*, A.P. Sinnett tried to explain the link, as he "... endeavored to ... emphasise the reason why I dwell upon the phenomena which exhibit these [extraordinary] faculties. Rightly regarded, these are the credentials of the spiritual teaching which their authors supply. Firstly, indeed, in themselves abnormal phenomena accomplished by the willpower of living men must be intensely interesting for every one endowed with an honest love of science. They open out new scientific horizons. It is as certain as the sun's next rising that the forward pressure of scientific discovery, advancing slowly as it does in its own grooves, will ultimately, and probably at no very distant date, introduce the ordinary

world to some of the superior scientific knowledge already enjoyed by the masters of occultism. Faculties will be acquired by exoteric investigation that will bring the outworks of science a step or two nearer the comprehension of some of the phenomena I have described in the present volume."

Phenomena from ancient to present times have been labeled "jugglery" and "charlatanry" by many skeptics. Believers have called them "miracles" and "super-natural." H.P.B. knew the former labels to be misused by so-called investigators. She detested the latter, saying phenomena were natural but outside the range of present-day abilities of John Doe and Mrs. Grundy. "We believe in no Magic which transcends the scope and capacity of the human mind, nor in 'miracle,' whether divine or diabolical, if such imply a transgression of the laws of nature instituted from all eternity. Nevertheless, we accept the saying of the gifted author of Festus, that the human heart has not yet fully uttered itself, and that we have never attained or even understood the extent of its powers. Is it too much to believe that man should be developing new sensibilities and a closer relation with nature? The logic of evolution must teach as much, if carried to its legitimate conclusion."

Madame B.'s brief work with the Societe Spiritual in Egypt was an attempt to bring some organized light to the spiritualism of the day. After that effort quickly failed, she was pointed to America and soon joined forces with Henry Olcott who was quite taken with mediumship and phenomena. H.P.B. quickly brought him around to her way of thinking with the help of her Masters and their "special effects."

But, the theosophical organization was limited in resources, funding and willing bodies, especially in the early days. Madame spent most of her time writing about ancient truths and secondarily about the occult. Colonel Olcott took on administrative chores, public speaking on Theosophy, magnetic treating ill natives in India, collecting a library of scriptures at Adyar, and rejuvenating Buddhism in southern Asia.

Little time and energy were left for specific efforts and due diligence in studies of the occult. Eventual "researches" were limited to the liberal sprinkling of H.P.B.'s articles and books with stories which are "fabulous" and "fantastic" to many readers. (*Isis Unveiled* is a cornucopia of documented magical narratives.) Those tales attracted many followers as did Madame's liberal exhibition of her own phenomena in the early years of the Theosophical Society.

Still, Helena did much more than write. She exposed the western world to the effects of the Inner Light through the demonstrations of her own phenomena. Her unusual practices continued until the benefits began to be out-weighed by the costs. Madame could channel so much energy to produce so many "tricks" for only so long. Eventually, her health paid the price. Furthermore, phenomena were never meant to be the "main course" of theosophy and of the Theosophical Society. Still, H.P.B. used them with students to teach occult principles. For others, they were hints of potentials and possibilities. For still others, they were offered as gifts and trinkets and mementos.

It seems clear, as her nemesis Solovyov remarked, that H.P.B. was herself the truest *phenomenon* -- a living one. Olcott said she was a veritable wonder in many ways, but most obviously because of the amazing and magical things she did. Often, they appeared to be accomplished by little or no effort. But, appearances can be deceiving.

After her very being, Madame's writing accomplishments may have been her greatest manifestations. She was "... endowed with a courage without bounds and a power of continuous mental concentration that has scarcely been equalled, she floundered on through weeks and months towards her goal, the fulfillment of her Master's orders. This literary feat (*Isis*) of hers surpasses all her phenomena."

Few got as close to her as Countess Wachtmeister who recognized the keen choices H.P.B. had to make to produce any of her works.

One day a temptation came to her in the form of a large yearly salary if she would write for the Russian papers. She might write, she was told, on occultism or any other subject which pleased her, if she would only contribute to their columns. Here was a promise of comfort and ease for the remainder of her life. Two hours' labour every day would be ample to satisfy all demands made on her time; but then no Secret Doctrine *would be written. I spoke of a compromise, and asked her if it would not be possible for her to accept this engagement, and, at the same time, continue her Theosophical work. "No -- a thousand times no"' she answered. "To write such a work as* The Secret Doctrine *I must have all my thoughts turned in the direction of that current. It is difficult enough even now, hampered as I am with this sick and worn-out old body, to get all I want, how much more difficult, then, if I am to be continually changing the currents into other directions. I have no longer the vitality or the energy left in me. Too much of it was exhausted at the time when I produced my phenomena."*

"Why, then, did you make these phenomena?" I asked her.

"Because people were continually bothering me," she replied. "It

was always, 'Oh, do materialise this,' or, 'do let me hear the astral bells,' and so on, and then I did not like to disappoint them. I acceded to their request. Now I have to suffer for it!" So the letter was written to Russia containing the refusal of the splendid offer, and one more sacrifice was made in order that the Theosophical Society might live and prosper.

Many people have remarked to me, at different times, how foolish it was that 'phenomena' should ever have been connected with the Theosophical Society or that H.P.B. should ever have wasted her time over such trivialities. To these remarks H.P.B. has invariably given the same answer, namely, that at the time when the Theosophical Society was formed it was necessary to draw the attention of the public to the fact, and that phenomena served this object more effectually than anything else could have done. Had H.P.B. given herself out in the first instance as simply a teacher of philosophy, very few students would have been drawn to her side.... But having once introduced this element of the marvelous, it was difficult to get rid of it when it had served its turn. All came eager to have their sense of wonder gratified, and, when disappointed, went away wrathful and indignant.

The phenomena which H.P.B. displayed and shared surely were bought with a price. But, they riveted attention. The names of Helena Petrovna Blavatsky and the Theosophical Society came to the fore in the 19th century. Her phenomena left trails for others to follow, experiments for researchers to study, and clues to human potential.

Regardless of motives or effects, H.P. Blavatsky produced a web of phenomena, not equalled by any figure in recorded history. This book only scratches the surface of the talents she carried and the magic she displayed. Favorite events and episodes are passed on for the reader to consider. Would that we could review H.P.B. "at work in the astral light" as she composed her books and created her moments of magic. Or, that we might "read" her as she did others. Ah, someday we will do as she did.

In the meantime, we borrow from Madame Blavatsky's contemporaries who saw and remembered her in action. Sometimes, they just gawked. Sometimes, they trembled and ran away. Other times, they gazed and learned.

Charles Johnston gathered many things on an early visit with her. H.P.B. moved from words and ideas to exposition and experience as she gave him a "reading lesson" he surely never forgot.

... we came back to the question of magical powers. In August, 1888, H.P.B. had a visit from her old chum, Colonel H.S. Olcott. He was writing, at a side table. H.P.B. was playing Patience, as she did nearly every evening, and I was sitting opposite her, watching, and now and then talking about the East, whence Colonel Olcott had just come. Then H.P.B. got tired of her card game, which would not come out, and tapped her fingers slowly on the table, half unconsciously. Then her eyes came to focus, and drawing her hand back a foot or so from the table, she continued the tapping movement in the air. The taps, however, were still perfectly audible -- on the table a foot from her hand. I watched, with decided interest. Presently she had a new idea, and turning in my direction, began to send her astral taps against the back of my hand. I could both feel and hear them. It was something like taking sparks from the prime conductor of an electric machine; or, better still, perhaps, it was like spurting quick-silver through your fingers. That was the sensation. The noise was a little explosive burst. Then she changed her direction again and began to bring her taps to bear on the top of my head. They were quite audible, and, needless to say, I felt them quite distinctly. I was at the opposite side of the table, some five or six feet away, all through this little experiment in the unexplained laws of nature, and the psychical powers latent in man....

When the last word is said, she was greater than any of her works, more full of living power than even her marvellous writings. It was the intimate and direct sense of her genius, the strong ray and vibration of that genius itself, which worked her greatest achievements and won her greatest triumphs. Most perfect work of all, her will carried with it a sense and conviction of immortality. Her mere presence testified to the vigour of the soul.

Personal experiences are well known to captivate attention. We generally admit that. "Experience is the best teacher." Madame B. gave many such gifts to all manner of friends and associates, strangers and passersby. W.Q. Judge recalled H.P.B. and her arts in both ordinary and extraordinary display.

I was one day, about four o'clock, reading a book by P.B. Randolph, that had just been brought in by a friend of Colonel Olcott. I was sitting some six feet distant from H.P. Blavatsky, who was busy writing. I had carefully read the title-page of the book, but had forgotten the exact title. But I knew that there was not one word of writing upon it.

As I began to read the first paragraph I heard a bell sound in the air, and looking saw that Mme. Blavatsky was intently regarding me.
"What book do you read?" said she.
Turning back to the title-page, I was about to read aloud the name, when my eye was arrested by a message written in ink across the top of the page which, a few minutes before, I had looked at and found clear. It was a message in about seven lines, and the fluid had not yet quite dried on the page -- its contents were a warning about the book. I am positive that when I took the volume in my hand, not one word was written in it.

Judge remembered other episodes from his treasury of H.P.B. phenomena: "But all that paled and grew dim before the glorious hours spent in listening to the words of those illuminated Ones who came often late at night when all was still, and talked to H.S.O. and myself.... It was after twelve midnight until 4 A.M. that I heard and saw most while with her in New York."

Madame Blavatsky had an unusual taste for jewelry and was happy to show her *charming* talents to others. She shared them in recovering lost jewels, duplicating rings, and even adding stones to settings, etc. All in moments, often as quick as the blink of the eye. Such episodes occurred round the world - America, Asia, Europe - as H.P.B. demonstrated the simple yet extraordinary wonders of materialization. Brooches, rings, necklaces vanished and reappeared, often being transformed along the way. And, they sometimes vanished again, as when, "her three-stoned sapphire ring was taken off, given to a lady who wanted it to wear for a while, taken away by her, and yet on her departure the real ring remained on HPB's finger, only an illusion was taken by the lady."

Helena Blavatsky had many uncanny abilities, some of them quite inimitable. She was well known to be able to locate almost any lost object and recover or reproduce it when she deemed appropriate. A *New York Times* reporter, writing in 1889 (two years before H.P.B.'s death) after a visit to London, told of some of those abilities.

Madame Blavatsky now very seldom gives any manifestation of her occult powers except to intimate friends; but I had while over there several evidences that she can do things quite inexplicable by any laws of exact science. Two years ago I lost here in New York a paper that was of considerable interest to me, and I certainly mentioned to no one

that I had lost it. One evening a little over a fortnight ago, while I was sitting in Madame Blavatsky's parlour (in London) with Mr. B. Keightley and several other persons, I happened to think of that paper. Madame got up, went into the next room, and, returning, almost immediately handed to me a sheet of paper. I opened it and found it an exact duplicate of the paper that I had lost two years before. It was actually a facsimile copy, as I recognised at once. I thanked her, and she said:
"Well, I saw it in your head that you wanted it.'"

It was not a thing to astonish anyone acquainted with the laws of nature as comprehended by occultists, who understand clearly how consciousness of my thought was possible, how the reproduction of a thing once within my knowledge was necessarily facsimile, and how that reproduction could be effected by a simple act of volition on her part, but it would puzzle materialists to explain it in accordance with the facts.

Many of Madame's magical feats were simply utilitarian. Her ability to duplicate inanimate objects came in handy. A *Hartford Daily Times* reporter told the story of H.P.B. "creating things from nothing."

Madame, my friend, and myself were out one day looking about the stores, when she said she desired some of these illuminated alphabets which come in sheets, like the painted sheets of little birds, flowers, animals, and other figures, so popular for decorating pottery and vases. She was making a scrap-book, and wished to arrange her little page in these pretty colored letters. Well, we hunted everywhere but could not find any, until at last we found just one sheet, containing the twenty-six letters, somewhere on Sixth Avenue. Madame bought that one and we went home. She wanted several, of course, but not finding them proceeded to use what she could of this. My friend and I sat down beside her little table, while she got her scrap-book and busily began to paste her letters in. By and bye she exclaimed, petulantly, "I want two S's, two P's, and two A's." I said, "Madame, I will go and search for them downtown. I presume I can find them somewhere.

"No, you need not," she answered. Then, suddenly looking up, said, "Do you wish to see me make some?"

"Make some? How? Paint some?"

"No, make some exactly like these."

"But how is that possible? These are printed by machinery."

"It is possible -- see!"

She put her finger upon the S and looked upon it. She looked at it with infinite intensity. Her brow ridged out. She seemed the very spirit of will. In half a minute she smiled, lifted her finger, took up two S's exactly alike, exclaiming, "It is done!" She did the same with the P's.

Then my friend thought: "If this is trickery, it can be detected. In one alphabet can be but one letter of a kind. I will try her." So he said: "Madame, supposing this time, instead of making two letters separately, you join them together thus A--A--?"

"It makes no difference to me how I do it," she replied indifferently, and placing her finger on the A, in a few seconds she took it up, and handed him two A's, joined together as he desired. They were as if stamped from the same piece of paper. There were no seams or (artificial) joinings of any kind. She had to cut them apart to use them. This was in broad daylight, in the presence of no one but myself and friend, and done simply for her own convenience.

We were both astounded and lost in admiration. We examined these with the utmost care. They seemed as much alike as two peas. But if you wish, I can show you the letters this moment.

"Madame, may we take your scrap-book to look at?"

"Certainly, with pleasure," returned Madame, courteously. We waited impatiently until Mr. P. could open the volume. "There ... those are the letters she used, and this is the one she made." There was no difference in them.

The page was beautifully arranged and read thus in brilliant letters:

THIRD VOLUME, SCRAP-BOOK OF THE
THEOSOPHICAL SOCIETY
New York, 1878
THEIR TRIBULATIONS and TRIUMPHS

H.P. Blavatsky did not only materialize mundane items for trivial projects. She also brought forth copies of books and papers from distant libraries and archives. Not just for the eyes to see, but also at times for hands to touch and hold. Colonel Olcott recalled such wonders being performed during the busy time when he helped Madame B. to compose *Isis Unveiled*. "I remember well two instances when I, also, was able to see and even handle books from whose astral duplicates she had copied quotations into her manuscript, and which she was obliged to 'materialise' for me, to refer to when reading the proofs, as I refused to pass the pages for the 'strike-off' unless my doubts as to the accuracy of her copy were satisfactory. One of these was a French work on physiology and psychology; the other, also by a French author, upon some branch of neurology. The first was in two volumes, bound in half calf, the other in pamphlet wrapper. It was when we were living at 302 West 47th street -- the once-famous 'Lamasery' and the executive headquarters of the Theosophical Society. I said: 'I cannot pass this quotation, for I am sure it cannot read as you have it.' She said: 'Oh don't bother; it's right; let it pass.' I refused, until finally she said: 'Well, keep still a minute and I'll try to get it.' The far-away look came into her eyes, and presently she pointed to a far corner of the room, to an etagere on which were kept some curios, and in a hollow voice said: 'There!' and then came to herself again. 'There, there; go look for it over there!' I went, and found the two volumes wanted, which, to my knowledge, had not been in the house until that very moment. I compared the text with H.P.B.'s quotation, showed her that I was right in my suspicions as to the error, made the proof correction and then, at her request, returned the two volumes to the place on the etagere from which I had taken them. I resumed my seat and work, and when, after awhile, I looked again in that direction, the books had disappeared! After my telling this (absolutely true) story, ignorant sceptics are free to doubt my sanity; I hope it may do them good. The same thing happened in the case of the *apport* of the other book, but this one remained, and is in our possession at the present time."

Even in the long past 19th century, Helena Blavatsky previewed modern inventions which would appear generations after her death. (Her instant duplicating process detailed above has itself yet to be *duplicated*.) From fax machines to copiers and audio recordings to directory assistance, H.P.B., using mind and will only, accomplished works hardly dreamed of in the 1800s. "On one occasion the address of a business firm in Philadelphia was needed for the purpose of sending a letter through the mail, and no one present could remember the street or number, nor could any directory of Philadelphia be found in the neighborhood. The business being very urgent, it was proposed that one of us should go down nearly four miles to the General Post Office, so as to see a Philadelphia directory. But H.P.B. said: 'Wait a moment, and perhaps we can get the address some other way.' She then waved her hand, and instantly we heard a signal bell in the air over our heads. We expected no less than that a heavy directory would rush at our heads from the empty space, but no such thing took place. She sat down, took up a flat tin paper-cutter japanned black on both sides and without having any painting on it. Holding this in her left hand, she gently stroked it with her right, all the while looking at us with an intense expression. After she had rubbed thus for a few moments, faint outlines of letters began to show themselves upon the black, shining surface, and presently the complete advertisement of the firm whose address we desired was plainly imprinted upon the paper-cutter in gilt letters, just as they had had it done on slips of blotting paper such as are widely distributed as advertising media in America -- a fact I afterwards found out. On a close examination, we saw that the street and number, which were the doubtful points in our memories, were precipitated with great brilliancy, the other words and figures being rather dimmer. Mme. Blavatsky said that this was because the mind of the operator was directed almost entirely to the street and number, so that their reproduction was brought about with much greater distinctness than the rest of the advertisement, which was, so to speak, dragged in in a rather accidental way."

Henry Olcott also described his Chum Helena at work as the western world's very first photocopying machine. "What a strange woman she was, and what a great variety in her psychical phenomena! We have seen her duplicating tissues, let me recall incidents where letters were doubled. I received one day a letter from a certain person who had done me a great wrong, and read it aloud to H.P.B. 'We must have a copy of that,' she exclaimed, and, taking the sheet of note-paper from me, held it daintily by one corner and actually peeled off a duplicate, paper and all, before my very eyes! It was as though she had split the sheet between its two surfaces. Another example, perhaps even more interesting, is the following: Under date of December 22, 1877, Stainton Moses wrote her a five-paged letter of a rather controversial, or, at any rate, critical, character. The paper was of square, full letter size, and bore the embossed heading 'University College, London' and near the left-hand upper corner his monogram, -- a W and M interlaced and crossed by the name 'STAINTON' in small capitals. She said we must have a duplicate of this too, so I took from the desk five half-sheets of foreign letter-paper of the same size as Oxon's [Moses's pseudonym] and gave her them. She laid them against the five pages of his letter, and then placed the whole in a drawer of the desk just in front of me as I sat. We went on with our conversation for some time, until she said she thought the copy was made and I had better look and see if that were so. I opened the drawer, took out the papers, and found that one page of each of my five pieces had received from the page with which it was in contact the impression of that page. So nearly alike were the original and copies that I thought them ... exact duplicates."

Stainton Moses, a Church of England cleric and spiritualist as well, was an esteemed friend of Blavatsky and Olcott. He therefore got special treatment: "One evening, in the autumn of 1876, she and I were working, as usual, upon *Isis*, at opposite sides of our writing-table, and dropped into a discussion of the principles involved in the conscious projection of the Double. Through lack of early familiarity with those subjects, she was not good then at explaining scientific matters, and I found it difficult to grasp her meaning. Her fiery temperament made her prone to abuse me for an idiot in such cases, and this time she did not spare her expressions of impatience at my alleged obtuseness. Finally, she did the very best thing by offering to show me in a picture how Oxon's evolution was proceeding, and at once made good her promise. Rising from the table, she went and opened a drawer from which she took a small roll of white satin ... and laying it on the table before me, proceeded to cut off a piece of the size she wanted; after which she returned the roll to its place and sat down. She laid the piece of satin, face down, before her, almost covered it with a sheet of clean blotting-paper, and rested her elbows on it while she rolled for herself and lighted a fresh cigarette. Presently she asked me to fetch her a glass of water. I said I would, but first put her some question which involved an answer and some delay. Meanwhile I kept my eye upon an exposed edge of the satin, determined not to lose sight of it. Soon noticing that I made no sign of moving, she asked me if I did not mean to fetch her the water. I said: 'Oh, certainly.' 'Then what do you wait for?' she asked. 'I only wait to see what you are about to do with that satin.' I replied. She gave me one angry glance, as though seeing that I did not mean to trust her alone with the satin, and then brought down her clenched fist upon the blotting-paper, saying: 'I shall have it now -- this minute.' Then, raising the paper and turning over the satin, she tossed it over to me. Imagine, if you can, my surprise! On the sheeny side I found a picture, in colours, of a most extraordinary character. There was an excellent portrait, of the head only, of Stainton Moses as he looked at that age, the almost duplicate of one of his photographs that hung 'above the line' on the wall of the room, over the mantel-shelf. From the crown of the head shot out spikes of golden flame; at the place of the heart and the solar plexus were red and golden fires, as it might be bursting forth from little craters; the head and the place of the thorax were involved in rolling clouds of pure blue aura, bespeckled throughout with flecks of gold; and the lower half of space where the body should be was enwrapped in similarly rolling clouds of pinkish and greyish vapour, that is, of auras of a meaner quality than the superior cumuli."

Madame's "artistic and magical talents" took another turn one evening when Olcott and she sat with Wong Chin Fu, a Chinese lecturer, well known at the time in the United States. "We three were chatting about the pictures of his country as lacking the elements of perspective, whereupon he said how admirable were the figure-paintings of their artists, how rich in colour and bold in drawing. H.P.B. concurred and, in the most casual way, as it seemed, opened the drawer where she kept her writing-paper, and drew forth a finely-executed painting of a Chinese lady dressed in full Court robes. I am sure as I can be that it was not there before, but as Wong Chin Fu was not specially interested in the occult science which for us had so great a charm, I made no remark. Our visitor took the picture in his hand, looked at it, remarked upon its beauty, but said: 'This is not Chinese, Madam; it has no Chinese writing in the corner. It is probably Japanese.' H.P.B. looked at me with an amused expression, returned the picture to the drawer, shut it for a moment, and then re-opening it, drew forth a second picture of a Chinese lady, but wearing different coloured robes, and handed it to Wong Chin Fu. This he recognised as unmistakably from his country, for it bore Chinese lettering in the left-hand lower corner, and he at once read it!"

On another occasion, Helena and Henry hosted a French woman named Liebert with supposed spirit photographic abilities. By the end of several weeks, both were frustrated with their guest.

All these weeks and months that the two series of experiments were going on, Mlle. Liebert lived with us, and almost every evening she used to bring out and lovingly con over a handful of so-called spirit photographs that she had collected in divers places. The ignominious collapse of her hopes as to the test trials in progress seemed to make her dote upon what the poor deluded creature regarded as past successes ... H.P.B. had naturally but small pity for intellectual weaklings, especially little for the stubborn dupes of mediumistic trickery, and she often poured out the vials of her wrath upon the ... purblind old maid.

One cold evening (Dec. 1, 1875), after a fresh day of failures at Mr. Mason's laboratory, Mlle. Liebert was, as usual, shuffling over her grimy photographs, sighing and arching her eyebrows into a despairing expression, when H.P.B. burst out: "Why will you persist in this folly? Can't you see that all those photographs in your hand were swindles on you by photographers who did them to rob you of your money? You have had every possible chance now to prove your pretended power, -- more than one hundred chances have been given you, and you have not been able to do the least thing. Where is your pretended guide, Napoleon, and the other sweet angels of Summer land; why don't they come and help you? Pshaw! it makes me sick to see such credulity. Now see here: I can make a 'spirit picture' whenever I like and of any-body I like. You don't believe it, eh? Well, I shall prove it on the spot!"

She hunted up a piece of card-board, cut it to the size of a cabinet photograph, and then asked Mlle. Liebert whose portrait she wished. "Do you want me to make your Napoleon?" she asked. "No," said Mlle. L., "please make for me the picture of that beautiful M. Louis." H.P.B. burst into a scornful laugh, because, by Mrs. Britten's request, I had returned to her through the post the Louis portrait three days previously, and it being by that time in Boston, 250 miles away, the trap set by the French lady was but too evident. "Ah!" said H.P.B., "you thought you could catch me, but now see!" She laid the prepared card on the table before Mlle. Liebert and myself, rubbed the palm of her hand over it three or four times, turned it over, and lo! on the under side we saw (as we then thought) a facsimile of the Louis portrait. In a cloudy background, at both sides of the face were grinning elemental sprites, and above the head a shadowy hand with the index-finger pointing downward. I never saw amazement more strongly depicted on a human face than it was upon Mlle. Liebert's at that moment. She gazed in positive terror at the mysterious card, and presently burst into tears and hurried out of the room with it in her hand, while H.P.B. and I went into fits of laughter.

After a half hour she returned, gave me the picture, and on retiring for the night I placed it as a book-mark in a volume I was reading in my own apartment. On the back I noted the date and the names of the three witnesses. The next morning I found that the picture had quite faded out, all save the name "Louis," written at the bottom in imitation of the original: the writing, a precipitation made simultaneously with the portrait and the elves in the background.

Seemingly even more amazing events -- simply because they happened outdoors -- occurred when the "Twins" relocated to India in 1879. A.P. Sinnett, a great chronicler of theosophical wonders, recorded numbers of Madame Blavatsky's phenomena in *The Occult World*. His writings stimulated his Anglo-Indian peers as well as later readers around the globe. The "teacup incident" at Simla may be the most well known and possibly the most fascinating to readers 130 years after the event.

We set out at the appointed time next morning. We were originally to have been a party of six, but a seventh person joined us just before we started. After going down the hill for some hours a place was chosen in the wood near the upper waterfall for our breakfast: the baskets that had been brought with us were unpacked, and, as usual at an Indian picnic, the servants at a little distance lighted a fire and set to work to make tea and coffee.

Concerning this some joking arose over the fact that we had one cup and saucer too few, on account of the seventh person who joined us at starting, and some one laughingly asked Madame Blavatsky to create another cup and saucer. There was no set purpose in the proposal at first, but when Madame Blavatsky said it would be very difficult, but that if we liked she would try, attention was of course at once arrested. Madame Blavatsky, as usual, held mental conversation with one of the Brothers, and then wandered a little about in the immediate neighbourhood of where we were sitting - that is to say, within a radius of half-a-dozen to a dozen yards from our picnic cloth - I closely following, waiting to see what would happen. Then she marked a spot on the ground, and called to one of the gentlemen of the party to bring a knife to dig with.

The place chosen was the edge of a little slope covered with thick weeds and grass and shrubby undergrowth. The gentleman with the knife - let us call him X - as I shall have to refer to him afterwards - tore up these in the first place with some difficulty, as the roots were tough and closely interlaced. Cutting then into the matted roots and earth with the knife, and pulling away the debris with his hands, he came at last, on the edge of something white, which turned out, as it was completely excavated, to be the required cup. A corresponding saucer was also found after a little more digging. Both objects were in among the roots which spread everywhere through the ground, so that it seemed as if the roots were growing round them. The cup and saucer both corresponded exactly, as regards their pattern, with those that had been brought to the picnic, and constituted a seventh cup and saucer when brought back to where we were to have breakfast.

The gentleman called X had been a good deal with us during the week or two that had already elapsed since Madame Blavatsky's arrival. Like many of our friends, he had been greatly impressed with much he had seen in her presence. He had especially come to the conclusion that the Theosophical Society, in which he was interested, was exerting a good influence with the natives, a view which he had expressed more than once in warm language in my presence. He had declared his intention of joining this Society as I had done myself. Now, when the cup and saucer were found most of us who were present, X among the number, were greatly impressed, and in the conversation that ensued the idea arose that X might formally become a member of the Society then and there. I should not have taken part in this suggestion - I believe I originated it - if X had not in cool blood decided, as I understood, to join the Society; in itself, moreover, a step which involved no responsibilities whatever, and simply indicated sympathy with the pursuit of occult knowledge and a general adhesion to broadly philanthropic doctrines of brotherly sentiments towards all humanity, irrespective of race and creed....

The proposal that X should then and there formally join the Society was one with which he was quite ready to fall in. But some documents were required - a formal diploma, the gift of which to a new member should follow his initiation into certain little Masonic forms of recognition adopted in the Society. How could we get a diploma? Of course for the group then present a difficulty of this sort was merely another opportunity for the exercise of Madame's powers. Could she get a diploma brought to us by 'magic?' After an occult conversation with the Brother who had then interested himself in our proceedings, Madame told us that the diploma would be forthcoming. She described the appearance it would present - a roll of paper wound round with an immense quantity of string, and then bound up in the leaves of a creeping plant. We should find it about in the woods where we were, and we could all look for it, but it would be X, for whom it was intended, who would find it. Thus it fell out. We all searched about in the undergrowth or in the trees, wherever fancy prompted us to look, and it was X who found the roll, done up as described.

Colonel Olcott filled in some details regarding the latter incident at Simla. "After luncheon, H.P.B. did another wonder which surprised me more than any of the rest. One of the gentlemen said that he was ready to join our Society if H.P.B. could give him his diploma then, and there duly filled out! This was, certainly, a large order but the old lady, nothing daunted, made a sweep of her hand, and pointing to a bush at a little distance, told him to see if he could not find it there; trees and bushes having often served as letter-boxes. Laughingly, and in apparent confidence that his test would not be complied with, he walked over to the bush -- and drew forth a diploma of membership filled in with his name and that day's date, together with an official letter from myself, which I am quite sure I never wrote, but which was still in my handwriting!"

In later years, Henry Olcott tried to categorize Madame's magic. "When we come to analyse the psychical phenomena of or connected with Mme. Blavatsky, we find that they may be classified as follows:
1. Those whose production requires a knowledge of the ultimate properties of matter, of the cohesive force which agglomerates the atoms.
2. Those which relate to the powers of the elementals when made subservient to human will.
3. Those where hypnotic suggestion through the medium of thought-transference creates illusive sensations of sight, sound, and touch.
4. Those which involve the art of making objective images, pictorial, or scriptory -- first purposely created in the adept-operator's mind ...
5. Those pertaining to thought-reading and retrospective and prospective clairvoyance.
6. Those of the intercourse at will between her mind and the minds of other living persons equally or more perfectly gifted, psychically, than herself....
7. Those, of the highest class, were by spiritual insight, or intuition, or inspiration ... she reached the amassed stores of human knowledge laid up in the registry of the Astral Light."

The phenomena which Madame produced for many could be seen as magical and wonderful, engaging and even educational. They were the natural outgrowths of her spiritual evolution. "Seek ye first the kingdom of God, and all these things shall be added unto you." Her development and expansion of consciousness drew her into more fulsome rapport with Universal Mind and made it possible for her to accomplish great good for the planet and humanity. H.P.B. expressed many of the siddhis which are emblems and talents of the Raj Yogin.

From another view, her exhibitions appeared to some onlookers as playing to the crowd and quite probably detracting from the real work.

Writing to Mr. Sinnett, Madame's Master M. said, "Also try to break thro' that great maya against which occult students, the world over, have always been warned by their teachers -- the hankering after phenomena. Like the thirst for drink and opium, it grows with gratification. The Spiritualists are drunken with it; they are thaumaturgic sots. If you cannot be happy without phenomena you will never learn our philosophy. If you want healthy, philosophic thought, and can be satisfied with such -- let us correspond. I tell you a profound truth in saying that if you (like your fabled Shloma) but choose wisdom all other things will be added unto it -- in time. It adds no force to our metaphysical truths that our letters are dropped from space on to your lap or come under your pillow. If our philosophy is wrong a wonder will not set it right. Put that conviction into your consciousness and let us talk like sensible men. Why should we play with Jack-in-the-box; are not our beards grown."

Beyond entertaining favors, H.P.B.'s phenomena became focal points of discord, attack and lies. People not only fawned on Madame because of her unusual gifts, but numbers also became envious and spiteful. They lusted for what they could not have or feared what they could not understand. Then, they turned against her wreaking all kinds of havoc. From the Coulombs to Solovyov, sad pictures of human weakness rose to the surface in the eyes and words and actions of people she had offered the hands of friendship.

Madame's intimates readily wrote of her inexplicable exploits and extraordinary phenomena. Even her enemies attested to the wonders she performed. Vsevolod Solovyov sent the following letter to the St. Petersburg Rebus. In later years, the "eye-witness" explained away the occurrence by "psychological glamour of the witnesses." Yet, he found the phenomenon worthy enough to send a Letter to the Editor in 1884.

INTERESTING PHENOMENON: A LETTER TO THE EDITOR.
Several persons, among that number myself, met casually H.P. Blavatsky (the founder of the Theosophical Society, then on a visit to Paris) about 10 A.M. in the forenoon. A postman entered and brought, among others, a letter for a relative of Mme. B., then on a visit to the latter, but owing to the early morning hour still absent in her bedroom. From the hands of the postman the letter passed on, in the presence of all present, upon the table in the parlour, where we were all gathered. Glancing at the postmark and the address of that particular letter, both Mme. Blavatsky and her sister, Mme. Jelihowsky, remarked that it

came from a mutual relative then at Odessa. The envelope was not only completely closed on all its flaps, but the post-stamp itself was glued on the place where the seal is habitually placed -- as I got convinced by carefully examining it myself. H.P. Blavatsky, who was on that morning, as I had remarked, in very high spirits, undertook, unexpectedly for all of us, with the exception of her sister, who was the first one to propose it and to defy Mme. B. to do it, to read the letter in its closed envelope. After this she placed it on her forehead, and with visible efforts began to read it out, writing down the pronounced sentences on a sheet of paper. When she finished, her sister expressed her doubts as to the success of the experiment, remarking that several of the expressions read out and written down by Mme. B. could hardly be found in a letter from the person who had written it. Then H.P.B. became visibly irritated by this, and declared that in such case she would do still more. Taking the sheet of paper again she traced upon it with red pencil, at the foot of the sentences supposed to be contained in the closed letter, noted down by her, a sign, then she underlined a word, after which, with a visible effort on her face, she said: 'This sign that I make must pass into the envelope at the end of the letter, and this word in it be found underlined, as I have done it here.'

When the letter was opened, its contents were found identical with what Mme. B. had written down, and, at the end of it, we all saw the sign in red pencil correctly repeated, and the word underlined by her on her paper was not only there, but equally underlined in red pencil. After that an exact description of the phenomenon was drawn up, and all of us, the witnesses present, signed our names under it. The circumstances under which the phenomenon occurred in its smallest details, carefully checked by myself, do not leave in me the smallest doubt as to its genuineness and reality. Deception or fraud in this particular case are entirely out of question.

Vs. SOLOVIOF. PARIS. 10 (22) June 1884.

Solovyov eventually disputed this bit of H.P.B.'s magic, as others did on different phenomenal moments and for a wide range of reasons. No one, either friend or foe, ever came up with plausible causes for the wonders she performed. It was easy to throw out broad, demeaning and cheap accusations. Still, both supporters and detractors knew so little about Helena Blavatsky, neither what she was really about nor how she did what she did. Few understood her true work, so how could they make sense of the phenomena which sprang from it. Self-described experts from the Society for Psychical Research and media mavens alike had just the barest hints of any of the "miracles" they investigated because they lacked understanding of basic principles of nature. They were not even novices in the effort to grasp forces which can take lifetimes to develop and master.

Solovyov and the SPR were hardly the only ones who misunderstood H.P.B. and her works. Without a sense of the Big Picture, many got lost in her phenomena, distracted by her temper, or disturbed by her doctrine. A.P. Sinnett was very close to Madame for years, received piles of correspondence from her and the Masters, and saw wonders upon wonders. Yet, it seems he failed to "get it." H.P.B. did the wonders. She also accomplished the work. Blavatsky was the greatest public phenomenon of her century and millennium, and quite possibly of all time.

One of Madame's Teachers attempted to explain the paradoxical state of affairs which existed with their star chela. "She can and did produce phenomena, owing to her natural powers combined with several long years of regular training and her phenomena are sometimes better, more wonderful and far more perfect than those of some high, initiated chelas, whom she surpasses in artistic taste and purely Western appreciation of art -- as for instance in the instantaneous production of pictures ... Thus, while fathering upon us all manner of foolish, often clumsy and suspected phenomena, she has most undeniably been helping us in many instances; saving us sometimes as much as two-thirds of the power used, and when remonstrated -- for often we are unable to prevent her doing it on her end of the line -- answering that she had no need of it, and that her only joy was to be of some use to us. And thus she kept on killing herself inch by inch, ready to give -- for our benefit and glory, as she thought -- her life-blood drop by drop, and yet invariably denying before witnesses that she had anything to do with it."

Baba
(Russian for Grandmother, Hindi for Grandfather)

> "H.P.B. was born so great an aristocrat as
> to be at ease in the highest society,
> and so thorough a democratic altruist as
> to give cordial hospitality to the humblest caller."
> Henry Olcott

Helena Blavatsky was known to be a wonderful storyteller. One of her best is recorded in *From the Caves and Jungles of Hindustan*. As all writing is autobiographical, the tale of "The Donkey and the Elephant" provides another portrait of one who was kin to all.

It is remarkable that the elephants, creatures with great ambition and easily offended, never fight each other when living in the towns, though they often destroy one another in their native habitat. It is also remarkable that while they show each other signs of mutual respect, they never become friends, but frequently choose as object of their passionate and fiery attachment dogs, donkeys and other smaller animals.

One such elephant becoming attached to a donkey took it under his protective care. The elephant was free and belonged to a pagoda, while the donkey was hired out for work.

Once an English soldier, who had hired it, mounted it and began to hit its sides with his heavy boots. The elephant stood at the gate of the stable where his friend lived and, observing the abuse of his favorite, took hold of the British warrior with his trunk and gave him such a shaking that the latter, upon freeing himself, wanted, in his rage, to shoot the elephant on the spot.

He was persuaded not to do it because the other elephants standing near would sooner or later certainly kill him, so astounding is the esprit de corps *of the elephants. Interested by what he had heard, he forgave the elephant and, as a peace offering, gave him a piece of sugar cane.*

The elephant stood over it for a while, thought a bit and then, taking the luscious morsel, went straight to the donkey and, with his trunk, put it into the mouth of the abused creature, then turned around and went his way 'without looking at me, like a man who had been offended,' said the soldier who related the circumstance to us himself.

To nourish the seed of a Universal Brotherhood through service to humanity was the third and most important mission of the Theosophical Society. It was also its most difficult task, whether attempted inside or outside the Society. Human differences are hard barriers to bridge. Traditions, good or not so good, change slowly and often take other casualties along with them. Religions get stuck in unshakeable dogma. All belong to the personality world, the outer shell of things, which is often very hard to budge or crack. Minds get set in many ways and can become immovable. That is why we have "mindsets."

The fractions and frictions of H.P.B.'s era have changed little into our own times. Despite the leveling and cleansing of the World Wars and the fall of the Iron Curtain, stark dualities continue to shape life on Earth. The struggles between capital and labor, the rich and the poor, the powerful and the impotent, guns versus butter persist. "The poor (and the rich) will always be with you." Ancient ideals and modern fads, racial divides and religious unrest continue to confront each other all over the world.

The Theosophical Society had a high calling. Active Goodwill to All topped its pyramid of works. "The Chiefs want a 'Brotherhood of Humanity,' a real Universal Fraternity started; an institution which would make itself known throughout the world and arrest the attention of the highest minds." The Society and its founders were presented with the simple command for another holy crusade. H.P.B. and H.S.O. thence took up the torch and marched onward little thinking how huge a chore was set before them. Still, the TS Founders themselves were keen examples of true and persistent unselfishness.

The Brotherhood which the Mahatmas so deeply intended was hardly a new aspiration. In many ways, it was a simple restatement of the Golden Rule: Love one another, Do unto others ... "To all, whether Chohan or Chela, who are obligated workers among us the first and last consideration is whether we can do good to our neighbour, no matter how humble he may be; and we do not permit ourselves to even think of the danger or any contumely, abuse of injustice visited upon ourselves. We are ready to be 'spat upon and crucified' daily -- not once -- if real good to another can come of it."

The Great Commandment has been known as an essential ideal of most all the world's creeds and religions. Dreams of Utopia born and reborn from Plato to More. How far had they ever gotten? How could they evolve as the planet was languishing in materialistic self-interest as it trudged through the early centuries of the Iron Age (Kali Yuga)?

The Elder Brothers resurrected the dream and handed it to the Twins to pursue. "The term 'Universal Brotherhood' is no idle phrase. Humanity in the mass has a paramount claim upon us ... It is the only secure foundation for universal morality. If it be a dream, it is at least a noble one for mankind; and it is the aspiration of the true adept." "For it is 'humanity' which is the great Orphan, the only disinherited one upon this earth, my friend. And it is the duty of every man who is capable of an unselfish impulse to do something, however little, for its welfare. Poor, poor humanity! It reminds me of the old fable of the war be-tween the Body and its members: here, too, each limb of this huge 'orphan' -- fatherless and motherless -- selfishly cares but for itself. The body uncared for suffers internally, whether the limbs are at war or at rest. Its suffering and agony never ceases."

Writing about past and passing cycles in 1889, H.P.B. recalled Victor Hugo's prophecy that the coming century might bring such advancement as to demonstrate an "innate and holy love of humanity which constitutes an apostolate, and opens up a prophetic vista into the future. In the twentieth, war will be dead, the scaffold will be dead, animosity will be dead, royalty will be dead, and dogmas will be dead, but man will live. For all there will be but one country -- that country the whole earth; for all, there will be but one hope -- that hope the whole heaven."

H.P.B.'s enthusiasm and optimism in this arena seemed almost unbounded, even as she visioned other more likely scenarios for the coming times.

If Theosophy prevailing in the struggle, its all-embracing philosophy strikes deep root into the minds and hearts of men, if its doctrines of Reincarnation and Karma, in other words, of Hope and Responsibility, find a home in the lives of the new generations, then, indeed, will dawn the day of joy and gladness for all who now suffer and are outcast. For real Theosophy IS ALTRUISM, and we cannot repeat it too often. It is brotherly love, mutual help, unswerving devotion to Truth. If once men do but realize that in these alone can true happiness be found, and never in wealth, possessions, or any selfish gratification, then the dark clouds will roll away, and a new humanity will be born upon earth. Then, the GOLDEN AGE will be there, indeed. But if not, then the storm will burst, and our boasted western civilization and enlighten-ment will sink in such a sea of horror that its parallel History has never yet been recorded.

Look around you and behold! Think of what you see and hear, and draw therefrom your conclusions. The age of crass materialism, of Soul insanity and blindness, is swiftly passing away. A death struggle between Mysticism and Materialism is no longer at hand, but is already raging. And the party which will win the day at this supreme hour will become the master of the situation and of the future; i.e., it will become the autocrat and soul disposer of the millions of men already born and to be born, up to the latter end of the XXth century. If the signs of the times can be trusted it is not the Animalists who will remain conquerors.

The Theosophical Society was not just intended to be about studying Eastern philosophy, experimenting with phenomena, and meditating for enlightenment. Nor was it meant to fall to "preaching the Brothers more than the Brotherhood." But, the latter happened in later years and especially after the passing of Helena Blavatsky.

That failure came glaringly to H.P.B.'s awareness time and again. She reminded Mr. Sinnett of the predicament while she took responsibility for her part in it. "The Master K. H. wrote to you himself namely, that the T.S. is first of all a universal Brotherhood, not a society for phenomena and occultism. The latter must be held secret etc. I know that owing to my great zeal for the cause and your assurances that the society would never prosper unless the occult element was introduced into it and the Master proclaimed I am more guilty than any for having listened to this. Still all of you have now to suffer Karma."

Recognition of the Oneness of ALL beings through the Soul was the essential teaching of Theosophy and the Theosophical Society. Thus, the doors of the Theosophical Society were open to all. The TS began with extended arms and generous hearts. Dues were modest and could be waived. At times, they were even abolished, Olcott and Blavatsky and other donors making up shortfalls.

The Society, even in Asia, generally attracted more educated and endowed applicants. But, no obstacle or bar was set to entry. Like the Lodges of Freemasonry, all members were intended to "meet upon the level and part upon the square." Still, theosophical thought required a developing mind and character.

Material wealth did make for more opportunities to contact and engage the Theosophical Society in one place or another. But, there are two sides to every coin. Gazing deeply at the state of things, H.P.B.

saw that money in a man's pockets is not always a boon. Poverty can have its own advantages. "The motto of the Headquarters of the T.S. should be -- 'rigid justice to all.' If it is right to care for the poor and those who suffer, it is as right to care for the rich and all those who will unavoidably be brought to far greater sufferings, unless warned and shown the true cause of all such Karmic sorrows. The poorer a man, the more sad his life, the nearer he is to the end of his punitive Karma; the richer his neighbour, the more is full of pleasures his life, the nearer he is -- unless he acts in the right path -- [to] his Karmic doom. Help the poor, but pity the ignorant rich."

As repeatedly stated, Helena Blavatsky was the heart and soul of the Theosophical Society. Henry Olcott acted as its brains and brawn. He bore the brunt of the work in the outer world. H.S.O. did most of the "leg work" and was incredibly active in bridging differences once the TS had become headquartered in India. Olcott, occasionally with H.P.B. at his side, traveled far and wide lecturing and conversing with people of all races, creeds, and religions. He spurred the establishment of Buddhist schools in Ceylon (Sri Lanka) and used theosophical teachings to connect past and present, science and philosophy, religion and religion.

Politics used as an avenue toward human rights and equality was not intended to be part of the TS mission and both founders turned away from any such arena. Of their own free will and accord, other theosophists stepped into social and political roles in India to promote causes on behalf of the native population. After parting ways with the Theosophical Society, A.O. Hume was instrumental in founding the Indian National Congress which sounded the call for more Indians in the colonial government prior to the 20th century. Annie Besant, who followed Olcott as TS President, eventually pressed for Home Rule.

Hume had received much and grasped enough of H.P.B. and H.S.O. to bear testimony to the outstanding Theosophical ideal. "This much I have gathered about the Society, viz. that one primary and fundamental object of its existence is the institution of a sort of brotherhood in which, sinking all distinction of race and nationality, caste and creed, all good and earnest men, all who love science, all who love truth, all who love their fellowmen, may meet as brethren, and labor hand in hand in the cause of enlightenment and progress. Whether this noble ideal is ever likely to germinate and grow into practical fruition; whether this glorious dream, shared in by so many of the greatest minds in all ages, is ever destined to emerge from the shadowy realms of Utopia into the broad sunlight of the regions of reality, let no one now pretend to decide. Many and marvelous are the changes and developments that the past has witnessed; the impossibilities of one age have become the truisms of the next; and who shall venture to predict that the future may not have as many surprises for mankind as has had the past, and that this may not be one amongst them. Be the success, however, great or little of those who strive after this grand ideal, one thing we know, that no honest efforts for the good of our fellowmen are ever wholly fruitless. It may be long before that fruit ripens; the workers may have passed away long ere the world discerns the harvest for which they wrought; nay, the world at large may never realize what has been done for it, but the good work itself remains, imperishable, everlasting. They who wrought it have necessarily been by such efforts purified and exalted, the community in which they lived and toiled has inevitably benefitted directly or indirectly, and through it, the world at large. On this ground, if on no other, we must necessarily sympathize with the Theosophists."

Education and social influence took center stage in Theosophical activities. Olcott was keenly instrumental in bringing about rapprochement between diverse religious groups in various locations in South Asia through his personal endeavors. H.S.O. also helped convene meetings and celebrations between Buddhist and Hindu groups in India. Truth was the guiding light of the TS and religious dogmas were to be set aside. Local theosophical societies appeared which included Buddhists, Christians, Sikhs, Hindus, Parsis, Muslims and agnostics in their membership. Some charters were granted to societies which had specific religious leanings. But, each group was expected to search for theosophical truths within their own home framework.

Madame Blavatsky largely remained in the background in such work. Olcott hit the road, rode the waves, and made uncounted journeys to aid any group intent on raising Asian living and learning standards. H.S.O. was on the hoof promoting and proselytizing in venues with large numbers. H.P.B. spent most of her time holding her prolific pen to paper and meeting the public one-on-one at Bombay and Madras while in India and later in Europe and Britain.

That arrangement suited the temperaments of the two TS founders well. Colonel Olcott reveled in rubbing elbows with rajahs and princes and dewans. And, he was equally proud to stand before audiences, often many hundreds of Indian listeners, who were thrilled to contact a white man who offered them respect, interest, and brotherly care.

At one stage of Olcott's career in India, he was drawn into healing work using simple mesmeric methods. He was amazed at the results and so were the natives. Over a period of many months, the Colonel was often swamped with lines of ill and injured pleading to be treated by his magnetic methods. Hundreds were cured of major ailments for which the physicians of the day were baffled in diagnosis and ineffective in treatment. His work began quietly and suddenly, and persisted for several months. The Masters apparently shuttled healing forces through his outstretched hands. Then, just as suddenly he was told to turn off the spigot.

Madame did most of her work either alone or with intimate groups. She had done healing work on human bodies in her younger days. But in her latter years, the healing she administered occurred at much more subtle levels as she touched minds, hearts and souls. Interestingly while H.P.B. shied away from "dealing with bodies" as she aged, her own shell became more and more enfeebled and ravaged.

Many of her greater works involved fraternizing with her fellows at the depths of their beings -- sometimes when they may have been consciously unaware of the proceedings. On the outer level, she wished to act as brother, sister, parent and friend to all. But, no one has ever been able to long fill that position. Even Jesus and Gautama met enemies and detractors simply because they drew to the surface the truth in all beings -- good, bad and indifferent -- whom they met.

Helena Blavatsky was the Old Horse to her Teachers, the Old Lady to Olcott. She was even the Old Man to others who saw her through their own glasses of varied colors. Woman, man or "horse" it was all the same. H.P.B. was kin to humanity and all of nature. She wished for others to take on that way of thinking and living as well.

H.P.B.'s benevolence and love for humanity was set early in life -- if not before -- as the result of a painful incident. Colonel retold how, "In childhood her temper was practically unrestrained, her noble father petting and idolising her after the loss of his wife. When, in her eleventh year, the time came for her to leave his regimen and pass under the management of her maternal grandmother, she was warned that such unrestrained liberty would no longer be allowed her, and she was more or less awed by the dignified character of her relative."

But on one occasion, in a fit of temper at her nurse, a faithful old serf who had been brought up in the family, she struck her a blow in the face. This coming to her grandmother's knowledge, the child was sum-

moned, questioned, and confessed her fault. *The grandmother at once had the castle bell rung to call in all the servants of the household of whom there were scores, and when they were assembled in the great hall, she told her that she had acted as no lady should, in unjustly striking a helpless serf who would not dare defend herself; and she ordered her to beg her pardon and kiss her hand in token of sincerity.*

The child at first, crimson with shame, was disposed to rebel, but the old lady told her that if she did not instantly obey she would send her from her house in disgrace. She added that no real noble lady would refuse to make amends for a wrong to a servant, especially one who by a lifetime of faithful service had earned the confidence and love of her superiors.

Naturally generous and kind-hearted towards the people of the lower classes, the impetuous child burst into tears, kneeled before the old nurse, kissed her hand, and asked to be forgiven. Needless to say she was thenceforth fairly worshipped by the retainers of the family. She told me that the lesson was worth everything to her, and it had taught her the principle of doing justice to those whose social rank made them incapable of compelling aggressors to do rightly towards them.

In later years, H.P.B. became instant "family" to any and all who met her penetrating gaze and lion heart with bits of their own authentic selves. She accepted all regardless of station, race, nation, or religion. Madame was neither vain nor judgmental. Her tasks were to share Truth wherever found, to unmask the unreal and replace it with the Real, and to bow to the sacred Soul in all. She desired to pass those aspirations on to her students, associates and future generations.

"That splendid impersonality which was, to a pre-eminent degree, H.P.B.'s, is a quality of the Soul and hard to attain by lesser beings. She came to show us ourselves; our weaknesses, perhaps. Yes, but above and beyond all else, to show us our inherent god-like potentialities. And ever she insisted that the only path thereto was the practice of Brotherhood, to 'live the life,' which is -- and has ever been -- the sole condition for becoming one with the 'God within.'"

As a parent who can see goodness and also accept the opposite in children of her own breast, H.P.B. automatically peeled the layers of all who came before her. She read others at a distance, much as the Masters and the saints who followed after them. And, she recognized that the personal struggles of humans around her were ultimately little different than her own.

Colonel Olcott recalled another telling incident which occurred as the result of Madame's precipitate voyage to the United States in 1873. He noted how it brought "into high relief one trait of her many-angled character -- her impulsive generosity."

She had bought a first-class ticket from Havre to New York [with only a few dollars extra for the crossing], and had gone to the quay to either see or embark on the steamer, when her attention was attracted by a peasant woman, sitting on the ground with a child or two beside her, and weeping bitterly. Drawing near, H.P.B. found she was from Germany on her way to America to rejoin her husband, but a swindling emigrant runner at Hamburg had sold her bogus steamer tickets, and there she was, penniless and helpless: the steamship company could do nothing, of course, and she had neither relative nor acquaintance in Havre. The heart of our kind H.P.B. was so touched that she said: 'No matter, good woman, I will see if something cannot be done.' She first vainly tried her powers of persuasion (and objurgation) upon the blameless agent of the company, and then, as a last expedient -- her own funds being insufficient for the purpose -- had her saloon ticket changed for a steerage berth for herself, and for the difference got steerage tickets for the poor woman and her children! Many 'proper' and 'respectable' people have often expressed horror at H.P.B.'s coarse eccentricities, including profanity, yet I think that a generous deed like this would cause whole pages of recorded solecisms in society manners to be washed away from the Book of Human Accounts! If any doubt it, let them try the steerage of an emigrant ship.

H.P.B. settled in New York City in 1873 at a time in the western world when women were restricted to home turf and a few trades like teaching and sewing. The Russian-born noblewoman took up residence with forty others in a cooperative experiment for women who wished to live unconventionally. Their home was a rented tenement at 222 Madison Street, a two-storey house with front and back yard.

Madame immediately became part of the co-op family as well as one of its central fixtures. Helena had a room on the second floor and shared a common sitting room which doubled as office-meeting place. "Mme Blavatsky sat in the office a large part of her time, but she seldom sat alone; she was like a magnet, powerful enough to draw round her everyone who could possibly come. I saw her, day by day, sitting there rolling her cigarettes and smoking incessantly. She has a conspicuous tobacco pouch, the head of some fur-bear animal, which she wore round the neck. She was certainly an unusual figure. I think she must have been taller than she looked, she was so broad; she had a broad face and broad shoulders; her hair was a lightish brown and crinkled like that of some Negroes. Her whole appearance conveyed the idea of power.

"In mental or physical dilemma, you would instinctively appeal to her, for you felt her fearlessness, her unconventionality, her great wisdom and wide experience and hearty good will -- her sympathy with the underdog."

Such incidents on the steamer and in the tenement house were hardly the first times H.P.B. extended herself to help widows and orphans, the down and out. In the late 1860s while Helena crisscrossed southern Europe, she cared for a child named Yury. The disabled and sickly boy became her ward for five years. Yet, the details of Yury's story remain a secret. Madame B. never spoke of him more than to say that her actions were taken to "protect the honor of another." The child's few years were spent in ill health even as Helena endeavored to save his life. She eventually made a short visit to Russia to bury the boy without telling her family.

H.P.B. was more willing to tell parts of the story of Agardi Metrovitch, a man maligned even as Madame was. Her loyalty to friends and willingness to stand fearlessly for decent treatment of fellows shows forth clearly in this sketch of Metrovitch's last days.

Agardi Metrovitch was my most faithful devoted friend ever since 1850. With the help of Count Kisseleff I had saved him from the gallows in Austria. He was a Mazzinist, had insulted the Pope, was exiled from Rome in 1863 -- he came with his wife to Tiflis, my relatives knew him well and when his wife died a friend of mine too -- he came to Odessa in 1870. There my aunt, miserable beyond words, as she told me, at not knowing what had become of me begged of him to go to Cairo as he had business in Alexandria and to try and bring me home. He did so.

There some Maltese instructed by the Roman Catholic monks prepared to lay a trap for him and to kill him. I was warned by Illarion, then bodily in Egypt -- and made Agardi Metrovitch come direct to me and never leave the house for ten days. He was a brave and daring man and could not bear it, so he went to Alexandria quand meme *and I went after him with my monkeys, doing as Illarion told me, who said*

he saw death for him and that he had to die on April 19th (I think)....
Now whether he was poisoned, poor man, as I had always suspected
or died of typhoid fever, I cannot say. One thing I know. When I arrived
to Alexandria, to force him to go back on the steamer that brought him,
I arrived too late. He had gone to Ramleh on foot, had stopped on his
way to drink a glass of lemonade at the hotel of a Maltese who was
seen talking with two monks and when he arrived at Ramleh fell down
senseless. Mme. Pashkoff heard of it, and telegraphed to me.

I went to Ramleh and found him in a small hotel, in typhoid fever I
was told by the doctor, and with a monk near him. I kicked him out
knowing his aversion to priests -- had a row and sent for the police to
drag away the dirty monk, who showed me his fist. Then I took care of
him for ten days -- an agony incessant and terrible, during which he
saw his wife apparently and called loudly for her. I never left him for I
knew he was going to die as Illarion had said and so he did.

Then no Church would bury him, saying he was a larbonar. I
appealed to some Free Masons, but they were afraid. Then I took an
Abyssinian -- a pupil of Illarion and with the hotel servant we dug him
a grave under a tree on the sea shore and I hired fellahs to carry him
in the evening and we buried his poor body. I was then a Russian
subject and had a row for it with the Consul at Alexandria (the one at
Cairo was always my friend). Then I took up Mme. Sebir, my monkeys
and went back to Odessa. That's all. The Consul told me that I had no
business to be friends with revolutioniers and Mazzinists and that
people said he was my lover. I answered that since he (Ag. Metrovitch)
had come from Russia with a regular passport, was a friend of my
relatives and had done nothing against my country I had a right to be
friends with him and with whomsoever I chose.

Helena Blavatsky's family and homelands encompassed large
sectors of Europe, Asia and North America. She was born in Ukrainian
Russia, naturalized a citizen of the U.S.A., and died in London, United
Kingdom. But, her revered Masters circled around India and there she
seemed most magnetized and at home. Still, like Socrates, she was a
"citizen of the world."

H.P.B. was compelled by world work to become an American
citizen after exactly five years living in the USA. To do so, she was
required to renounce allegiance to the emperor of Russia and obedience to its government. "I was awfully scared when pronouncing this
black-guardly recantation of Russia and the emperor. And so I am not

only an apostate to our beloved Russian Church, but a political renegade. A nice scrape to get into, but how am I to manage to no longer love Russia or respect the emperor? It is easier to say a thing than to act accordingly."

Her Russian Motherland held large allegiance from her. Through "... learning to love one's country one but learns to love humanity the more." H.P.B. relished letters and newspapers from home. She was thrilled to be visited by old friends and family and most any Russian with whom she could converse in her original language.

During the Russo-Turkish War (1877-78), H.P.B. gave away practically all her income to benefit Russian soldiers. All she earned from her Russian newspaper articles along with first royalties from *Isis Unveiled* was sent to Odessa and Tiflis for wounded soldiers and their families, or to the Red Cross Society.

When Alexander II was assassinated in 1881, Helena was as devastated as her Russian kinsmen. (The Tsar had emancipated the serfs twenty years earlier.) "Good heavens, what is this new horror? Has the last day fallen upon Russia?... How sorry I am for the Imperial family, for the Tsar martyr, for the whole of Russia. I abhor, I despise and utterly repudiate these sneaking monsters -- Terrorists. Let every one laugh at me if they choose, but the martyr-like death of our sovereign Tsar makes me feel - though I am an American citizen -- such compassion, such anguish, and such shame that in the very heart of Russia people could not feel this anger and sorrow more strongly."

On seeing a picture of the dead Emperor in his coffin, H.P.B. wrote, "Would you believe it, the moment I glanced at it something went wrong in my head; something uncontrollable vibrated in me, impelling me to cross myself with the big Russian cross, dropping my head on his dead hand. So sudden it all was that I felt stupified with astonishment. Is it really I who during eight years since the death of father never thought of crossing myself, and then suddenly giving way to such sentimentality? It's a real calamity: fancy that even now I cannot read Russian newspapers with any sort of composure! I have become a regular and perpetual fountain of tears; my nerves have become worse than useless."

While hardly a follower of any church, H.P.B. still revered the Orthodox Church. "People call me, and, I must admit, I also call myself, a heathen. I simply can't listen to people talking about the wretched Hindus or Buddhists being converted to Anglican Phariseeism or the Pope's Christianity: it simply gives me the shivers. But when I read about the spread of Russian orthodoxy in Japan, my heart rejoices. Explain it if you can. I am nauseated by the mere sight of any foreign clerical, but as to the familiar figure of a Russian pope I can swallow it without any effort.... I told you a fib in Paris, when I said I did not want to go to our Church; I was ashamed to say that I went there before your arrival, and stood there, with my mouth wide open, as if standing before my own dear mother, whom I have not seen for years and who could not recognise me!... I do not believe in any dogmas, I dislike every ritual, but my feelings towards our own church service are quite different. I am driven to think that my brains lack their seventh stopper.... Probably, it is in my blood ... I certainly will always say: a thousand times rather Buddhism, a pure moral teaching, in perfect harmony with the teachings of Christ, than modern Catholicism or Protestanism. But with the faith of the Russian Church I will not even compare Buddhism. I can't help it. Such is my silly, inconsistent nature."

Helena Blavatsky's loyalties went wide and deep because all men (in the generic sense) were her brothers. She considered all other creatures on Earth either younger kin or Elder Brothers. Her adoration for her physically distant Masters was unbounded as has been shown many times in earlier pages. And having real experience with the Universal Soul, helped make her the tenacious but loving Tartarian termagant who gave and forgave.

More vignettes of Madame's wholly philanthropic nature survive. We know that she and Colonel Olcott dug deeply into their pockets to "cover expenses" even before the first day the Theosophical Society "opened its doors." They took Baron de Palm into their apartments in New York City in his own dying days. Many thought the Baron was rich and was helping the Society. But it was rather the Twins who took him in, fed him, cared for him in his latter days, and paid for his cremation -- the first ever in America.

Helena and Henry extended themselves to numerous spiritualists and mediums. They practically bankrolled Mr. Gerry Brown and *The Spiritual Scientist* in Boston for several months until his fledgling journal went bankrupt and their investment disappeared. They brought numerous other "spiritual scientists" into their home and attempted to shepherd their gifts and interests in an often hostile climate.

Both Blavatsky and Olcott defended the Eddy and the Holmes mediums. When they were pilloried by the press and manipulated by self-serving interests, the TS founders did their best to support them in newsprint and in person at seances. "I went to the Holmeses and helped by M ∴ and his power, brought out the face of John King and Katie King in the astral light, produced the phenomena of materialization and—allowed the Spiritualists at large to believe it was done thro' the mediumship of Mrs. Holmes. She was terribly frightened herself, for she knew that this once the apparition was real. Did I do wrong? The world is not prepared yet to understand the philosophy of Occult Sciences—let them assure themselves first of all that there are beings in an invisible world, whether 'Spirits' of the dead or Elementals; and that there are hidden powers in man, which are capable of making a God of him on earth."

H.P.B. took Drs. George Beard and William Hammond (former Surgeon General) to task for their biting criticisms in New York newspapers of the disabled Mollie Fancher. Fancher was a young woman who had suffered injuries from a trolley car accident. She was eventually bedridden although attended by numbers of physicians who couldn't understand her predicament yet vouched for the genuineness of her condition as well as her subsequent phenomenal activities. When Madame Blavatsky wrote in her defense, Miss Fancher had been living without eating for YEARS. "This extraordinary girl never sleeps -- her frequent trances being the only rest she obtains; she reads sealed letters as though they were open; describes distant friends; though completely blind, perfectly discriminates colours; and finally, though her right hand is rigidly drawn up behind her head, by a permanent paralysis, makes embroidery upon canvas, and produces in wax, without having taken a lesson in the art, and with neither a knowledge of botany nor even models to copy, flowers of a most marvellously natural appearance."

Mollie lived to the age of 70 while restricted to bed for over 50 of those years and passed decades neither eating nor manifesting other "natural functions." She told her attendants that she "received nourishment from a source of which they [physicians and attendants] were ignorant."

Mollie was clairvoyant and predicted future events while demonstrating five different personalities. At times, she lost the sense of pain along with other bodily senses. Fancher, like H.P.B., had the ability to read books without use of her eyes.

Mollie Fancher was an "accidental" phenomenon worthy of study a century after her death. Still, her fascinating talents only approximated a few of Madame Blavatsky's many gifts.

H.P.B. accomplished many chores while abstracted from the body. Helena Blavatsky worked "after hours" tending to business, conferring with her fellows, and teaching brothers on the inner planes "I work all the twenty-four hours; in this body all day, in another [more ethereal] one, all night." H.P.B. surely has continued doing so since parting her most incarnation in 1891.

Jasper Niemand never saw Madame in the flesh yet was taken on as a student across the ocean and treated much like the Masters had done with H.P.B. Although coming from unremarkable background and common lifestyle, the newcomer felt the presence not only of a teacher but also a family member - maybe even as her own mother. "After H.P.B. accepted me as a pupil, no rules were laid down, no plans formulated. I continued my daily routine, and at night, after I fell into a deep sleep, the new life began. On waking in the morning from a sleep so profound that the attitude of the previous night was still retained, I would vividly remember that I had gone, as it were, to H.P.B. I had been received in rooms which I could and did describe to those who lived with her -- described, even to the worn places or holes in the carpet. On the first occasion of this kind she signified to me her acceptance of me as a pupil and in no other way. After that, she would receive me in varying fashion, showing me pictures which passed like panoramas across the walls of the room.... All the expressions of H.P.B.'s face became familiar to me. I can see her now, her old bedgown -- what dingy old gown was ever so cherished? -- folded about her, as she opened out space before me, and then, too, expanded into her own real being."

H.P. Blavatsky was passionate about sharing Truth and stimulating friends and onlookers with phenomena. But, the practices she displayed and also demanded were that of the highest morality based on the Oneness of beings. "He who would profit by the Wisdom of the Universal Mind has to reach it through the whole of Humanity."

Helena Blavatsky, with all her imperfections, emulated her Mahatmas in so many ways. Most especially in regards to all her brothers. "Realize, my friend, that the social affections have little, if any, control over any true adept in the performance of his duty. In proportion as he rises towards perfect adeptship the fancies and antipathies of his former self are weakened: he takes all mankind into his heart and regards them in the mass."

"Men cannot all be Occultists, but they can all be Theosophists. Many who have never heard of the Society are Theosophists without knowing it themselves; for the essence of Theosophy is the perfect harmonizing of the divine with the human in man, the adjustment of his god-like qualities and aspirations, and their sway over the terrestrial or animal passions in him. Kindness, absence of every ill feeling or selfishness, charity, goodwill to all beings, and perfect justice to others as to oneself, are its chief features. He who teaches Theosophy preaches the gospel of goodwill; and the converse of this is true also -- he who preaches the gospel of goodwill, teaches Theosophy."
Helena Petrovna Blavatsky

"DUTY that which is due to Humanity -- to our fellowmen, neighbors, family - and especially that which we owe to all those who are poorer and more helpless than we are ourselves. This is a debt which, if left unpaid during life, leaves us spiritually insolvent and moral bankrupts in our next incarnation, Theosophy is the quintessence of duty."
H.P. Blavatsky

"First Humanity, and then the Theosophical Society, and last myself."
H.P.B.

The Millennial Man

"The most extraordinary woman of our century, or any century ..."
Saladin

Helena Blavatsky was the one and only candidate who could fill the unique job of Light bringer for the 19th century. She became "the best and truest of Teachers, the most faithful and untiring of Messengers." Furthermore, H.P.B. was the most amazing being to ever stand on the public stage for a whole lifetime, expressing "a whole group of the most extraordinary manifestations emanating from a single source ..."

She was really quite incomparable. Many humans can do one or two things well. H.P.B. was a grand exception who excelled in many, many areas. She began as a prodigy doing the most incredible things which led her to be the "most remarkable medium" en route to become a chela, magician and yogi. Helena circled the world thrice to study, learn and teach with Great Ones all round the planet. She returned to the outer worlds to "do battle" in the name of Truth, to write volumes in which were contained "revolutions," and to Light the Path for all.

H.P. Blavatsky possessed many more extraordinary qualities. It is hard to take them all in without an open mouth or sneering grimace -- depending on the viewer. Encomiums were abundant before and after Madame died in 1891. In life, newspaper editor and investigative journalist W.T. Stead bowed to her "transcendent genius." On her death, writer and publisher William Stewart Ross (Saladin) saw her as "an oracle, a sphinx, ... a sibyl" who was also "simply an upright and romantically honest giantess." Socialist and activist Herbert Burrows was convinced that "a more unconventional *woman* never lived." Indian writer R. Jagannathia gathered her disparate aspects together to say, "She was a *woman* in body, a man in speech, earthly in appearance, celestial in reality."

Another Indian journalist Rai Laheri wrote that, "There is not the least doubt that H P.B. is a woman of mysterious and wonderful occult powers, and must have acquired them, I believe, with great, very great difficulty and drawbacks; for now-a-days it is very rare to find out, than to recognise, a powerful Yogi in India, and especially to succeed in getting anything out of him; the more so by a *woman* born of Mlecha (foreign) tribe."

Nonetheless, Madame Blavatsky was the perfect *woman* for the work to be done for she had the "restless power of a rushing river," was like unto "a whirlwind, a very cyclone," and embodied "the energies of an immortal."

Still looking back over past and continuing times of patriarchal dominance, it seems amazing that a WOMAN was chosen to occupy the role of Messenger and Light bringer. How many molds did Mme. Blavatsky have to break, obstacles to overcome, barriers to force? In the nineteenth-century world, women and cattle often ranked equally. They were considered *chattel*.

Helena Petrovna Blavatsky helped prepare the way for many movements and organizations, ideas and individuals in the twentieth century. Her *female* nature was part of the package. A true forerunner, she was about clearing the way as a teacher, messenger and *woman*.

To this we might answer by repeating the fable told by brother Joseph N. Nutt, 'Grand Master' of the Masonic Lodge for Women in the United States, to show what women can do if they are not shackled by males -- whether as men or as God:

A lion passing a monument representing an athletic and powerful figure of a man tearing the jaws of a lion said: "If the scene which this represents had been executed by a lion the two figures would have changed places!"

The same remark holds good for woman. If only she were allowed to represent the scenes of human life, she would distribute the parts in reverse order. She it was who first took man to the Tree of Knowledge, and made him know Good and Evil; and, if she had been let alone and allowed to do what she wished, she would have led him to the Tree of Life and thus rendered him immortal.

Madame Helena Blavatsky carried the Lighted torch for her century, as well as later ones. It was predicted that another harbinger would follow her in the last quarter of the 20th as in prior centuries. But, no such person appeared. That Messenger was not a single person or group, but manifested as diverse Movements in the likes of feminism, holistic health, parapsychology, civil rights, ecumenism. Essential ingredients for all those 20th-century trends can be found in the Theosophical Movement for which Madame Blavatsky readily stands as an emblem because she was the Soul of her time. H.P.B. planted the seeds for many wonders of the past 125 years and more yet to come.

Regardless of her phenomena, power and goodness, she was largely misunderstood in her life. Would that the media and the people of the day had chosen "wisdom over phenomena." To the present, evidence suggests that the lies and falsifications spread about her during her life are hard to dissipate. It may be possible that this small book can right some of those continuing misrepresentations.

Three essential problems made it so that, "There never was a woman more unjustly abused than H.B." First, she was not allowed to tell all that she knew. Second, H.P.B. -- in person and in phenomena -- towered much higher than her fellows. Third, even "thinkers" of the time could not fathom what she had to give. Twenty-first century humanity persists in a state of relative darkness.

First: Madame Blavatsky had so much to share, offer and teach. And yet, even more was left unsaid and undemonstrated. Master M. wrote that, "The Old Woman is accused of *untruthfulness, inaccuracy* in her statements. 'Ask no questions and you will receive *no lies.*' *She is forbidden* to say what she knows. You may cut her to pieces and she will not tell. Nay -- she is ordered *in cases of need* to *mislead people*; and, were she more of a natural born *liar* -- she might be happier and won her day long since by this time. But that's just where the shoe pinches, Sahib. She is *too truthful, too outspoken, too incapable* of *dissimulation*: and now she is being daily crucified for it."

That situation was a simple matter of fact, but one which few of her time or the present might handle comfortably. The plain truth was that like other earlier Teachers, H.P.B. was bound to be misunderstood and abused. More information and ideas, phenomena and philosophy could have been given out. But, how many might have been able to take it in. The Buddha and the Christ are at best poorly understood by their intent devotees even after millennia of study and worship.

Second: The ancient adage goes, "Seeing is believing." But, many who chased -- in one way or another -- after H.P. Blavatsky seemed to disprove that grand motto -- in respect to truth as well as phenomena. Henry Olcott, one of the fortunate exceptions, explained the situation this way. "It is beyond dispute that phenomena, exhibited under thoroughly satisfactory conditions to persons intelligent enough to comprehend their significance, create an effect in awakening a thirst for the study of occult philosophy that no other appeal can produce. But it is equally true, though at the first glance this may not be so apparent, that to minds, quite unprepared by previous training to grasp the operation of occult forces, the most perfectly unimpeachable phenomenon will be received rather as an insult to the understanding than as a proof of the operation of occult power.

"Nothing is commoner than to hear people say: 'I can't believe in the reality of a phenomenal occurrence unless I see it for myself. Show it me and I shall believe in it, but not till then.' Many people who say this are quite mistaken as to what they would believe if the occurrence were shown to them. I have over and over again seen phenomena of an absolutely genuine nature pass before the eyes of people unused to investigating occurrences of the kind, and leave no impression behind beyond an irritated conviction they were somehow being taken in."

By her efforts and sacrifices, Madame Blavatsky was able to coax some few eyes to "look up." Still, she suffered from the problem which Mark Twain enunciated in her own era. "If it is a Miracle, any sort of evidence will answer, but if it is a Fact, proof is necessary."

Facts caused H.P.B. known in various quarters as the "champion impostor of the age." But, she was really quite the opposite. Saladin experienced and knew better: "She was almost the only mortal I have ever met who was not an impostor."

Third: The ultimate problem lay in the undeveloped minds of H.P.B.'s brethren. Though we have created wonders in the material world, we have yet to scratch the surface of the inner realms of mind and spirit. H.P. Blavatsky was a veritable denizen of those spaces, amphibious with physical and ethereal environs. She lived in two worlds and tried to bridge them for her fellows.

Many people sought to reveal her, to interpret her, to emulate her. But, who was up to the task? "Those who do not understand her had better not try to explain her."

To accomplish that huge task would require self (soul) knowledge. But, so few were and are aware of their inner selves. In a world ignorant of self, H.P.B. came to "SHOW what the self is."

"Aye, there is the rub," as well as the opportunity which Helena Blavatsky brought for the Millennium and the New Age. Her message was not at all new, but it was one which requires open eyes and warm hearts and generous hands. It was built on similar ones carried from the past. It had been told for ages that the Divine dwells within all creatures and most especially human ones. All in God, and God in all. If it is so, then the powers of God also reside in every human being.

All of us have latent powers: "there are hidden powers in man, which are capable of making a God of him on earth." For H.P.B. to have been properly received, her readers and listeners and sitters had to be like her. "We know that when he appears we shall be like him, because we shall see him as he is."

"This power is 'latent in MAN,' and not just in solitary units of the human family only, though this mystery of dual life in every man, woman and child may remain unknown to them ninety-nine times out of a hundred. This ignorance is due to our Western modes of life.

"Whether rich or poor, educated or illiterate -- we, of the civilized nations, are born, live and die under an artificial light; a false light which, distorting our real selves like a mirror cracked in all directions, distorts our faces, and makes us see ourselves not as we are, but as our religious superstitions and social prejudices show us to ourselves....

"For who of us knows, or has any means of knowing Self, while he lives in the lethal atmospheres of whether Society or Proletariat? Who, taught from babyhood that he is born in sin, helpless as a reed, whose only true support is the 'Lord' -- can think of testing his own powers -- when even their presence in him is a thought that never could enter his mind? Between the eternal struggle for more gold, more honours, more power in the higher classes, and the 'struggle for existence,' for bread and life, in the lower ones, there is no time or room for the manifestation of the "inner man" in us. Thus, from birth to death that EGO slumbers, paralyzed by the external man, and asserts itself only occasionally in dreams, in casual visions, and strange 'coincidences' -- unbidden and unheeded. The Psychic or HIGHER SELF as it is called in United [book by A.P. Sinnett], has to be, first of all, entirely ridden of the soporific influence of Personal Self, before it can proclaim obviously its existence and actual presence in man."

When the personal self is set aside, as it was in Helena Blavatsky, the Light of Life shines on the world and its Powers begin to show forth. H.P.B.'s magical gifts proved -- if such is provable -- her place as a Teacher and Leader in the quest for God in all creation. "Man-spirit proves God-spirit, as the one drop of water proves a source from which it must have come. ... prove the soul of man by its wondrous powers -- you have proved God!"

The works of Madame and her Masters have been submerged over recent decades. Yet, they most certainly live on in many ways including the writings of H.P. Blavatsky, remembrance of her phenomenal nature, and the great movements her life spawned. The spirit of Helena Petrovna Blavatsky persists. Her gifts and goodness shall not be forgotten. One day, she will be rightfully recognized not just as *The Phenomenon* but also as THE MILLENNIUM MAN.

No one can render
a greater service to humanity
than to proclaim
the Unity of Eternal Truth ...

Albert de Pouvourville

The name of Helena Blavatsky
will become increasingly famous with time....
Justice will one day be rendered
to her deeds and her work.

Marc Semenoff

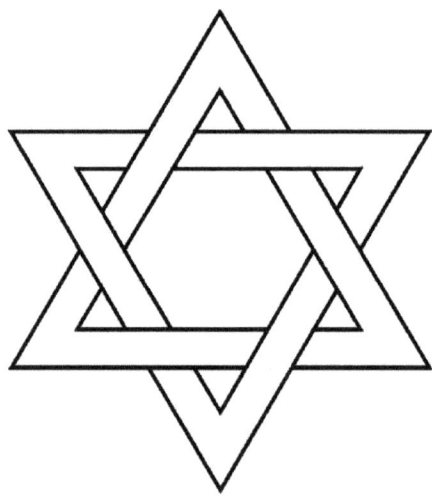

Learn more about

THE PHENOMENON
and
THE MILLENNIUM MAN

at

www.phenom1000man.com

This expanding site has

- Maps of world travels
- Bios of contemporaries and followers
- Sketches and artwork
- Glossary of terms
- Bibliography and references
- Links to Ageless Wisdom sites
- Links to relevant literature

Visit the author's other websites:

theportableschool.com
peoplemedicine.net
rockymountainastrologer.com

Email him:

theportableschool@gmail.com

www.ingramcontent.com/pod-product-compliance
Lightning Source LLC
Chambersburg PA
CBHW052018290426
44112CB00014B/2288